The Billy Graham Christian Worker's Handbook

A Layman's Guide for Soul Winning and Personal Counseling

Original material compiled by
the Christian Guidance Department of the
Billy Graham Evangelistic Association
in conjunction with the
Counseling and Follow-Up Department
Edited by Charles G. Ward

World Wide
PUBLICATIONS

1303 Hennepin Avenue
Minneapolis, Minnesota 55403

Material for this book has been selected from many of
Mr. Graham's sermons, letters, articles, and books.
The following sources have been used:

Blow, Wind of God © 1975 Baker Book House
The Challenge © 1969 Billy Graham
The Holy Spirit © 1978 Billy Graham
How To Be Born Again © 1977 Billy Graham
The Jesus Generation © 1971 Billy Graham
My Answer © 1960 Doubleday
The Quotable Billy Graham © 1966 Droke House
Till Armageddon © 1981 Billy Graham
World Aflame © 1965 Billy Graham

Published by World Wide Publications
1303 Hennepin Avenue
Minneapolis, Minnesota 55403

ISBN #0-89066-042-5

Printed in U.S.A.

93 94 95 96 97 – 13 12 11 10 9 8 7

TABLE OF CONTENTS

FOREWORD

The need is apparent. Look around. Read the newspaper, or watch the evening news telecast. Listen to your friends and family members as they share their hurts, their sorrows, their questions.

You will be deeply touched by the lost, helpless, hopeless people existing in all parts of the world. The spiritual need is overwhelming, but—praise God—there is an answer in the person of Jesus Christ. He alone can meet any need man faces. The Gospel is "Good News" for people to hear and understand. God's Word is Truth and it sets man free.

We at the Billy Graham Association believe in the power of the Holy Spirit to transform lives. Over the years, millions of people around the world have written to us searching for answers and meaning in life. Because of the tremendous need we see for biblical solutions to man's problems, this book is presented to you—not as an exhaustive reference volume, but to help you as you minister to others.

THE BILLY GRAHAM CHRISTIAN WORKER'S HANDBOOK was originally compiled and designed for use in a ministry of telephone counseling during Mr. Graham's crusade telecasts. In several cities of the United States, counseling centers have been developed with the express purpose of meeting the needs of people who watch the Billy Graham Crusades on television. Some wish to make a commitment to Christ. Many are uncertain about their salvation. There are always those who have serious problems and are seeking specific counsel.

A tool for the volunteer counselors was desperately needed, and so this book is the result. The topics selected are those which our Spiritual Counseling department has dealt with over and over throughout the years of this ministry.

Mr. Graham and all of us who work with him are convinced that the Holy Spirit works most effectively and powerfully through the written Word of God. We have carefully searched for Scripture verses which deal specifically with each topic. We believe that the last thing you should leave with anyone you counsel is God's Word. The Truth is indeed a powerful tool and no words of man will change the heart as the Word of God will.

We pray that as you use THE BILLY GRAHAM CHRISTIAN WORKER'S HANDBOOK, God's love will touch many lives.

—Charles Riggs, Director of Counseling

INTRODUCTION

We realize that not all problems in life are of a spiritual nature, but the ultimate problem is. Without a personal relationship to Jesus Christ, we cannot expect any real solutions in our search to be restored to fellowship with God. However, as we experience new life in Christ — forgiveness, freedom from guilt and fear, a sense of fulfillment and completeness, a new motivation towards righteousness, etc., we receive power and a new perspective to face realistically and positively the issues of this life.

As we witness to the transforming power of a relationship with Jesus Christ, we must remember that *attitude* can make the difference between a positive or a negative impact. We may not always be successful in securing a commitment, but we should be kind and empathetic in order to encourage and reassure the inquirer. This will leave the door open for another time when he may make a positive decision. That is more likely to occur if he remembers that he talked to a caring, concerned person who did not put him down, but who left him with a warm feeling and a favorable attitude toward God.

As part of such conditioning of attitude, the Christian witness should cultivate the art of sympathetic listening. So many are crying out: "Look at me. I'm hurting. Won't somebody listen to me? I want help!" The right kinds of questions will help bring the problems of the inquirer to the surface. Many attempts at witnessing are unsuccessful because of efforts to offer solutions that are not relevant to the needs of the person concerned.

The *BACKGROUND* of each chapter is a brief description of persons and problems to be dealt with. It is hoped, of course, that the user of this book will become thoroughly familiar with the background in order to broaden his understanding of the human condition. Such knowledge will impel him to seek increased skills in witnessing and result in more relevant sharing of solutions.

The accompanying *COUNSELING STRATEGY* offers some guidelines in providing solutions. Though there may appear to be certain discernible patterns to human behavior, any attempt to follow an inflexible, stereotyped set of solutions will bring only frustration. Each individual is unique! Therefore, depend upon the strategies only to the degree that they are helpful. The Christian witness must trust the Holy Spirit for guidance in each instance, as He is the only One who can be trusted to apply effectively the Word of God to specific needs.

A continuing witness (otherwise known as "follow-up") is of inestimable value. The apostle Paul's practice was not only to "warn every man," but also to "teach every man," so that he might "present every man perfect in Christ Jesus" (cf., Colossians 1:28, KJV).

Our witness is not really complete until we have exposed the seeker to the excitement of becoming grounded in God's Word, to the discipline and joy of prayer, and to the responsibility of identifying with the Body of Christ — a local Bible-teaching church — for the purposes of worship, fellowship and witness.

Finally, we need to realize that deeply imbedded behavioral problems often need special attention. It is not a negation of the Gospel or of God's power to act in human life for you to suggest professional counseling if the need is apparent. A qualified pastor, a Christian psychologist, psychiatrist, or some type of counseling service may be recommended. We emphasize "Christian" professionals with a firm conviction that solutions to behavioral problems will be found only as they are dealt with in the light of God's Word. The Christian professional can also be an instrument of God to effect spiritual change.

If the seeker begins to receive attention from a Christian professional, this does not mean that your responsibility toward him has ended. Your support as a spiritually concerned friend must continue as long as possible, certainly until he has gained sufficient maturity and stability to walk alone. (See Ephesians 4:14 to 5:21.)

You will notice that the "Counseling Strategy" often refers to a booklet called *Living In Christ*. This follow-up booklet for adults is used by the Billy Graham Evangelistic Association in all its ministries. The corresponding children's booklet is called *Following Jesus*. Both booklets can be purchased from Grason, Box 1240, Minneapolis, MN 55440 or your local Christian bookstore.

The first edition of this book was compiled from the resources of the Billy Graham Spiritual Counseling Department for use in the telephone counseling ministry. Much of the original material has been rewritten and much has been added. I am grateful to all the staff for their time, resources, feedback and encouragement to me as I worked on this project.

This book has been written for use in the extensive ministries of the Billy Graham Evangelistic Association and to encourage believers everywhere to share Jesus Christ as the Lord and Savior of life.

— Charles G. Ward

STEPS TO PEACE WITH GOD

NOTE: *If the individual is immediately ready to receive Christ, skip the four steps and go directly to the section between the asterisks.*

1. GOD'S PLAN — PEACE AND LIFE

God loves you and wants you to experience His peace and life.
The BIBLE says ... "For God so loved the world that he gave his only begotten Son, that whosoever believeth in him should not perish, but have everlasting life." John 3:16 (KJV)

2. MAN'S PROBLEM — SEPARATION

Being at peace with God is not automatic because you by nature are separated from God.
The BIBLE says ... *"For all have sinned and fall short of the glory of God." Romans 3:23 (NIV)*

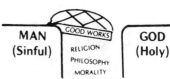

Man has tried to bridge this separation in many ways ... without success.

3. GOD'S REMEDY — THE CROSS

God's love bridges the gap of separation between God and you. When Jesus Christ died on the Cross and rose from the grave, He paid the penalty for your sins.
The BIBLE says ... "He personally carried the load of our sins in his own body when he died on the cross ..." 1 Peter 2:24 (TLB)

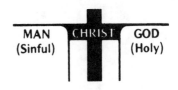

4. MAN'S RESPONSE—RECEIVE CHRIST

You cross the bridge into God's family when you receive Christ by personal invitation.
The BIBLE says ... "But as many as received Him, to them He gave the right to become children of God, even to those who believe in His name ..." John 1:12 (NASB)

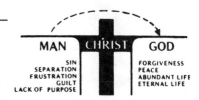

* To receive Christ you need to do four things:
1) ADMIT your spiritual need. "I am a sinner."
2) REPENT and be willing to turn from your sin.

3) BELIEVE that Jesus Christ died <u>for you</u> on the cross.
4) RECEIVE, through prayer, Jesus Christ into your heart and life.

The Bible says (Christ is speaking), "Behold, I stand at the door and knock; if any man hear my voice, and open the door, I will come in . . ." Revelation 3:20, (KJV)

"Everyone who calls on the name of the Lord will be saved." Romans 10:13 (NIV)

WHAT TO PRAY:

Dear Lord Jesus:
I know I am a sinner. I believe you died for my sins. Right now, I turn from my sins and open the door of my heart and life. I receive you as my personal Lord and Savior. Thank you for now saving me. Amen.

* *After leading the inquirer in the above prayer, confirm his decision by sharing the next page.*

CONFIRMING THE DECISION TO RECEIVE CHRIST

You prayed, committing your life to Christ. What does the Bible say happened?

1. You are saved
Jesus said, *"I am the door; if any one
enters by me, he will be saved."* John 10:9 (RSV)

What did Jesus say about Himself?

I am _____ _____ (to eternal life).

What will happen when a person enters (receives Christ)?

He will _____ _____.

*The BIBLE says... "Behold, I stand at the door ad knock; if any man hear my
voice, and open the door, I will come in to him, and will sup with him, and he
with me." Revelation 3:20 (KJV)*

*The BIBLE says... "Everyone who calls on the name of the Lord will be saved."
Romans 10:13 (NIV)*

2. You are a Child of God:
*The BIBLE says, "But as many as received Him, to them He gave the right to
become children of God, even to those who believe in His name."
John 1:12 (NASB)*

What happened when you received Him?

I became a _____ _____ _____.

3. You have eternal life.
*The BIBLE says, "For God so loved the world that he gave his only Son, that
whoever believes in him should not perish but have eternal life."
John 3:16 (RSV)*

Now that you believe in Jesus Christ, what can you say with assurance?

I have _____ _____.

To summarize, emphasize the following questions and answers:

How do you know ...
   you are saved?
   you are a child of God?
   you have eternal life?

I know because...
   God said it ... in His Word
   I believe it ... in my heart
   that settles it ... in my mind

After sharing Christ and confirming the decision, point out these follow-up steps:

1. Take a firm stand for Christ. Tell someone about your decision.

2. Read and study God's Word.

3. Pray every day.

4. Identify with a Bible-teaching church for worship, fellowship, and service.

5. We would like to send you our Bible study booklet, *Living in Christ*, which will help you in your Christian life. What is your name and address?

FINDING ASSURANCE OF SALVATION
(For a person who has received Christ, but has doubts.)

CLAIM THESE PROMISES

1. *The BIBLE says . . . "For God so loved the world, that he gave <u>his</u> only begotten <u>Son</u> that whosoever <u>believeth</u> <u>in</u> Him should not perish, but have <u>everlasting life.</u>" John 3:16 (KJV)*

What did God give to make everlasting life possible? _____ _____.

What must you do to possess everlasting life? _____ _____ _____.

What does God promise you? _____ _____.

2. *The BIBLE says, "Whoever has God's Son has life, . . . I have written this to you who believe in the Son of God, so that you may know that you already have <u>eternal life.</u>" (TLB) 1 John 5:12,13*

If you believe in Christ, what can you know with certainty?

I have _____ _____.

3. *The BIBLE says . . . "My sheep hear my voice, and I know them, and they follow me: and I give unto them <u>eternal life:</u> and they shall <u>never perish,</u> neither shall any man <u>pluck</u> them out of my <u>hand.</u> My Father which gave them me is greater than all: and no man is able to <u>pluck</u> them out of my Father's <u>hand,</u>" John 10:27-29 (KJV)*

What are you promised?

a. And I give unto them _____ _____.

b. And they shall _____ _____.

c. Neither shall any man _____ them out of my _____.

d. No man is able to _____ them out of my Father's _____.

To summarize, emphasize the following questions and answers:

How do you know . . .
you have life eternal?
you will never perish?
you are safe in God's Hand?

I know because. . .
God said it . . . in His Word
I believe it . . . in my heart
that settles it . . . in my mind

After sharing the above on assurance, point out these follow-up steps:

1. Take a firm stand for Jesus Christ; make your life count. Tell someone about your decision.

2. Read and study God's Word.

3. Pray every day.

4. Identify with a Bible-teaching church for worship, fellowship, and service.

5. We would like to send you our Bible study booklet, *Living in Christ*, which will help you in your Christian life and future witness. What is your name and address?

SEEKING FORGIVENESS AND RESTORATION

(For a person who has received Christ, but has failed Him and now seeks forgiveness.)

1. REPENT AND CONFESS TO GOD
The BIBLE says . . . "If we <u>confess</u> <u>our</u> <u>sins,</u> he is faithful and just to <u>forgive</u> us <u>our sins,</u> and to cleanse us from all unrighteousness." 1 John 1:9 (KJV)

What must we do to be forgiven? _____ _____ _____.

What does God say He will do if we confess? _____ _____ _____.

Confess means "to agree" with God . . . I lied, I cheated, I was unkind, I lost my temper. Right now be specific with God . . . silently confess your sins to Him.

Note: Sin takes us off God's pathway and results in alienation. Confession puts us back on God's pathway to peace and joy.

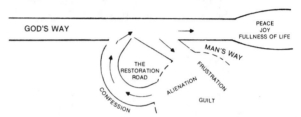

2. DETERMINE TO FORSAKE KNOWN SIN
The BIBLE says, "He that covereth his sins <u>shall</u> <u>not</u> <u>prosper;</u> but whoso confesseth and <u>forsaketh</u> them shall have mercy." Proverbs 28:13 (KJV)

What happens if we cover our sins?

We _____ _____ _____.

Following confession we must _____ our sins.

3. MAKE RIGHT ANY WRONGS
It is important not only to confess and forsake sin, but also to make things right with those whom we may have wronged.

The BIBLE says. . . "And herein do I exercise myself, to have always a conscience void of offence toward God and toward men." Acts 24:16 (KJV)

4. RENEWED FELLOWSHIP WILL BE THE RESULT
The BIBLE says. . . "But if we walk in the light, as he is in the light, we have fellowship with one another, and the blood of Jesus, his Son, purifies us from all sin." 1 John 1:7 (NIV)

"We proclaim to you what we have seen and heard, so that you also may have fellowship with us. And our fellowship is with the Father and with his Son, Jesus Christ." 1 John 1:3 (NIV)

How do you know . . .
   you are forgiven?

I know because. . .
   God said it . . . in His Word

you are cleansed?	I believe it . . . in my heart
you are restored?	that settles it . . . in my mind

After guiding the inquirer to spiritual renewal, share these follow-up steps:

1. Now that you are restored to fellowship with Christ, take a firm stand for Him. Tell someone about your decision.

2. Read and study God's Word faithfully.

3. Pray every day.

4. Identify with a Bible-teaching church for worship, fellowship, and service.

We would like to send you our Bible study booklet, *Living in Christ,* which will help you in your Christian life and future witness. What is your name and address?

UNSURE OF ONE'S RELATIONSHIP TO CHRIST.

Start by asking the basic question: "Has there ever been a time in your life when you trusted Jesus Christ as your personal Lord and Savior?"

1. If the answer is YES, ask him to tell you about it in order to determine just where he really is.
   A. If you feel that he has made a commitment, but is uncertain, go over assurance, page 9.
   B. If he seems firm in his commitment, perhaps he will need help with some other spiritual problem. Go over the section called Seeking Forgiveness and Restoration, page 11.

2. If the answer is NO, then share "Steps to Peace with God," page 5.

3. If the answer is vague: "I have doubts," "I'm not sure," then ask the question: "If you were to die tonight, would you go to heaven?"
   A. If he doesn't know, share "Steps to Peace with God," page 5.
   B. If he believes that he would go to heaven, then share "Assurance." page 5.
   C. If he is still vague, using such phrases as "I have always attended church," or, "I'm doing the best I can," or, "I try to be a moral person," etc., then say:
      (1) "Let me share with you how you can know for sure that if you died tonight you would go to heaven."
      (2) Share "Steps to Peace with God," page 5.

4. Always close your conversation with prayer. Remember to offer the Bible study booklet, "Living In Christ," which will help him in his Christian life and future witness.

ABORTION

Background

Most evangelical Christians feel that no medical doctor or practitioner has the right to play God in terminating human life through abortion. No woman has the "right" over her own body to the extent that she has the freedom to destroy arbitrarily her unborn child. The embryo growing inside her body is more than just another part of her. It has separate existence. It is another life!

The Scriptures place the highest value on human life. It is sacred and of inestimable worth to God, who created it "in his own image" (Genesis 1:26,27), who sustains it ("In whose hand is the soul of every living thing, and the breath of all mankind" Job 12:10, KJV), and who redeemed it (2 Corinthians 5:19).

Abortion is wrong because the Bible says, "Thou shalt not kill" (Deuteronomy 5:17, KJV). It is wrong because every fetus has the potential of becoming a fully developed person, ultimately accountable before God. David wrote thousands of years ago, "You saw me before I was born and scheduled each day of my life before I began to breathe. Every day was recorded in your Book" (Psalm 139:16, TLB).

Counseling Strategy

This problem has many facets. Two which you may have to deal with are the woman who is considering having an abortion and the guilt of one who has already gone through with it. These need to be treated differently. Counselors may also deal with parents of a pregnant girl, father of a baby, medical personnel who have to help with or perform abortions, etc.

The Person Considering an Abortion:

1. Encourage her. Tell her that she has done well in sharing her anxiety. You are happy to talk with her, and you hope you can share some insights which will help her make a final decision.

2. Tactfully remind her that she quite possibly has strong feelings about the moral implications of abortion or she wouldn't have called.

   Avoid being judgmental about her situation. For example, if she is young and unmarried, her pregnancy could be the result of having sought love, attention, and affection which she never received at home. At the same time, avoid minimizing the wrongness of her conduct, because it is sin.

3. Question her about her feelings on abortion.

   What prompted you to call about your problem?
   What are your real feelings about abortion?
   Was there something in Dr. Graham's message that spoke to you? What was it?

4. Whether or not she admits to the wrongness of abortion, gently but firmly present the biblical side. (See BACKGROUND)

5. Ask her to consider the alternatives. If she is considering having an abortion because of the stigma of having an illegitimate child, she will complicate her situation and compound the guilt. Taking the life of her unborn child will turn a bad dream into a nightmare! Suggest that she consider having the child, asking God to bring good from the experience. He can do this as she commits herself and her problem completely to him. "And we know that in all things God works for the good of those who love Him" (Romans 8:28, NIV).

   If she is concerned about not being able to care for or support the child, ask her to consider placing it for adoption. There are many couples looking for a child to adopt, and they are able to provide love and a good home. There are many organizations to which she may turn for help. Suggest that she seek the counsel and advice of a local evangelical pastor, who should be able to initiate the process of arranging for adoption.

6. Ask her if she has ever received Jesus Christ as her Lord and Savior. If indicated, use *Steps to Peace with God*, page 5.

7. Counsel her to start reading the Bible. In order to restructure her life along biblical principles, she needs to read and study God's Word. Offer to send her *Living in Christ* to help her get started.

8. Ask her if she has a church home. She should attempt to identify with a Bible-teaching church where she can find fellowship, encouragement, and Christian growth.

The Person Who Has Had an Abortion and Suffers From Guilt:

1. Encourage her by saying that she is in touch with the right place. We care and want to help in any way we can. God has an answer to every human situation and she can trust Him to work for her good.

2. Don't make an issue of her sin; at the same time, don't minimize it. The fact that she is willing to share her guilt is an indication that God is speaking to her.

3. Dwell on God's forgiveness for those who are willing to repent and confess their sins to the Lord.

   To the woman taken in the act of adultery, Jesus said, "Neither do I condemn thee: go, and sin no more" (John 8:11, KJV).

4. Should confession result, do not dwell on the past (see Philippians 3:13,14).

5. Inquire if she has ever received Jesus Christ as her *personal* Savior. If indicated, share *Steps to Peace with God*, page 5.

6. Counsel her to seek fellowship with God through Bible reading and prayer.

   Forgiveness is immediate, but a sense of restoration and acceptance will come in due time. Through commitment to this important discipline of prayer and Bible study, she will grow in her relationship to God.

7. Counsel her to seek, or restore, fellowship with a Bible-teaching church.

There she can counsel with a pastor, hear God's Word taught, and find strength through Christian relationships.

8. Pray with her.

Ask God for forgiveness, commitment and strength for the future.

Scripture

The Wonder of Life:

"Children are an heritage of the Lord: and the fruit of the womb is his reward."

Psalm 127:3, KJV

"You made all the delicate, inner parts of my body, and knit them together in my mother's womb. Thank you for making me so wonderfully complex! It is amazing to think about. Your workmanship is marvelous — and how well I know it. You were there while I was being formed in utter seclusion! You saw me before I was born and scheduled each day of my life before I began to breathe. Every day was recorded in your Book!"

Psalm 139:13-15, TLB

Forgiveness:

"If we confess our sins, he is faithful and just to forgive us our sins, and to cleanse us from all unrighteousness." 1 John 1:9, KJV

"He forgives all my sins and heals all my diseases; he redeems my life from the pit and crowns me with love and compassion."

Psalm 103:3,4, NIV

Psalm 32:1-5 (These verses were written by one guilty of adultery and murder.)

Courage and Strength to Carry on:

"But they that wait upon the Lord shall renew their strength; they shall mount up with wings as eagles; they shall run and not be weary; and they shall walk, and not faint." Isaiah 40:31, KJV

"Why are you downcast, O my soul? Why so disturbed within me? Put your hope in God, for I will yet praise him, my Savior and my God."

Psalm 42:11, NIV

THE ABUSED WIFE/HUSBAND

Background

The abused wife, husband, girlfriend or boyfriend represents one of the uglier aspects of our society. Only a small percentage of such cases is ever brought to light. The abuse — physical and sexual as well as verbal and emotional — may continue for years. The abused spouse or friend can be found in all socio-economic levels, and in all educational, racial and age groups. And, Christians are not immune.

The abuser often masters the "art" of the put down, foul and abusive language, and threats. At times this abuse is so destructive of personality that the victim feels deserving of any physical battering which follows.

He/she is characterized by low self-esteem, depression, and a variety of stress related disorders and psychosomatic illnesses. He/she is trapped and vulnerable, confused and uncertain. It is impossible to assess objectively one's position or to make decisions. There is a martyr-like endurance and frustration: responsibility for the mate's behavior will often be assumed by the victim. The vague hope exists that change is "just around the corner," and that "someone will soon come and get me out of all this." At the same time, there is emotional isolation and no real contact with the family.

In the case of a wife, it may take from three to four months of counseling before she can begin to heal emotionally, even after she has been separated from her tormentor. Once she and the children are in a safe place (where he cannot reach them because he doesn't know where they are) and she has had time to reflect and sort out her feelings, she may be very angry.

The abuser of spouse and family seldom changes unless exposed and subjected to legal action.

Counseling Strategy

1. Reassure and encourage.

   He/she is doing the right thing in talking about the problem. We want to be of help and are happy to listen. He/she is not alone: many others are experiencing the same treatment.

2. Ask questions. It is quite common for abused persons to have difficulty in expressing their feelings. Ask:

   How do you feel about the way you are treated?
   How long has this been going on?
   Tell me about your husband/wife. What is he/she like?
   How do you feel about yourself at this point?
   What do you think you can do about all this?

   Based on the background of the abused and the emotional damage suffered, the counselor may have to formulate other questions. The goal is to lead the victim to express herself/himself and to make them realize that they have some God-given rights as a woman/man, and wife/husband.

3. Inform him/her not to feel deserving of such treatment. He/she *does not have to be a victim any longer.* Even though the spouse blames her or him and attempts to justify the abuse, it is *not* his/her fault.

4. Inform him/her that he or she doesn't have to take the abuse anymore. It must stop! He/she must be decisive and firm. The spouse's conduct is illegal. He/she can be punished for what he/she is doing, even put in jail.

5. In order to break the cycle of abuse, the victim must contact a local pastor or family services office and tell her or his story. They will be able to help the victim sort things out, suggesting legal action if necessary. Separation from the tormentor may be in order.

6. Suggest that further counseling and emotional support is a must. Arrangements must be made with a qualified pastor, a Christian professional, or a counseling service. Impress upon the victim that decisions must be made urgently and decisive action taken. The counselor may make suggestions, but concrete steps will have to be taken by the person involved.

   NOTE: *The Counseling Department of the Billy Graham Association has limited contacts in some cities for referrals. Ask the counselee if he/she would like to make contact with an organization in his or her area and if he or she needs help. If the answer is in the affirmative, the Billy Graham Association will attempt to contact someone. Please do not promise help. Only say that we will do the best we can. However, any initiative he/she could take on his/her own would be better for all concerned.*

7. Tell the individual that God loves him/her. Better than anyone else, He understands what he/she has been going through. Does he/she realize that Jesus was verbally and physically abused? Has he/she ever received Jesus Christ as his/her personal Savior and Lord? If not, share "Steps to Peace with God," page 5. If the response is affirmative, share ASSURANCE, page 9.

8. Counsel him/her to start Bible reading and study for solace and spiritual strength. (We will send *"Living In Christ,"* if he or she so desires.)

9. Explain the benefits of a good church relationship for him/her and the family. Emotional and spiritual support will be forthcoming as a result of corporate worship, Bible teaching, fellowship and witness. Counseling might also be arranged in those churches offering such a service.

10. Pray with him/her for strength and understanding. Commit him/her to God's special love and care.

Scripture

"Come unto me, all ye that labor and are heavy laden, and I will give you rest."
Matthew 11:28, KJV

"I sought the Lord and he answered me; he delivered me from all my fears. Those who look to him are radiant; their faces are never covered with shame."
Psalm 34: 4,5, NIV

"Cast all your anxiety on him because he cares for you."

1 Peter 5:7, NIV

"You will keep in perfect peace him whose mind is steadfast, because he trusts you. Trust in the Lord forever, for the Lord, the Lord, is the Rock eternal."

Isaiah 26:3,4, NIV

"Trust in the Lord with all your heart and lean not on your own understanding; in all your ways acknowledge him, and he will make your paths straight."

Proverbs 3:5,6, NIV

Other suggested Scripture: Psalm 23; Psalm 42:11.

THE ABUSIVE PERSON
Background

The abusive person is found in all socio-economic levels, in all educational, racial, and age groups. There are abusive women as well as abusive men. The following could be applied to either. Though there are similarities in the characteristics of the abuser, we shall briefly list three categories:

The Wife/Husband Abuser:

Although case histories vary, there are similar threads running through each. The abuser has a very "low boiling point" and knows of only one way to vent anger: abuse. He has little self-esteem, often considers himself a failure, relates poorly to people, is jealous, and accuses his mate of being non-supportive or unfaithful. He attempts to control all her activities and even spies on her, believing that his behavior actually promotes the good of the family, often offends without feeling, and admits no guilt on the emotional level even after admitting his problem.

Abusers tend to justify themselves, either feeling that their partners goad them to the point of abuse or denying that they are abusive. Frustration will trigger abuse: He can't punch his boss at work, so he takes it out on his wife and children at home. Alcoholism and drug abuse are sometimes causes of the explosive mistreatment.

The Child Abuser:

Most of the above symptoms are present in the child abuser. Add to this that he is very demanding, wanting to be obeyed blindly and immediately. He is extremely impatient and often vents his frustrations, the hurts and pains of his childhood on his own children. His expectations are far too high for them, so he often berates them or puts them down. Often his verbal abuse, accompanied by foul and obscene language, will be so devastating that the children begin to accept passively the physical abuse with a feeling that they deserve it. They become victims. Alcohol and drugs are involved in many cases.

The Sexual Abuser (incest):

NOTE: Girls are not the only ones being abused. There is much abuse of boys.

The characteristics of the wife abuser are generally true of the sexual abuser. He is emotionally isolated, although he may appear to be emotionally whole. He seems to be passive, but exercises a growing, rigid control over his daughter's actions as she grows up. He is callous, egocentric, self-indulgent, and sees people only as objects. Alcohol and drug addiction often are related to incest.

Sexual abuse is usually long-term and repetitive, accompanied by intimidation and coercion. When confronted, the abusive adult will deny involvement or responsibility and tends to blame the victim. In all probability, he was sexually abused as a child.

A wife who has failed to protect a child from sexual abuse (when she is actually aware of it), will remain passive and, more often than not, support her husband's denials or rationalizations. When caught, the offender often prommises "not to do it again." Such promises are not to be trusted!

From the above, you can readily understand that dealing with such an individual is difficult. However, perhaps the following will be helpful.

Counseling Strategy

1. Speak in love.

    Do not be judgmental or accusatory. As you are able to get the conversation around to it, let the Word of God reproach and convict.

2. Encourage him by telling him that he has done the right thing in sharing his problem.

    You are happy to talk with him because the Bible has answers to human problems, especially those regarding family relationships.

3. Tell him that he must be willing to face the reality of what he has done or of what is happening.

    His wife and child (children) have the God-given right to be treated decently and with love and concern for their highest welfare. He must realize that he is destroying them. What he is doing is against the law, and he can be punished severely for it. But he can control himself with God's help.

4. Ask him if he has ever received Jesus Christ as his Lord and Savior.
    Share "Steps to Peace with God," page 5.

    NOTE: He must be willing to confess his abusive behavior as sin and look to God for correction and deliverance. God will forgive sin; this is why He sent His Son to the Cross. If indicated, share page on assurance.

5. Suggest that he read and study the Bible.

    The Bible has answers to all the problems in the range of human behavior. Offer to send him *Living In Christ*, which will help him get started in Bible study.

6. Encourage him to learn to pray.

    If there is any rapport left in the family, prayer will help restore the broken cords of relationship.

7. Counsel him to get into a good, Bible-teaching church.

    There, the teaching of the Word of God and fellowship with God's people can be healing and corrective factors.

8. Counsel him to maintain a close contact with the pastor of his church. The pastor can continue to counsel and monitor behavior in the family.

9. Recommend serious commitment to professional counseling for both the offender and his family.

    If one is available in the community, a Christian psychologist or family counseling center should be contacted. The abusive husband-father has a serious, often deep-rooted problem which can be helped only through prolonged counseling. The effects on the family should also be treated professionally.

Scripture

"Husbands, love your wives, even as Christ also loved the church, and gave himself for it . . . So ought men to love their wives as their own bodies. He that loveth his wife loveth himself. For no man ever yet hated his own flesh; but nourisheth it and cherisheth it, even as the Lord the church."   Ephesians 5:25,28,29, KJV

"Fathers, do not exasperate your children; instead, bring them up in the training and instruction of the Lord."   Ephesians 6:4, NIV

"Do not be deceived: Neither the sexually immoral nor idolaters nor adulterers nor male prostitutes nor homosexual offenders nor thieves nor the greedy nor drunkards nor slanderers nor swindlers will inherit the kingdom of God. And that is what some of you were. But you were washed, you were sanctified, you were justified in the name of the Lord Jesus Christ and by the Spirit of our God."

1 Corinthians 6:9-11, NIV

"The Spirit, however, produces in human life fruits such as these: love, joy, peace, patience, kindness, generosity, fidelity, tolerance and self-control — and no law exists against any of them."   Galatians 5:22, Phillips

1 Peter 3:7

ADULTERY

Background

God's Word makes it clear that marriage is a commitment for life to that one individual chosen to be one's mate. This commitment means that "we forsake all others."

"For this reason a man will leave his father and mother and be united to his wife, and the two will become one flesh." (Matthew 19:5, NIV)

Sexual unfaithfulness, however, on the part of both husbands and wives, has become epidemic, according to polls and reports on sexual practices. Adultery is both forbidden and condemned by God in His Word, which states clearly that His wrath will fall upon those who practice it.

"Marriage should be honored by all, and the marriage bed kept pure, for God will judge the adulterer and all the sexually immoral." (Hebrews 13:4, NIV)

"Do you not know that the wicked will not inherit the kingdom of God? Do not be deceived: Neither the sexually immoral nor idolaters nor adulterers . . . will inherit the kingdom of God." (1 Corinthians 6:9,10, NIV)

"Flee from sexual immorality. All other sins a man (woman) commits are outside his body, but he who sins sexually, sins against his own body." (1 Corinthians 6:18, NIV)

Consider some of the consequences:

- Emotional: guilt, fear, anxiety, loss of self-esteem, shattered personalities, depression, etc.
- Physical: illegitimate pregnancies and births, venereal disease, and abortions.
- Spiritual: loss in this life and in that which is to come.

Mr. Graham writes: "How many homes are broken because of men and women who are unfaithful! What sin is committed every day at this point. God will not hold you guiltless! There is a day of reckoning. 'Be sure your sin will find you out' (Numbers 32:23). They will find you out in your own family life here in your relationship with your mate; they will find you out in the life to come."

Adultery is sin, but it is also a symptom that all is not well in a marriage. There are many reasons for adultery. Some are:

- Our own sinful, selfish desires.
    "But every man is tempted when he is drawn away of his own lust, and enticed." (James 1:14, KJV)

- Lack of maturity.

  50% of teen-age marriages come apart in the first five years; however, age is not the only criterion. Immature selfishness at any age can lead to unfaithfulness. Another sign of immaturity is a lack of willingness to accept the responsibility of a family.
- Demanding, critical, scolding, nagging husbands or wives.
- Lack of sexual satisfaction on the part of either mate.
- Transferring to one's mate hostility felt towards a mother or father.
- Meddlesome in-laws who smother a husband and wife with criticism or well-intentioned advice.
- Lack of adequate sex education.

You should expect no easy solutions in dealing with the problem of adultery. However, God can work the miracle of the new birth for the non-Christian and spiritual renewal for His own who have fallen away. If you are successful in securing a commitment to Christ, you can be confident that this will bring a new perspective, making it easier to mend lives and to reach permanent solutions.

Counseling Strategy

For the Partner Who is Involved in Adultery:

1. Attempt to project yourself as a caring, concerned person without being patronizing. You are glad to share, and hope that some solution can be reached.
2. Don't be judgmental or assume a "holier than thou" attitude. Don't start out with Scriptures that condemn; these will emerge normally as you share Christ at the appropriate time.
3. Encourage him or her to talk about the situation so that you can get a complete picture of circumstances. At the same time, don't press for too much detail.
4. When you feel that enough information has been given, tell him or her that you want to work on solutions. However, you would like to return to solutions in a few minutes. In the meantime, you would like to ask if he or she has ever received Jesus Christ as his personal Lord and Savior.

   If not, share "Steps to Peace with God," page 5.

   If the person is a fallen Christian, share "Restoration," page 11. Pray with him or her in this renewed commitment, and then proceed.
5. After praying with him or her, ask what solution he or she might suggest for the problem of adultery.
6. Make a transition to the Scriptures. Point out that God not only demands that we confess adultery as sin, but that we put it out of our lives.

   "He that covereth his sins shall not prosper; but whoso confesseth and forsaketh them shall have mercy." (Proverbs 28:13, KJV)
7. Suggest that the caller probe his or her mind for possible reasons for this

infidelity and share them with you. You might mention some of the "Reasons for Adultery" from the BACKGROUND to stimulate thinking.

Suggest that he or she share these reasons with the spouse. An honest effort to communicate is the only way that things can be brought to light and the climate provided which will lead to solutions. To begin with, the unfaithful partner must demonstrate remorse and ask for forgiveness.

8. Counsel him or her to begin to read and study God's Word with his or her spouse. This will illuminate them both as to their responsibilities and fortify them against temptation and sin. Also, encourage them to pray together.

9. Encourage them to seek out and identify with a Bible-teaching church. This will provide strength as they fellowship, worship, and study the Bible. Becoming committed Christians should be their goal. The absence of a vital relationship with Christ is the chief factor in this problem.

10. Advise him or her to seek out the pastor for encouragement and counseling. If he or she doesn't find the needed help through the pastor, he or she should make a commitment to serious, professional counseling with a Christian psychologist or psychiatrist.

For the Partner of the Adulterer:

He or she often feels betrayed, rejected and hurt. Although only one person may be guilty of unfaithfulness, often both partners in a marriage *contribute* to it.

1. Encourage the person to ask himself or herself:

   A. How may I have contributed to my mate's infidelity?
   Am I critical?
   Supportive?

   B. What circumstances have been present in our marriage which might have contributed to the problem?
   Parents?
   Ignorance?
   Work schedules, or absences from home?
   Lack of communication?

   C. How may I help to provide a solution to save our relationship?

2. Help the inquirer to determine the best course of action:

   A. Forgiveness. Things can never be worked out unless there is forgiveness. This may be very difficult, but a way can be found. Those involved must ask for God's grace and wisdom to face it. Your love and concern will be most evident at this point. The guilty spouse must also seek God's forgiveness and the spouse's forgiveness.

   B. Communication. The couple must make a determined effort to communicate with each other in order to discuss freely all facets of the issue. Lack of communication may have been a contributing factor to the problem. Now is the time to correct this.

C. Prayer. The couple should pray together and trust God to work things out so that the marriage may be saved and grow stronger.

D. Counseling. They should be willing to consider serious professional counseling with a qualified pastor or a Christian psychologist or psychiatrist. It may take time to work things out.

Scripture

"If we confess our sins, he is faithful and just and will forgive us our sins and purify us from all unrighteousness."   1 John 1:9,NIV

(Jesus is speaking to the woman accused of adultery).
"Then neither do I condemn you, Jesus declared. Go now and leave your life of sin."   John 8:11, NIV

"Marriage should be honored by all, and the marriage bed kept pure, for God will judge the adulterer and all the sexually immoral."
                                                        Hebrews 13:4, NIV

"The husband should fulfill his marital duty to his wife, and likewise the wife to her husband. The wife's body does not belong to her alone but also to her husband. In the same way, the husband's body does not belong to him alone but also to his wife."   1 Corinthians 7:3,4, NIV

"Take your evil deeds out of my sight! Stop doing wrong, learn to do right! Seek justice, encourage the oppressed. Defend the cause of the fatherless, plead the case of the widow. 'Come now, let us reason together,' says the Lord. 'Though your sins are like scarlet, they shall be as white as snow; though they are red as crimson, they shall be as wool.' "
                                                        Isaiah 1:16-18, NIV

1 Corinthians 6:15-20

ALCOHOLISM

Background

Habitual use of alcohol often can result in addiction. The drinker's inadequacies, faults and problems become intensified, and often personality changes result. Though feeling confident when under the influence of alcohol, he is often immature, insecure, and afflicted by guilt and depression. He does not feel good about himself. He cannot face his addiction and the problems which this creates, so he denies he has a problem. He is dishonest in his attempt to cover up the alcoholism and will blame family members, his boss, his parents, or the "bad breaks" he has had in life. The deviousness and pretense lead to a masquerade in life that at times assumes almost comic, though tragic, overtones.

Alcoholics desperately need help. Alcoholics Anonymous maintains that until alcoholics hit rock bottom, admitting their life is out of control, there is little hope of any change. Admitting that there is a problem is the first step on the road to recovery. There is hope! God is able to deliver from alcoholic addiction.

Billy Graham writes: "The Bible teaches that there is deliverance from the things that come upon the world . . . not by chemicals, but by Christ, bringing the mind and heart into harmony with God through submission to His will and accepting His forgiveness . . . In Christ alone there is deliverance from man's tortured thoughts and freedom from the sordid habits which are destroying so many people. Why does the Bible so clearly denounce drunkenness? Because it is an enemy of human life. Anything that is against man and his welfare, God is against."

Counseling Strategy

1. If the inquirer is drunk or on a "high," any counsel is lost time, a conversation with the alcohol and not with the person, and could even be counterproductive for the alcoholic. Arrange a meeting or have him telephone the following day when he is sober. If he appears out of control, get him to a detox center. If he has telephoned, ask that he surrender the phone to another, and ask that person to get him to a center.

2. Because alcoholics are often dishonest and deceivers (con artists), the counselor must evidence a "tough love" in dealing with them. Ask if he really wants help. Or did he just get in touch in order to "bleed on me," do a "snow job," excusing himself, blaming other things and people, hiding his real self and the problem?

   In taking a tough stance, avoid being judgmental and do not censure him with Bible texts. The texts will come out naturally as you present the

Gospel. Assure him that he is in touch with the right person because you care and are glad to speak with him (unless he is drunk).

3. Emphasize that he must admit that he has a problem he can't cope with. The alcohol is much bigger than he is and he can't defeat it alone.

   Is he willing to make a commitment to quit for good? Nothing short of this will do! He must stop the masquerade once and for all. He is personally responsible for his condition and his problems.

4. This might be the time to ask him if he has ever received Jesus Christ as his Lord and Savior. Christ went to the Cross specifically for him in order to save him and to change him. Share "Steps to Peace with God," page 5.

5. Return to the reasoning of point number 3:
   A. He must never again use alcohol. Living one day at a time, he must learn to trust God's promise in regard to temptation. (1 Corinthians 10:13 — See under SCRIPTURE).
   B. He must sever all relationships that keep him enslaved to his pattern of behavior.
      "Do not be misled. Bad company corrupts good character" (1 Corinthians 15:33, NIV).
   C. He must establish new relationships:
      Seek out a local chapter of Alcoholics Anonymous or other support groups. They are listed in the telephone book.
      Identify with a local, Bible-teaching church where he can worship, study the Bible and have fellowship which can also provide spiritual support.
   D. Be honest with him in stating that he may have relapses, but all is not lost. Renewal may be sought on the basis of 1 John 1:9, and the steps of point 5 must be practiced a day at a time.
   E. Pray with him for deliverance from the compulsion and bondage he is under, that he may experience a transformation of his mind and life by the power of God (see Romans 12:1-2). Urge him to cultivate a life of prayer.

6. If your inquirer is a Christian who has become a victim of alcohol, use the above steps. Then share "Restoration," page 11, emphasizing 1 John 1:9 and 2:1.

7. In both cases, urge him to seek further counseling from a pastor or psychologist who understands alcoholism or chemical dependence. Many times it is necessary to deal with the underlying causes of the addiction, such as insecurity, guilt, failure, stress, deviate sexual behavior, etc.

Scripture

"Therefore, if anyone is in Christ, he is a new creation; the old has gone, the new has come."   2 Corinthians 5:17, NIV

"If the Son therefore shall make you free, ye shall be free indeed."
                                                        John 8:36, KJV

"No temptation has seized you except what is common to man. And God is faithful; he will not let you be tempted beyond what you can bear. But when you are tempted, he will also provide a way out so that you can stand up under it."

1 Corinthians 10:13, NIV

"He that covereth his sins shall not prosper; but whoso confesseth and forsaketh them shall have mercy."

Proverbs 28:13, KJV

"If we say that we have no sin, we deceive ourselves, and the truth is not in us. If we confess our sins, he is faithful and just to forgive us our sins, and to cleanse us from all unrighteousness."

1 John 1:8,9, KJV

"Thou wilt keep him in perfect peace, whose mind is stayed on thee, because he trusteth in thee."

Isaiah 26:3, KJV

Matthew 11:28
2 Corinthians 2:14
John 3:16
Galatians 5:22,23
Romans 12:1,2
Romans 14:11,12

ANGER

Background

Anger is an emotion, an involuntary reaction to a displeasing situation or event. As long as anger is limited to this involuntary, initial emotion, it may be considered a normal reaction. It is when we respond improperly to anger — when we lose our temper (let anger get out of hand) or store it up so that it makes us bitter, resentful, or hostile — that it becomes dangerous. It is here that the Bible calls us to account.

In approaching the subject of anger, we must realize that not all anger is wrong. When the Bible deals with anger, it may be focusing on several different emotions. For example:

1. Moses' anger burned when he saw the unfaithfulness and idolatry of his people. (Exodus 32:19)
2. On healing the man with the "withered hand," it is recorded that Jesus "looked around at them in anger" because he was disturbed at their (the Pharisees') stubborn hearts. (Mark 3:5, NIV)
3. Though not explicitly stated, anger is implied in the attitude and actions of our Lord as He drove the profiteers from God's House. (Mark 11:15,17)
4. Anger is somehow involved in our attitudes and treatment of sin. "Be ye angry, and sin not." (Ephesians 4:26, KJV)

It Is Scriptural To Control Anger:

"A fool gives full vent to his anger, but a wise man keeps himself under control" (Proverbs 29:11, NIV). On attempting to control our anger, we must realize that each person has the right to his own opinions, and his life should be characterized by dignity and respect. At the same time, and in order to keep things in proper perspective, let us not forget that if Jesus had demanded His "rights," He wouldn't have gone to the Cross. There is a fine line of distinction here. The thing to remember is that the Christian must be careful of his responses, remembering that our position may be right but our attitudes wrong.

Billy Graham writes: "The Bible does not forbid displeasure, but it sets up two controls. The first is to keep anger clear of bitterness, spite or hatred. The second is to check daily on whether we have handled malevolent feelings. There is an old Latin proverb, 'He who goes angry to bed has the devil for a bedfellow.' Of course, there are many irritations in life. They become prime opportunities for Satan to lead us into evil passion."

Anger Is Excessive or Uncontrolled If:

1. It results in outbursts of temper and/or bad language.
2. It results in bitterness, resentment, and hostility (the urge to "get even").
3. It is spiritually debilitating, causing inner turmoil, unsettles one's tranquillity and sense of well-being. Do I have the feeling that my attitude is displeasing to God or that I am "giving place to the devil" (Ephesians 4:27, KJV)?
4. It results in harm to other people. Does it negatively affect my testimony as others observe my bad responses? Are they victims of those responses?

How Can We Learn to Control Excessive Anger?

1. Try not to interpret everything as a personal offense, oversight, hurt, etc. At the same time, attempt to pinpoint the things that cause you to become excessively angry.
2. Make your attitudes and responses a matter for serious prayer. We ought also to take the irritating behavior of others to the Lord, realizing that God uses people and circumstances to refine our character. One may have many rough edges that need to be filed down!
3. Cultivate the practice of confessing excessive anger as sin. The importance of "immediacy" in this matter of seeking forgiveness is to be interpreted in the words of the Apostle Paul, "Do not let the sun go down while you are still angry" (Ephesians 4:26, NIV). Learn to balance the books at least by the end of the day.
4. Realize that the Christian must learn to cope with two natures, each striving for supremacy. We must learn to practice the "put-off," "put-on" principle of Ephesians 4:22-24 (NIV):
   A. "Put-off" the old self which is being corrupted by its deceitful desires (verse 22).
   B. "Put-on" the new self, created to be like God in true righteousness and holiness (verse 24).
   C. The effect of practicing the "put-off," "put-on" principle is to "be made new in the attitude of your minds" (verse 23). This is the way to validate 2 Corinthians 5:17.
5. Strive to focus your anger away from yourself to the problems that are causing it.
6. Surrender each day to the Holy Spirit.
   "Live by the Spirit, and you will not gratify the desires of the sinful nature." (Galatians 5:16, NIV)
7. Let the Word of God permeate your life as you read, study, and memorize it.
   "Let the word of Christ dwell in you richly as you teach and admonish one another with all wisdom . . ." (Colossians 3:16, NIV)

Counseling Strategy

1. A personal relationship to Jesus Christ is basic to solving any spiritual problem.

   Ask the inquirer if he has entered into this relationship. Share "Steps to Peace with God," page 5.

2. Ask questions of your Christian inquirer to determine where he is in reference to unresolved or excessive anger.

   Share with him from the BACKGROUND, emphasizing attitudes of the Christian, daily confession, and the components of the "put-off," "put-on" principle. Have him write down points and Scripture references to help him remember them.

3. Pray with him. Pray that he may have a "conscience void of offense before God and man," and the faith to trust God for continued victory.

Scripture

"My dear brothers, take note of this: Everyone should be quick to listen, slow to speak and slow to become angry, for man's anger does not bring about the righteous life that God desires."   James 1:19,20, NIV

"A gentle answer turns away wrath, but a harsh word stirs up anger."
Proverbs 15:1, NIV

"But now you must rid yourselves of all such things as these: anger, rage, malice, slander, and filthy language from your lips."   Colossians 3:8, NIV

"A fool gives full vent to his anger, but a wise man keeps himself under control."   Proverbs 29:11, NIV

"You were taught, with regard to your former way of life, to put off your old self, which is being corrupted by its deceitful desires; to be made new in the attitude of your minds; and to put on the new self, created to be like God in true righteousness and holiness."   Ephesians 4:22-24, NIV

See also Bitterness and Resentment

ANXIETY, WORRY AND TENSION

Background

The term anxiety covers a wide range of problems which result because of unfounded fears. Someone has said that the anxious and the worrier are so preoccupied about what may happen in the future that they forget to cope with the present. It is characteristic of them to worry about anything. They build mountains of "mole hills," as insignificant matters assume great importance in their lives. They are anxious about imagined shortcomings, the future, their health, their families, and their work. They are often unable to pinpoint the reasons for their anxieties and fears.

Many anxious people suffer physical difficulties such as nervousness, sleeplessness, headaches, difficulty in breathing, excessive sweating, etc. Inability to find relief for anxiety can lead to more serious consequences, such as a "nervous breakdown." Obviously, such persons need our sympathy, our prayers, and whatever help we may be able to give them.

Billy Graham comments: "Man has always been beset by worry, and the pressures of modern life have aggravated the problem . . . many of you are filled with a thousand anxieties. Bring them to Jesus Christ by faith . . . I am learning in my own life, day by day, to keep my mind centered on Christ; the worries and anxieties and concerns of the world pass, and nothing but 'perfect peace' is left in the human heart."

Counseling Strategy

1. Offer encouragement.
   The Lord can help! ("Why are thou cast down, O my soul? And why art thou disquieted within me? *Hope thou in God;* for I shall yet praise him for the help of his countenance" (Psalm 42:5, KJV). The fear of God is the only fear that conquers all other fears.

2. Help the inquirer discover the reason for his anxiety.
   The counselor should seek to offer more than a palliative (an easing of pain without a cure) which might bring temporary relief but not touch the problem. As much as possible, seek to get at "root causes."

   Avoid probing too deeply. Limited time for counseling and the possibility that his anxieties are based on traumatic experiences of the past should limit your questions only to those which will help to open the door for presenting Christ as Savior and sustainer.

Ask him:
> Why are you fearful about your job, your future, your
> family?
> Why are you nervous? Why do you have headaches? Why can't you
> sleep?
> Describe the way you feel. Do you feel guilty? Why?
> Are you running from something? What is really your problem?

If anxiety seems to have been brought on by true feelings of guilt, this could indicate wrong behavior that needs correction. This is helpful, because the problem is sin. It has a remedy! Experiencing God's forgiveness in Christ can remove guilt and guilt feelings, which will contribute to healing. Share "Steps to Peace with God," page 5.

Avoid telling people that if they "think right" they are bound to "feel right." Sometimes they need to be told that "right living" produces "healthy thinking." God alone is the source of positive thoughts. Facing the basic problem — sin — will eventually produce that kind of conduct which pleases God and will result in changes.

It is possible that anxiety about the future could reveal concern about death and future judgment. Again, this opens the door to present Christ.

3. Share the necessity of daily Bible study and prayer.

We must not only read the Bible, but must assimilate its teachings in such a way that they begin to mold life and character. Memorizing the Word is most important. "Thinking God's thoughts" will take the place of worried, anxious concerns of self and self's nagging problems.

Prayer is the companion of Bible study. According to the Bible, we should be anxious for nothing, but "by prayer and supplication, with thanksgiving, make our requests known to God" (Philippians 4:6, KJV).

4. Share some of the promises of God's Word.

God can be trusted to keep His promises. See SCRIPTURE at end of section.

5. Counsel the inquirer to get involved with a Bible-teaching church.

Thinking of and serving with others can be an antidote to negative and unhealthy introspection.

6. Pray with the inquirer for genuine solutions.

"I sought the Lord, and He heard me, and delivered me from all my fears." (Psalm 34:4, KJV)

If you detect deeper problems than you can deal with, suggest that he consider counseling with a Christian psychologist.

Scripture

"I sought the Lord, and he answered me; he delivered me from all my fears."   Psalm 34:4, NIV

"Cast all your anxiety on him, because he cares for you."
                                                              1 Peter 5:7, cf., RSV

"Do not be anxious about anything, but in everything, by prayer and petition, with thanksgiving, present your requests to God. And the peace of God, which transcends all understanding, will guard your hearts and your minds in Christ Jesus."   Philippians 4:6,7, NIV

"But seek first his kingdom and his righteousness, and all these things will be given to you as well. Therefore do not worry about tomorrow, for tomorrow will worry about itself."   Matthew 6:33,34, NIV

"Why are you downcast, O my soul? Why so disturbed within me? Put your hope in God, for I will yet praise him, my Savior and my God."
                                                    Psalm 42:5, NIV

Psalm 55:22, NIV
Proverbs 3:5,6, KJV
Philippians 4:13, NIV
Philippians 4:19, NIV
Romans 8:28, NIV

ASSURANCE OF SALVATION

Background

Assurance is the awareness of belonging to Christ and having complete confidence in Him.

Many Christians lack assurance. Because of ambivalence about their relationship to Him, they don't really experience the joy of the Lord. The only thing they are entirely sure of is that they have doubts. Uncertainty can stem from one of the following:

- *Not being truly converted.*

    A Christian is a person who has trusted in Jesus Christ as his Lord and Savior. "That if thou shalt confess with thy mouth the Lord Jesus, and shalt believe in thine heart that God hath raised him from the dead, thou shalt be saved. For with the heart man believeth unto righteousness; and with the mouth confession is made unto salvation" (Romans 10:9,10, KJV).

    A person who lacks this experience cannot possibly be certain about eternal life. Salvation is not based on our own performance, but on our relationship to Jesus Christ. Confident Christians can say, "For I know whom I have believed, and am persuaded that he is able to keep that which I have committed unto him against that day" (2 Timothy 1:12, KJV).

- *Trusting feelings rather than God's Word.*

    Some persons expect a sustained, emotional elation, and when this is missing or lags, doubts come.

    Our eternal relationship to God cannot be based only on emotion. We must rest on facts based on the Word of God. We are to commit ourselves to the finished work of Christ on the Cross. Having trusted Him, we continue this relationship confident that "He which hath begun a good work in you will perform it until the day of Jesus Christ" (Philippians 1:6, KJV).

- *Sin and disobedience in the life of the Christian.*

    These will result in ambivalence and uncertainty. "A double-minded man is unstable in all his ways" (James 1:8, KJV). Sin must be acknowledged and confessed in order to maintain unbroken fellowship.

    The Christian who does not nurture his life in the Word of God, prayer, fellowship, and witness will dry up, opening the way to uncertainty and doubts. The biblical admonition to "grow in grace, and in the knowledge of our Lord and Savior Jesus Christ" (2 Peter 3:18, KJV), is not just an idle phrase. We grow or we die!

Counseling Strategy

1. The inquirer who is not sure of his salvation.

    If the inquirer does not know that he has trusted Jesus as Savior and Lord due to misunderstanding the true nature of Christian conversion or dependence on his own performance, share "Steps to Peace with God," page 5. Emphasize that salvation means relationship to Christ through the new birth (John 1:12 and 3:3), not our own efforts (Ephesians 2:8-9).

2. The inquirer who has been depending upon his feelings.

   Our experience must rest on the biblical facts of the Gospel, not on emotion. Share "Assurance," page 9.

3. The Christian who is disobedient, harboring sin in his life.

   Share "Restoration," page 11. Emphasize 1 John 1:9 and 2:1, and also Romans 12:1.

4. The immature Christian.

   If the uncertainty and doubt is the result of arrested spiritual development, point out that either we grow or we die. Share "Restoration," page 11.

5. With all the above, emphasize the need to pursue a vital, spiritual relationship with Christ.

   A. Read and study the Word of God.

      Offer to send *Living in Christ* to help the inquirer get started.

   B. Through prayer: we worship God

      we confess our sins to Him

      we express our gratitude and thanksgiving

      we remember the needs of others.

   C. Seek to develop relationships with other Christians through a Bible-teaching church. This will provide fellowship, Bible study, and opportunities for service to Christ — all necessary to develop the Christian life.

   D. Pray with the inquirer that he may begin to know a life of joy and assurance in Christ.

Scripture

Salvation:

"I tell you the truth, whoever hears my word and believes him who sent me has eternal life and will not be condemned; he has crossed over from death to life."

John 5:24, NIV

"But as many as received him, to them gave he the power to become the sons of God, even to them that believe on his name."   John 1:12, KJV

"For by grace are ye saved through faith; and that not of yourselves: it is the gift of God: not of works, lest any man should boast."

Ephesians 2:8,9, KJV

"When someone becomes a Christian he becomes a brand-new person inside. He is not the same any more. A new life has begun."

2 Corinthians 5:17, TLB

Fact Rather Than Feeling:

"For I am convinced that neither death nor life, neither angels nor demons, neither the present nor the future, nor any powers, neither height nor depth, nor anything else in all creation, will be able to separate us from the love of God that is in Christ Jesus our Lord."   Romans 8:38,39, NIV

". . . Yet I am not ashamed, because I know whom I have believed, and am convinced that he is able to guard what I have entrusted to him for that day."   2 Timothy 1:12, NIV

"And I am sure that God who began the good work within you will keep right on helping you grow in his grace until his task within you is finally finished on that day when Jesus Christ returns."   Philippians 1:6, TLB

"I write these things to you who believe in the name of the Son of God so that you may know that you have eternal life."   1 John 5:13, NIV

"For God took the sinless Christ and poured into him our sins. Then, in exchange, he poured God's goodness into us."   2 Corinthians 5:21, TLB

"And God, in his mighty power, will make sure that you get there safely to receive it (eternal life), because you are trusting him. It will be yours in that coming last day for all to see."   1 Peter 1:5, TLB

Confession of Sin for Restoration:

"If we confess our sins, he is faithful and just to forgive us our sins, and to cleanse us from all unrighteousness."   1 John 1:9, KJ

"He that covereth his sins shall not prosper, but whoso confesseth and forsaketh them shall have mercy."   Proverbs 28:13, KJ

"I waited patiently for the Lord, and he inclined unto me, and heard my cry. He brought me up also out of an horrible pit, out of the miry clay, and set my feet upon a rock, and established my goings. And he hath put a new song in my mouth, even praise unto our God; many shall see it, and fear, and shall trust in the Lord."   Psalm 40:1-4, KJ

BACKSLIDING, SPIRITUAL INDIFFERENCE

Background:

Webster's dictionary says that "backsliding" means to lapse morally or in the practice of religion. It has a deeper spiritual connotation than this would indicate. It means to lose one's fellowship with the Lord, to grow cold and indifferent to spiritual matters, or even to fall away (apostasy).

There are varying degrees of backsliding:

Apostacy: A falling away because of a conscious rejection of God's truth as revealed in His Word and in His Son.

Sins of the Flesh: Being "drawn away of his own lust and enticed" to sin. This would mean immorality, drunkenness, murder, etc.

Sins of the Spirit: (The most common among Christians). To head the list, we could speak of spiritual indifference — that lack of responsibility before God and the church which results in our being ineffective in life and witness as outlined in the Word. Also to be listed here are lying, cheating, gossip, envy, selfishness, jealousy, etc. (See Galatians 5:19-21.)

Things That Lead to Backsliding:

- Disappointment in the inconsistencies seen or imagined in other Christians.
- An indifferent relationship to Christ or "following afar off" and ignoring the place of God's Word, prayer, and witnessing in our Christian life.
- Ignorance of the true implications of spiritual responsibility and practice.
- Disobedience to God's revealed will for my life.
- Willful sin which remains unconfessed. We must realize that each person is responsible for his own acts before the Lord. This implies repentance and confession.

Billy Graham has wisely commented: "If you are a true believer in Christ, you are going to be at war. The lusts of the flesh, the influence of the world and the devil are going to war against your Christian life. The flesh will lust against the spirit, and the spirit against the flesh, and there will be constant conflict. The only time you will have perfect peace is when you are totally committed and yielded to Christ in every phase of your life. Too many people want to have one foot in the world and one foot in the kingdom of God, and it is like straddling a fence. You are not happy either way. Declare yourself for Christ."

Counseling Strategy

The counselor should seek true repentance, confession, and restoration of the inquirer so that his life might be renewed in love for Christ, for the Word, and for service.

In order to accomplish this goal, try to determine how the inquirer has lost his fellowship or relationship with the Lord. If he seems unsure about his original commitment to Christ, then review "Steps to Peace with God," page 5. If he is willing to face issues, then proceed as follows:

1. Ask him to confess to the Lord all known sin in the light of 1 John 1:9.
2. Lead him through the "Restoration" section on page 11. By confession he can be renewed. There is no sin that God will not forgive in Christ.
3. Urge him to start reading and studying the Bible and praying daily. Offer to send him *Living In Christ* which will help get him started in Bible study.
4. Urge him to get into a Bible-teaching church for fellowship, instruction, and service.
5. Urge him to make restitution, if necessary; to make right anything through which others might have been offended or taken advantage of.
6. Pray with him for full restoration and blessing.
7. Urge him to memorize Proverbs 3:5,6, and learn to lean on its truth in the days ahead.

Scripture

Repentance and Confession:

"If we confess our sins, he is faithful and just to forgive us our sins, and to cleanse us from all unrighteousness."   1 John 1:9, KJV

"He that covereth his sins shall not prosper; but whoso confesseth and forsaketh them shall (find) mercy."   Proverbs 28:13, KJV

"The sacrifices of God are a broken spirit; a broken and contrite heart, O God, thou wilt not despise."   Psalm 51:17, KJV

"I waited patiently for the Lord, and he inclined unto me, and heard my cry. He brought me up also out of an horrible pit, out of the miry clay, and set my feet upon a rock, and established my going. And he hath put a new song in my mouth, even praise unto our God; many shall see it, and fear, and shall trust in the Lord."   Psalm 40:1-4, KJV

Promise of Forgiveness:

"If my people, (who) are called by my name, shall humble themselves, and pray, and seek my face, and turn from their wicked ways, then will I hear from heaven, and will forgive their sin, and will heal their land."
                                              2 Chronicles 7:14, KJV

"Let the wicked forsake his way, and the unrighteous man his thoughts: and let him return unto the Lord, and he will have mercy upon him; and to our God, for he will abundantly pardon."   Isaiah 55:7, KJV

Spiritual Growth:

"That Christ may dwell in your hearts by faith; that ye, being rooted and grounded in love, may be able to comprehend with all saints what is the breadth, and length, and depth, and height; and to know the love of Christ which passeth knowledge, that ye (may) be filled with all the fullness of God."   Ephesians 3:17-19, KJV

"Let the word of Christ dwell in you richly in all wisdom; teaching and admonishing one another in psalms and hymns and spiritual songs, singing with grace in your hearts to the Lord."
Colossians 3:16, KJV

"Do not be anxious about anything, but in everything, by prayer and petition, with thanksgiving, present your requests to God. And the peace of God, which transcends all understanding, will guard your hearts and your minds in Christ Jesus."   Philippians 4:6,7, NIV

Trust in God for Daily Victory:

"Trust in the Lord with all thine heart and lean not unto thine own understanding. In all thy ways acknowledge him, and he shall direct thy paths."
Proverbs 3:5,6, KJV

"He that spared not his own Son, but delivered him up for us all, how shall he not with him also freely give us ALL things."   Romans 8:32, KJV

"Nay, in all these things we are more than conquerors through him that loved us."   Romans 8:37. KJV

BAD HABITS

Background

It has been said that human beings are creatures of habit. Many of our prac-tices become automatic: we are sometimes unaware that we do certain things or that we do them in a specific way.

The designation "Bad Habits" covers a wide range of negative behavior and could be defined as anything which inhibits Christian growth or offends others. We may be speaking of the so-called sins of the spirit, such as envy, jealousy, malice, gossip, lying, criticism of others, selfishness, impatience, quarreling, procrastination, etc. Or, we may be speaking of compulsive behavior: eating, drinking, spending, reading and viewing of pornography, excessive working, fantasizing and evil thoughts, masturbation, swearing, etc.

The subject of bad habits assumes special importance in the light of the scrip-tural demand that Christians "walk in newness of life" (Romans 6:4, KJV). As we surrender to the Lord, asking Him to search our hearts and reveal all that is displeasing to Him (Psalm 139:23,24), we will begin to see many ugly things that need to be dealt with. The most important things to remember in regard to bad habits are that they displease God, and with His help they can be broken and replaced with alternatives.

None of us is immune to change. The Gospel specializes in change (2 Corin-thians 5:17). We know that God can work in our lives in order to bring our con-duct into line with what pleases Him. "For we are God's workmanship, created in Christ Jesus to do good works, which God prepared in advance for us to do" (Ephesians 2:10, NIV).

Billy Graham comments, "The strength for our conquering and our victory is drawn continually from Christ . . . The Christian now has resources to live above and beyond the world. The Bible teaches that whoever is born of God does not practice sin."

Counseling Strategy

1. Commend the inquirer for being sufficiently interested in his spiritual life to seek solutions to problems related to bad habits.

   Change is possible for all persons, regardless of age or other limitations. "I can do all things through Christ (who) strengtheneth me" (Philippians 4:13,KJV). His help and the prospect of breaking the shackles of the self-life should provide the motivation for achieving ultimate victory.

2. Ask if the inquirer has ever received Jesus Christ as personal Savior and Lord.

One might assume that someone inquiring about conquering bad habits would be a Christian, but don't take it for granted. Is the caller confident that he has experienced that abiding relationship with Christ which will provide the power promised by God to bring about change? Share "Steps to Peace with God," page 5.

3. Suggest that the bad habit or habits (sins) be faced in specific terms.

    It is necessary to identify those areas that need changing. It is a challenge to be faced realistically, because habits are hard to break. They cannot be "wished" away. The use of pious phrases is of little help. We must work at it. The Apostle Paul put this in perspective when he said, "O wretched man that I am! Who shall deliver me from the body of this death?" (Romans 7:24, KJV). Cures are not instantaneous and easy.

4. Encourage him to confess his bad habits to the Lord as sin, and to seek forgiveness.

    At the same time, help him to make a covenant with God to work through to victory. A definite commitment at a given place and time will set the stage for change. Take a stand; be an overcomer. (See Joshua's statement in Joshua 24:15.)

5. Tell the inquirer that bad habits can be broken by practicing the principle of replacement or exchange.

    The Apostle Paul speaks of the "put-off," "put-on" principle. "You were taught, with regard to your former way of life, to put off your old self, which is being corrupted by its deceitful desires; to be made new in the attitude of your minds; and to put on the new self, created to be like God in true righteousness and holiness" (Ephesians 4:22-24, NIV). This can be thought of in terms of taking off an unclean garment and exchanging it for a clean one. Paul illustrates this principle as follows: "Therefore each of you must put off falsehood and speak truthfully . . ." (Ephesians 4:25, NIV); and, "He who has been stealing must steal no longer, but must work . . ." (Ephesians 4:28, NIV).

    Memorized Scripture can be a great help in practicing the "put off," "put on" principle of exchange. For the Christian afflicted with the inclination for swearing or bad language, a scripture such as the following would be helpful: "Let no corrupt communication proceed out of your mouth, but that which is good to the use of edifying, that it may minister grace unto the hearers" (Ephesians 4:29, KJV). At other times, one might use a word of praise, such as those found in Psalm 34 or 103.

    Assure your inquirer that there is a spiritual alternative for each bad habit which can be broken!

6. Suggest that daily Bible reading, study, memorization of Scripture and prayer are of great value. As God's thoughts invade our minds, things must begin to change.

7. Suggest that a fellowship link be established with another Christian for mutual sharing of problems, prayers and victories. This sort of "buddy system" has been very helpful to many persons.

8. Suggest that he seek opportunities to serve Christ.

As we begin to share ourselves, our experiences, and the fruit of our Bible study and personal victories, we are "fortified in the inner man."

9. If the inquirer is not already a member of an active Bible-teaching church, he should seek such a relationship.

This will give opportunity for fellowship, prayer, Bible study, and service.

10. Challenge him to select one habit to overcome and to set some immediate goals.

11. Pray with the inquirer for victory over the bad habit, to the glory of God.

Scripture

"Submit yourselves, then, to God. Resist the devil, and he will flee from you. Come near to God and He will come near to you." James 4:7,8, NIV

"Thy word have I hid in mine heart, that I might not sin against thee."
Psalm 119:11, KJV

"In the same way, count yourselves dead to sin but alive to God in Christ Jesus. Therefore do not let sin reign in your mortal body so that you obey its evil desires. Do not offer the parts of your body to sin, as instruments of wickedness, but rather offer yourselves to God, as those who have been brought from death to life; and offer the parts of your body to Him as instruments of righteousness. For sin shall not be your master, because you are not under law, but under grace." Romans 6:11-14, NIV

"No, in all these things we are more than conquerors through Him who loved us." Romans 8:37, NIV

"Then He said to them all: 'If anyone would come after Me, he must deny himself and take up his cross daily and follow Me.' " Luke 9:23, NIV

"For it is God who works in you to will and to act according to his good purpose . . . so that you may become blameless and pure, children of God without fault in a crooked and depraved generation, in which you shine like stars in the universe." Philippians 2:13,15, NIV

Jeremiah 17:9,10, NIV
Galatians 2:20, NIV
2 Timothy 2:15, NIV

THE BIBLE
Background

Some uninformed Christians or sincere doubters question the authority of the Bible. We may be challenged by those who state that the Bible is just a collection of myths and inaccuracies. Three things characterize almost everyone who has difficulty accepting the authority of the Scripture:

- They seldom, if ever, bother to read the Bible.
- They approach the Bible with prejudiced ideas learned from Bible critics and their writings.
- They are not acquainted with the "Author."

But, can we trust the Bible? Yes!

Billy Graham says: "Long ago I decided to accept the Bible by faith. This should not be difficult for anyone to do. Most of us do not understand nuclear fission, but we accept it. I don't understand television, but I accept it. I don't understand radio, but every week my voice goes out around the world, and I accept it. Why is it so easy to accept all these man-made miracles and so difficult to accept the miracles of the Bible?"

What is Our Authority for Believing the Bible?

1. The Bible itself claims to be the Word of God. "All Scripture is God-breathed and is useful for teaching, rebuking, correcting, and training in righteousness, so that the man of God may be thoroughly equipped for every good work" (2 Timothy 3:16,17, NIV).

   "Above all, you must understand that no prophecy of Scripture came about by the prophet's own interpretation. For prophecy never had its origin in the will of man, but men spoke from God as they were carried along by the Holy Spirit" (2 Peter 1:20,21, NIV).

2. Jesus and the Apostles confirmed its authenticity, quoting it scores of times in their writings and ministries. For example, Jesus' confirmation: "I tell you the truth, until heaven and earth disappear, not the smallest letter, nor the least stroke of a pen, will by any means disappear from the Law until everything is accomplished" (Matthew 5:18, NIV). Also, Peter quoted David's words to substantiate the resurrection of Jesus Christ. (See Acts 2:29-36).

3. The historical Church has recognized and used the Bible as God's inspired record of Himself and His will. There are quotations from the Church Fathers which go back to the end of the first century. The Bible has always been the ultimate rule of faith and practice for the true Church.

4. History and archeology combine to confirm the accuracy of the Bible. The historical record is obvious and indisputable. Many of the places mentioned in the Bible can easily be identified, even today. Hundreds of archeological sites have uncovered ample evidence to substantiate the Christian's claim that the Bible can be trusted. Ancient manuscripts of the Bible have been preserved to the present day. We mention three:

   The Dead Sea Scrolls contain either a fragment or the complete text of all the books of the Old Testament except the Book of Esther. Some of these texts go back to the second and third centuries before Christ.

   The Septuagint (Greek Translation) dates from 250 B.C.

   Codex Sinaiticus, discovered at the ancient monastery at the foot of Mt. Sinai, dates back to the earliest centuries of the Christian era.

   All of these documents, and many more, are available for examination.

5. Fulfilled Prophecies witness to the Bible's accuracy. A few examples from the life of Jesus illustrate the point:

   He would be born of a virgin: Isaiah 7:14 and Luke 2:26-35.

   He would be born in Bethlehem: Micah 5:2 and Luke 2:4-7.

   He would live a sinless life: Isaiah 53:9 and 2 Corinthians 5:21.

   He was to be killed (crucified): Isaish 53:5,7 and Matthew 27:35.

   He would cry from the Cross, "My God, my God, why hast thou forsaken me": Psalm 22:1 and Matthew 27:46.

6. The Bible's remarkable unity and coherence confirm it. It reveals a single author — the Holy Spirit — behind the diversity of its human writers. It is not just a jumble of characters, places, and dates. It has an amazing continuity, as both the facts and the message of the Bible are closely and amazingly interconnected to reveal God's Son, our Lord and Savior Jesus Christ and His part in human redemption and restoration. One Book, one Theme — Jesus Christ!

7. The Bible is confirmed by its power to transform lives. Its message exploded on the human scene in New Testament times to turn "the world upside down" (Acts 17:6, KJV). There is power in the message of the Word. From the Apostle Paul's time down to the present day, the power of the Gospel has changed lives. Only those countries affected by the evangelical message of the Bible have seen any real results in the uplifting of society: human rights, treatment of children and women, medical advances, freedom from slavery, etc. The Bible is the only book which gives answers to life's ultimate questions: Who am I? Where did I come from? Why am I here? Where am I going? What is the purpose of existence?

Counseling Strategy

Never argue! If the inquirer is open-minded enough to listen, present as much of the background as you can.

1. A person's acceptance of the Bible is directly related to his willingness to accept the Author. At some convenient point during the conversation, ask the inquirer if he has ever received Jesus Christ as his Lord and Savior. Share "Steps to Peace with God," page 5.

2. Counsel him to obtain a recent translation of the Bible to read and study. Approaching it with an open mind and asking God to reveal Himself, His will, and His eternal purposes, should result in a rewarding experience. Offer to send him *Living in Christ* to encourage him to start Bible reading and study.

3. Counsel him to find a Bible-teaching church where he can participate in worship, Bible study, and fellowship with others who take the Bible seriously.

4. Pray with him for spiritual illumination, for faith, and for fulfillment in his life through the power of the Word. "And now, brethren, I commend you to God and to the word of his grace, which is able to build you up, and to give you an inheritance among all them which are sanctified" (Acts 20:32, KJV).

Additional Suggestions:

1. If the inquirer admits to not having read much of the Bible, challenge him to get started at once. He should follow the same approach he would on any experiment: approach it impartially and give it a chance in his thinking. Suggest that he start with the Gospel of Luke, then go to Acts, then wherever he will.

2. Possible answers to questions that might be raised:

   A. The Bible says that man has been on the earth for only approximately 6,000 years.

      Answer: Nowhere does the Bible state that man has been here only 6,000 years. This misconception is probably due to Bishop Ussher's chronology, developed in the 1600's. The Bible doesn't say man is 6,000 years old, nor 60,000 nor 600,000. It does say, "In the beginning, God created the heaven and the earth" (Genesis 1:1, KJV).

   B. The Bible is filled with inaccuracies.

      In order to test the caller's knowledge, ask him, "What inaccuracies?" Should he bring up creation, Noah's ark, Joshua's long day, Jonah's fish, the Virgin Birth, etc., tell him that we can't explain these things, though we believe they are historical. We don't have to defend them. God has spoken. The Bible demands the exercise of faith! Quote Billy Graham from the BACKGROUND. Paul the Apostle said, in writing of those who have problems with the Scriptures, "The natural man receiveth not the things of the Spirit of God: for they are foolishness unto him: neither can he know them because they are spiritually discerned" (known only through the Holy Spirit) (1 Corinthians 2:14, KJV).

C. I find the Bible hard to believe, or I can't understand it.

Answer: Suggest that he purchase a modern translation of the Bible (New International Version, Good News for Modern Man, etc.) and try again. Quote Mark Twain: "It's not the things I don't understand about the Bible that bother me; it's the things I do understand that. bother me."

If the inquirer seems sincere in his doubts, suggest that he pray the prayer suggested by John Stott in his book "Basic Christianity": "God, if you exist (and I don't know if you do) and if you can hear this prayer (and I don't know if you can), I want to tell you that I am an honest seeker after the truth. Show me if Jesus is your Son and the Savior of the world. And if you bring conviction to my mind, I will trust Him as my Savior and follow Him as my Lord."

You may find it helpful to use D.L. Moody's approach to the Bible:

"I prayed for faith, and I thought that some day faith would come down and strike me like lightning. But, faith did not come! One day I was reading the 10th chapter of Romans: 'Faith cometh by hearing, and hearing by the word of God' (Romans 10:17, KJV). I had closed my Bible and prayed for faith. I now opened my Bible, and began to study, and faith has been growing ever since."

Scripture

"The word of God is living and active. Sharper than any double-edged sword, it penetrates even to dividing soul and spirit, joints and marrow; it judges the thoughts and attitudes of the heart."   Hebrews 4:12, NIV

"For this cause also we thank God without ceasing, because, when ye received the word of God which ye heard of us, ye received it not as the word of men, but as it is in truth, the word of God, which effectually worketh also in you that believe."   1 Thessalonians 2:13, KJV

"For whatsoever things were written aforetime were written for our learning, that we through patience and comfort of the scriptures might have hope."   Romans 15:4, KJV

2 Timothy 3:16,17
2 Peter 1:20,21
Acts 20:32

BITTERNESS AND RESENTMENT

Background

Bitterness is the product of intense animosity, characterized by cynicism and ill-will. Resentment is indignant displeasure and ill-will which results from a wrong, an insult or injury, either real, imagined, or unintentional. They often go together and are the result of unresolved anger.

Billy Graham says, "The Bible does not forbid displeasure, but it sets up two controls. The first is to keep anger clear of bitterness, spite and hatred. The second is to check daily to see if you have handled malevolent feelings. There's an old Latin proverb: 'He who goes angry to bed has the devil for a bedfellow.' Of course, there are many irritations in life. They become prime opportunities for Satan to lead us into evil passion."

Professional counselors reveal that a large percentage of those being counseled today are angry, embittered, and resentful. Bottled-up feelings eat away until some become emotional cripples and physically ill. Their ability to function is impaired, diminishing their effectiveness. They often have difficulty sleeping, and their personal relationships, both within and without the family, erode. Some become so obsessed with the urge to "get even" that they may kill someone. The individual who has deep-seated, unresolved anger is not a whole person.

A classic case of the "grudge and get even" syndrome is found in the story of Cain and Abel (Genesis 4:1-16). Cain was angry because his offering was not accepted but his brother's was. It really wasn't a matter between Cain and Abel at all, but between Cain and God. It was God who rejected his offering. But Cain became resentful and depressed ("his face fell"). Instead of repenting and asking forgiveness of the Lord, he turned on his brother.

Many times people will share problems of this nature because they are seeking sympathy or reinforcement. They will tell you how they have been misunderstood, maligned, and mistreated, never realizing the sinful implications behind their own behavior. As the story unfolds and you detect resentment and bitterness, treat it as sin.

God's Word says, "But now you must rid yourselves of all such things as these: anger, rage, malice, slander, and filthy language from your lips" (Colossians 3:8, NIV).

Counseling Strategy:

1. As your inquirer reveals the problem, remain neutral. Assure him that

God's Word has the solution to any problem.

2. Assure yourself that you are speaking with someone who has truly received Christ.

If this is not the case, then share "Steps to Peace with God," page 5.

3. If your inquirer has not yet realized that he has a problem with bitterness and resentment, or if he is aware of it and sincerely wants to find a solution, make sure he understands that he is dealing with sin in his life. To ignore this will prevent any real solution.

4. Repentance and confession will result in forgiveness and restoration to fellowship with God. Share "Restoration," page 11, emphasizing 1 John 1:9. Pray together, asking the inquirer to confess his bitterness and resentment.

5. If the above is accomplished, then steps toward reconciliation are in order, especially if there has been accusation, recrimination, criticism, and a rupture in relationship. Victory comes when matters are solved both on the vertical and horizontal planes. The prize is a "conscience void of offense toward God, and toward men" (Acts 24:16, KJV).

It is not necessary to make a public issue of it, but Jesus said, "First go and be reconciled to your brother" (Matthew 5:23, NIV). The Apostle Paul advised, "If it is possible, as far as it depends on you, live at peace with everyone . . . if your enemy is hungry, feed him; if he is thirsty, give him something to drink. In doing this, you will heap burning coals on his head. Do not be overcome by evil, but overcome evil with good" (Romans 12:18, 20-21, NIV). If there is reconciliation, God will be pleased and both parties will be spiritually healed. If, on the other hand, nothing positive happens, the inquirer will have done all God requires. He has been obedient and can thus live with a clear conscience.

6. Counsel your inquirer to pray that God will fill him with love for the other, whether or not reconciliation occurs. "Love . . . keeps no record of wrongs . . . does not delight in evil" (1 Corinthians 13:5,6, NIV).

7. If the bitterness and resentment are of long standing, and the inquirer stubbornly maintains the correctness of his position, give him Paul's admonition, "Get rid of all bitterness, rage and anger, brawling and slander, along with every form of malice. Be kind and compassionate to one another, forgiving each other, just as in Christ God forgave you" (Ephesians 4:31,32, NIV). Ask him to reflect on the verses and to pray for his enemies in the light of their truth.

8. Pray with the inquirer.

Scripture

"When they hurled their insults at him (Jesus), he did not retaliate; when he suffered, he made no threats. Instead, he entrusted himself to him who judges justly."   1 Peter 2:23, NIV

"For if you forgive men when they sin against you, your heavenly Father will also forgive you. But if you do not forgive men their sins, your Father will not forgive your sins."

Matthew 6:14,15, NIV

"Bless those who persecute you; bless and do not curse. Rejoice with those who rejoice; mourn with those who mourn. Live in harmony with one another. Do not be proud, but be willing to associate with people of low position. Do not be conceited. Do not repay anyone evil for evil. Be careful to do what is right in the eyes of everybody. If it is possible, as far as it depends on you, live at peace with everyone. Do not take revenge, my friends, but leave room for God's wrath, for it is written: 'It is mine to avenge; I will repay,' says the Lord."

Romans 12:14-19, NIV

"Make every effort to live in peace with all men and to be holy; without holiness no one will see the Lord. See to it that no one misses the grace of God and that no bitter root grows up to cause trouble and defile many."

Hebrews 12:14,15, NIV

See also Anger

CHASTENING

Background

Often, a Christian will admit to some sin or disobedience which has resulted in God's chastening. At other times, a conversation will reveal problems and troubles that seem to indicate that God is dealing with the caller.

Chastening from the Lord is Scriptural:

"Blessed is the man you discipline, O Lord, the man you teach from your law; you grant him relief from days of trouble." (Psalm 94:12,13, NIV)

"My son, do not despise the Lord's discipline AND DO NOT RESENT HIS REBUKE, because the Lord disciplines those he loves, as a father the son he delights in." (Proverbs 3:11,12, NIV)

Billy Graham comments on the subject: "The Bible says, 'Whom the Lord loveth He chasteneth.' If life were all easy, wouldn't we become flabby? When a ship's carpenter needed timber to make a mast for a sailing vessel, he did not cut it in the valley, but up on the mountainside where the trees had been buffeted by the winds. These trees, he knew, were the strongest of all. Hardship is not our choice; but if we face it bravely, it can toughen the fiber of our souls.

"God does not discipline us to subdue us, but to condition us for a life of usefulness and blessedness. In His wisdom, He knows that an uncontrolled life is an unhappy life, so He puts reins on our wayward souls that they may be directed into the paths of righteousness."

Chastening is Desirable, Considering the Alternatives:

"So he gave them what they asked for, but sent a wasting disease upon them" (Psalm 106:15, NIV).

"I beat my body and make it my slave so that after I have preached to others, I myself will not be disqualified for the prize ("Be a castaway," KJV) (1 Corinthians 9:27, NIV)

God Has Motives in Disciplining or Chastening:

1. He wants to lead us to repentance. "Yet now I am happy, not because you were made sorry, but because your sorrow led you to repentance. For you became sorrowful as God intended and so were not harmed in any way by us" (2 Corinthians 7:9, NIV)

2. He wants to restore us to fellowship. "That which we have seen and heard declare we unto you, that ye also may have fellowship with us: and truly

our fellowship is with the Father, and with his Son Jesus Christ" (1 John 1:3, KJV).

3. He wants to make us more faithful. "Now it is required that those who have been given a trust must prove faithful" (1 Corinthians 4:2, NIV).

4. He wants to keep us humble. "To keep me from becoming conceited because of these surpassingly great revelations, there was given me a thorn in my flesh, a messenger of Satan, to torment me. Three times I pleaded with the Lord to take it away from me. But he said to me, 'My grace is sufficient for you, for my power is made perfect in weakness'" (2 Corinthians 12:7-9, NIV).

5. He wants to teach us spiritual discernment. "But if we judged ourselves, we would not come under judgment. When we are judged by the Lord, we are being disciplined so that we will not be condemned with the world." (1 Corinthians 11:31,32, NIV).

6. He wants to prepare us for more effective service. "Therefore, my beloved brethren, be ye steadfast, unmoveable, always abounding in the work of the Lord, forasmuch as ye know that your labor is not in vain in the Lord" (1 Corinthians 15:58, KJV).

Counseling Strategy

1. Encourage the inquirer. He may be glad that the Lord has His disciplining hand upon him. By chastening or disciplining, God is not discarding His child or disowning him, but rather:

   A. He is confirming His love for you. "For whom the Lord loveth he chasteneth..." (Hebrews 12:6, KJV)

   B. He is confirming His relationship to you. "If you are not disciplined (and everyone undergoes discipline), then you are illegitimate children and not true sons" (Hebrews 12:8, NIV).

   C. He wants you to respond in obedience and faithfulness to Him. "Before I was afflicted I went astray, but now I obey your word" (Psalm 119:67, NIV).

2. Help the individual to open up to the Lord in the manner of the Psalmist: "Search me, O God, and know my heart; test me and know my anxious thoughts. See if there is any offensive way in me, and lead me in the way everlasting" (Psalm 139:23,24, NIV).

   Some questions might help. For example:

   Why do you feel that you are being chastened or disciplined?

   Do you feel that there is some disobedience or sin in your life that God is dealing with?

3. In no way minimize the sin or disobedience the person admits. This is the basis on which you can ask him to repent, confess, and be restored to fellowship.

4. Go over the section on "Restoration," page 11, especially emphasizing 1 John 1:9.

5. Encourage him to start and continue a daily devotional experience with God through reading His Word and praying.

6. Encourage the inquirer to seek God's direction in discovering His purpose for his life. From chastening, one goes on to obedience and blessing which lead to opportunities to live for and serve Christ.

7. Encourage him to find a good church where he can find a biblically oriented fellowship. Christian friends help to make us stronger!

8. Pray with him for complete restoration and renewal.

Scripture

Psalm 94:12,13
Proverbs 3:11,12
1 Corinthians 9:27

CHILD ABUSE

Background

"Child abuse is a great American tragedy," states a T.V. commentator. Children of domestic violence are found in all socio-economic, educational, racial and age groups. Violence patterns often run in families; the battered becomes the batterer! Abuse falls into three categories: verbal, physical and sexual. Any one of these can be so devastating in the life of a child that he may never recover from the damage.

Verbal abuse can be degrading, debasing the child. He may feel that any physical abuse that follows is deserved. The screaming parent, who often accompanies his tirades by swearing and foul language and his constant put downs "You can't do anything right," "Stop acting like a child," "You should be more like so-and-so," etc., will strip his child of all self-esteem, give him problems with identity, and may depress him to the point of becoming an emotional cripple.

Add physical punishment to this, and the child will be further denied that proper emotional development which results in a normal, responsible adult. It is easy for the abused child to slip into drugs, alcohol or deviate sexual behavior.

Such children often are depressed, do poorly in school, misbehave and are delinquent. They are frequently deceptive and lie, steal, cheat and violate the rights of others. Assuming violence to be a normal behavioral response, he reverts to it in order to solve problems in school, with peers and his family. He will often be suicidal and entertain thoughts of murdering his parents. A great percentage of our prison population is a product of family violence.

Proper emotional responses in such children are almost impossible, but a tender, loving attitude may at least begin to open a door to solutions.

Counseling Strategy

1. Be sensitive, patient and caring in your approach.
   You may be speaking to a child who is incapable of comprehension on the emotional level.

2. Reinforce his motive in calling.
   Tell him:
   We are glad you called.
   We are here to help you.
   God loves you and we love you.
   You are special to Him and to us.
   God knows what you are going through and will help.

3. Ask how he feels about himself.
   As he reports abuse which may have come from his father, mother or elder sibling, find out how he feels about the constant punishment. Such persons may feel that they deserve the physical punishment they have been receiving.

4. Reassure him that he is not necessarily bad.

     Sometimes parents do not realize that they are abusive. They do not necessarily need a motive for hurting a child. Seventy percent of abusers were themselves abused as children.

5. Tell him that Jesus loves him very much.

     Jesus died on the Cross for him. Jesus is the only one who is preparing a special kingdom for children ("For of such is the kingdom of heaven" Matthew 19:14, KJV).

6. Ask him is he has ever received Jesus as his Savior. If he has not, share "Steps to Peace with God," page 5.

7. Ask him if he has a Bible. Encourage him to start reading it. Offer to send him either *Living In Christ* (12 yrs. and above) or *Following Jesus* (under 12). This will help to get him started in his Bible reading.

8. Ask him if he goes to church.

     If he knows the pastor, encourage him to go and tell him about all that he is going through, even though it may be very embarassing. The pastor needs to know about the abuse if he is to help. The abusing parent is not likely to change unless faced with the legal implications of his behavior, thus the recommendation that the pastor be informed. He can confront the parents, arrange for counseling and contact the necessary authorities if need be.

9. Pray with the child to encourage him further.

Scripture

"Jesus said, 'Let the little children come to me, and do not hinder them.' "
Matthew 19:14, NIV

"Come to me, all you who are weary and burdened, and I will give you rest."
Matthew 11:28, NIV

"Let him have all your worries and cares, for he is always thinking about you and watching everything that concerns you."
1 Peter 5:7, TLB

THE CHURCH

Background

By definition, the Church is the "Body of Christ," that community of the redeemed of which He is the Head. "And He is the head of the body, the church: who is the beginning, the firstborn from the dead; that in all things he might have the preeminence" (Colossians 1:18, KJV)

The Church came into being because "Christ also loved the Church and gave himself for it" Ephesians 5:25, KJV). It is nurtured by His own dynamic life "That he might sanctify and cleanse it with the washing of water by the word" (Ephesians 5:26, KJV). Christ will come to claim it as his "bride, [as one] adorned for her husband" (Revelation 21:2, KJV), "that he might present it to himself a glorious church, not having spot, or wrinkle, or any such thing; but that it should be holy and without blemish" (Ephesians 5:27, KJV).

Its birth was confirmed by the coming of the Holy Spirit (Acts 2:1-11) who also provides the power for its self-perpetuation through witness to the world (Acts 1:8).

The Church is Both Visible and Invisible:

- The invisible Church is that larger body of believers who, down through the ages, have sincerely trusted Jesus Christ as Lord and Savior. "The Lord knoweth them that are his. And, let everyone that nameth the name of Christ depart from iniquity" (2 Timothy 2:19, KJV). One becomes a member of the invisible Church when he receives Jesus Christ as his Lord and Savior (John 1:12).

- The visible Church is the present-day universal Church, composed of local groups of Christians. In it are both the "wheat and tares" (Matthew 13:25-40) — the truly redeemed, and many who are not.

  Those churches who, down through the centuries, have denied "the faith which was once delivered" (Jude 3, KJV), would be identified as apostate.

  When a person experiences the new birth, he becomes a member of the invisible Church. He should seek to identify immediately with a local, biblical assembly of believers in order to take an active part in worship, fellowship, evangelism, Bible study, and prayer. This is a responsibility which the Bible teaches: "Let us not give up meeting together, as some are in the habit of doing, but let us encourage one another — and all the more as you see the Day approaching" (Hebrews 10:25, NIV).

Billy Graham writes: "The Church is primarily the Body of Christ ... The Bible says ... that it was Christ's love for the Church that caused Him to go to the Cross. If Christ loved the Church that much ... I must love it too. I must pray for it, defend it, work in it, pay my tithes and offerings to it, help to advance it, promote holiness in it, and make it the functional, witnessing body our Lord meant it to be. You go to church with that attitude this Sunday, and nobody will keep you away the next . . . The family of God contains people of various ethnological, cultural, class, and denominational differences. I have learned that there can be minor disagreements of theology, methods and motives, but that within the true Church there is a mysterious unity that overrides all divisive factors."

Counseling Strategy

1. Congratulate him on his interest in the church. We are being obedient to God when we identify with the local church. In church we are seeking the opportunity to worship, fellowship, evangelize, study the Bible, pray, and participate in the Lord's Supper.

2. Becoming a member of a local church does not save us. We identify with a church because we are saved and desire to be obedient. Jesus said, "I am the door: by me if any man enter in, he shall be saved" (John 10:9, KJV). Ask him if he has received Jesus Christ as his Lord and Savior. Share "Steps to Peace with God," page 5.

3. After trusting Christ, the inquirer should seek to identify immediately with a local church. Counsel him to pray for God's guidance in finding the right church, one which exalts Christ, preaches and teaches the Word of God, and evangelizes the lost.

4. Once a member of a church, he should be faithful in attendance.

5. He should seek a place of service in the church. Opportunities are always available if we offer ourselves in service to God.

6. Counsel him to support the church financially. Other Christian causes and ministries are worthy of our giving, but in order to function and grow, the local church should receive a substantial part of one's tithes and offerings.

Scripture

Revelation 21:2

Additional Scriptures

THE ACTS OF THE APOSTLES presents the birth of the church, its early growth and personalities involved.

THE EPISTLES were directed to the church, and provide its only guidelines for faith and practice, in the past, present, and future.

CULTS

Background

What is a cult? It is a group which teaches doctrines or beliefs which deviate from those held by the historical, evangelical Christian Church. They major on half-truths, or they distort truth. The little truth which they do use is often mixed with error and therefore dangerous; cults do succeed in deceiving many. This was spoken of by Paul: "For the time will come when men will not put up with sound doctrine.... They will turn their ears away from the truth and turn aside to myths" (2 Timothy 4:3,4, NIV). Jesus said, "For many shall come in my name, saying, I am Christ; and shall deceive many" (Mark 13:6, KJV).

What has Caused the Proliferation of Cults?

Cults thrive on ignorance and uncertainty. Christians who do not know whose they are, what they believe, or why they believe it are especially vulnerable. Churches are lax in their responsibility to teach God's Word and disciple Christians. Paul admonished Timothy to, "Preach the Word; be prepared in season and out of season; correct, rebuke and encourage — with great patience and careful instruction" (2 Timothy 4:2, NIV).

There are a Number of Features Common to all Cults:

- Extra-biblical or special revelation.
  To the sixty-six books of the Old and New Testaments they add their own revelations, which take precedence over the Bible. Or, a limited number of Scripture passages are used completely out of context resulting in erroneous interpretations.
  The Bible is explicit in defending its own integrity: "If anybody is preaching to you a gospel other than what you accepted, let him be eternally condemned" (Galatians 1:9, NIV). (See also Revelation 22:18,19.)

- Salvation by works.
  Any teaching that attempts to lead people into right relationship to God apart from the uniqueness of the person and work of the Lord Jesus Christ is in error. This can take the form of a complete rejection of Christ and His work, or a partial rejection that attempts to add to His work. The Gospel is of grace — plus nothing and minus nothing (See Ephesians 2:8,9).

- A denial of or lack of full recognition of Jesus Christ as God's Son.
  He is totally denied or relegated to a place that is less than He merits. "Who is a liar but he that denieth that Jesus is the Christ? He is antichrist that denieth the Father and the Son" (1 John 2:22, KJV).
  "For no other foundation can anyone lay than that which is laid, which is Jesus Christ" (1 Corinthians 3:11, RSV).
  "Christ is the exact likeness of the unseen God. He existed before God made anything at all, and, in fact, Christ himself is the Creator who made everything in heaven and earth" (Colossians 1:15,16, TLB).

"He is before all things, and in him all things hold together" (Colossians 1:17, RSV).

And the Word (Jesus) was made flesh and dwelt among us, (and we beheld his glory, the glory as of the only begotten of the Father,) full of grace and truth" (John 1:14, KJV).

"Neither is there salvation in any other; for there is none other name under heaven given among men, whereby we must be saved (Acts 4:12, KJV).

Counseling Strategy

1. The Christian who has been deceived into a cult.

   A. He needs to reassure himself about his personal relationship to Jesus Christ. Happy indeed is that believer who can say with the Apostle Paul "I know whom I have believed, and am persuaded that he is able to keep that which I have committed unto him against that day" (2 Timothy 1:12, KJV).

   B. He must constantly reaffirm his faith and commitment by adhering to the teachings of the Bible. "So then, just as you have received Christ Jesus as Lord, continue to live in him, rooted and built up in him, strengthened in the faith as you were taught, and overflowing with thankfulness. See to it that no one takes you captive through hollow and deceptive philosophy, which depends on human tradition and the basic principles of this world rather than on Christ" (Colossians 2:6-8, NIV).

   C. He needs to be sure he is identified with a local assembly of evangelical believers. Get involved in ministry, serving the Christ of the Word and reaching out to people in spiritual need. A person who has been redeemed from a cult can be a most effective witness to those who are still involved.

   D. Pray with him for definite deliverance from the cult and commitment to the Lord Jesus Christ and His Word.

2. If you counsel an agressive cultist, you will find it necessary to assume command of the conversation or he will attempt to overwhelm you with an endless defense of the cult's false doctrines and organization.

   You might interrupt with something like the following: "Yes, I understand that this is very meaningful to you, but let me ask you a few important questions."

   A. What do you think of Jesus? Is He God's Son? Is He the only Savior? (Use John 3:16 and Acts 4:12)

   B. What do you believe about sin? Are you a sinner? If you don't trust Jesus Christ for forgiveness, how will you find it?

   C. Whether you receive positive or negative answers to the above, ask the most important question of all:

Have you ever received Jesus Christ as your personal Savior? Or, do you know God's plan for peace and life? (Page 5).

D. Encourage the caller to take a definite stand for Christ by leaving the cult and former associations. There must be a break with the past.

E. Encourage him to get into a church that holds to the historic, evangelical Christian position where he can begin to study the Bible for what it actually says.

F. Pray with him for complete deliverance and for complete commitment to Christ and to the Word of God.

Scripture

False Teachers, False Doctrines Prophesied:

"But, dear friends, remember what the apostles of our Lord Jesus Christ foretold. They said to you, 'In the last times there will be scoffers who will follow their own ungodly desires.' These are the men who divide you, who follow mere natural instincts and do not have the Spirit."

Jude 17-19, NIV

"For such men are false apostles, deceitful workmen, masquerading as apostles of Christ. And no wonder, for Satan himself masquerades as an angel of light. It is not surprising, then, if his servants masquerade as servants of righteousness. Their end will be what their actions deserve."

2 Corinthians 11:13-15, NIV

2 Timothy 4:3-5, NIV

How To Discern Error:

"At that time if anyone says to you, 'Look, here is the Christ!' or, 'Look, there he is!' do not believe it. For false Christs and false prophets will appear and perform signs and miracles to deceive the elect — if that were possible. So be on your guard; I have told you everything ahead of time."

Mark 13:21-23, NIV

"Dear friends, do not believe every spirit, but test the spirits to see whether they are from God, because many false prophets have gone out into the world. This is how you can recognize the Spirit of God: Every spirit that acknowledges that Jesus Christ has come in the flesh is from God, but every spirit that does not acknowledge Jesus is not from God. This is the spirit of the antichrist, which you have heard is coming and even now is already in the world."

1 John 4:1-3, NIV

". . . Evil men and imposters will go from bad to worse, deceiving and being deceived. But as for you, continue in what you have learned and have become convinced of, because you know those from whom you learned it, and how from infancy you have known the holy Scriptures which are able to make you wise for salvation through faith in Christ Jesus."

2 Timothy 3:13-15, NIV

How To Resist Error:

"Study to show thyself approved unto God, a workman that needeth not to be ashamed, rightly dividing the word of truth."   2 Timothy 2:15, KJV

"That ye may approve things that are excellent; that ye may be sincere and without offence till the day of Christ; being filled with the fruits of righteousness, which are by Jesus Christ, unto the glory and praise of God."

Philippians 1:10,11, KJV

"Watch ye and pray, lest ye enter into temptation. The spirit truly is ready, but the flesh is weak."   Mark 14:38, KJV

"But you, dear friends, build yourselves up in your most holy faith and pray in the Holy Spirit. Keep yourselves in God's love as you wait for the mercy of our Lord Jesus Christ to bring you to eternal life. Be merciful to those who doubt; snatch others from the fire and save them; to others show mercy, mixed with fear — hating even the clothing stained by corrupted flesh."   Jude 20-23, NIV

See also False Doctrines

64

DEATH
Background

The Bible contains hundreds of references to death. It is a formidable foe: "the last enemy that shall be destroyed is death (1 Corinthians 15:26), but also a conquered foe: "death is swallowed up in victory" (1 Corinthians 15:54, KJV).

Jesus Christ has changed the meaning of death. The Scriptures amply support this premise.

At death, the spirit of the believing Christian enters immediately into the presence of the Lord. Physical death is but a transition from life on earth with Christ to life in heaven with Christ. Death does not alter the continuity of relationship; it only enriches it.

"To be with Christ is far better" (cf., Philippians 1:23, KJV). The Apostle confirms that the transition is immediate: We are confident, I say, and willing rather to be absent from the body, and to be present with the Lord" (2 Corinthians 5:8, KJV).

The Bible teaches that someday the "dead in Christ" are going to be resurrected, at which time we shall be given new bodies. We don't know exactly just what or how these new bodies will be, except that they will be spiritual, permanent, and glorious.

"And just as we have borne the likeness of the earthly man, so shall we bear the likeness of the man from heaven" (1 Corinthians 15:49, NIV). "But we know that when he (Christ) shall appear, we shall be like him, for we shall see him as he is" (1 John 3:2). (See also 1 Corinthians 15:51-58.)

Billy Graham writes of the "Resurrection that blasts apart the finality of death, providing an alternative to the stifling, settling dust of death and opens the way to new life."

At the Second Coming of the Lord Jesus, the believing dead will be resurrected and joined immediately to Him. "The dead in Christ shall rise first; then we which are alive and remain shall be caught up together with them in the clouds, to meet the Lord in the air; and so shall we ever be with the Lord" (1 Thessalonians 4:16,17, KJV).

We have hope beyond the grave! "If only for this life we have hope in Christ, we are to be pitied more than all men" (1 Corinthians 15:19, NIV). The reuniting of living believers with those who have died before the coming of our Lord is called our blessed hope (See Titus 2:13).

Thus, the Christian should be able to confront death realistically yet victoriously. Though inevitable and often unexpected, it should never completely catch us off guard. Death should never be the "great unknown" which produces fear and terror; it should be, rather, the moment when we no longer see "through a glass, darkly" but "face to face" (1 Corinthians 13:12, KJV).

Counseling Strategy

1. If the inquirer is a Christian, bear in mind that death and bereavement bring changes and adjustments.

    Attempt to be considerate and understanding. "Wherefore comfort one another with these words" (1 Thessalonians 4:18, KJV). As you share Scriptures from the BACKGROUND, suggest that they be noted and later reviewed and possibly memorized for added strength and encouragement. Be sensitive to guide him to new commitment and devotion to Christ. If there is any uncertainty about his relationship to Christ, share "Steps to Peace with God," page 5.

2. If the inquirer is not a Christian, emphasize that to be properly prepared for death a person must make the all-important decision about his eternal relationship during this lifetime.

    Invite him to receive Jesus Christ as his personal Lord and Savior. Share "Steps to Peace with God," page 5.

3. Encourage him to read and study the Bible and to cultivate habits of prayer.

4. Encourage him to become involved in a Bible-teaching church for fellowship, worship, and Bible study. This will also help him to be constantly reassured as to the "Blessed Hope."

Scripture

"Yea, though I walk through the valley of the shadow of death, I will fear no evil, for thou art with me; thy rod and thy staff they comfort me."
Psalm 23:4, KJV

"Let not your heart be troubled: ye believe in God, believe also in me. In my Father's house are many mansions: if it were not so, I would have told you. I go to prepare a place for you. And if I go and prepare a place for you, I will come again, and receive you unto myself; that where I am, there ye may be also."
John 14:1-3, KJV

"Jesus said to her, 'I am the resurrection and the life. He who believes in me will live, even though he dies.' "
John 11:25, NIV

"For to me to live is Christ, and to die is gain."   Philippians 1:21, KJV

"But as it is written, Eye hath not seen, nor ear heard, neither have entered into the heart of man, the things which God hath prepared for them that love him. But God hath revealed them unto us by his Spirit: for the Spirit searcheth all things, yea, the deep things of God."
1 Corinthians 2:9,10, KJV

"But our citizenship is in heaven. And we eagerly await a Savior from there, the Lord Jesus Christ, who, by the power that enables him to bring everything under his control, will transform our lowly bodies so that they will be like his glorious body."   Philippians 3:20, NIV

See also Grief

DEMONS

Background

In both the religious and secular worlds there is a growing recognition of, and interest in, demonic activity. The Bible recognizes the reality of this activity. "For our struggle is not against flesh and blood (human beings), but against the rulers, against the authorities, against the powers of this dark world and against the spiritual forces of evil in the heavenly realms" (Ephesians 6:12, NIV). Demons, also called in Scripture "familiar spirits" (1 Samuel 28:7), "unclean spirits" (Luke 4:36), and "seducing spirits" (1 Timothy 4:1, KJV), are invisible, disembodied, and superhuman in intelligence.

Like Satan, demons fell into condemnation through pride and are the adversaries of both God and man. Though real and active, the devil and his messengers (demons) are often blamed for many things for which they are not guilty. Some Christians tend to blame all erratic behavior on "demon possession" when, actually, most of it is the result of mankind's sinful, selfish nature. Also, sometimes individuals who are on drugs, who have been dabbling in the occult or eastern religions, or who are mentally ill will appear to be afflicted by demons.

The Christian who desires to be used by God to help people with spiritual problems might do well to heed the admonition of the Apostle John: "Beloved, believe not every spirit, but try the spirits (put them to the test) whether they are of God" or "that spirit of antichrist" (1 John 4:1,3, KJV). Thus, demons must be discerned, tested, resisted, and rejected by believers. (See 1 Corinthians 12:10; Ephesians 4:27; 6:10-18; 1 Peter 5:8,9; 1 John 4:1-6; James 4:7.)

Through the victory of Jesus Christ over Satan and his host, and in the mighty name of Jesus Christ and in the power of the Holy Spirit, the child of God can overcome Satan and his demons. (See Matthew 8:16,17; 12:28; Mark 16:17; Acts 19:15.)

Our resources against the hosts of wickedness are:
- Watchfulness (1 Peter 5:8).
- Prayer (John 15:7).
- The appropriation of the whole armor of God. (See Matthew 26:41 and Ephesians 6:10-18.)

Counseling Strategy

For the Non-Christian:

If the inquirer speaks of spiritual bondage or demonic activity or behavior, ask questions. Try to discern if the situation is truly as he describes it. "Tell me about it," is a phrase to be used and repeated until the actual problem emerges. Do not hesitate to press for answers.

1. Emphasize the efficacy of the sacrifice of Christ on the Cross to solve sinful problems. "The blood of Jesus Christ, (God's) Son cleanseth us from all

sin" (1 John 1:7, KJV).   Share "Steps to Peace With God," page 5.

2. If he receives Christ, encourage him to read and study the Word of God every day. Offer to send *Living In Christ* to help him get started.

   He should also pray daily. These two disciplines usually become established for the inquirer who gets into a local Bible-teaching church where he can fellowship, worship the Lord, study the Bible, and learn the joys of a consecrated life.

3. If you find that you are dealing with a person who is truly demonized, follow the steps outlined below in regard to "Dealing With A Legitimate Case Of One Demonized."

For the Christian:

If he fears demonic activity, proceed as follows:

1. Question him about the circumstances. Why does he think demons are involved? Sometimes fears are induced by other well-meaning but mistaken Christians.

2. Remind him that all God's resources are at our disposal:
   Satan is a defeated foe (1 John 3:8).
   Christ lives in the believer (Colossians 1:27).
   The Holy Spirit empowers him (Acts 1:8 and 2 Timothy 1:7).
   The Word of God guides him (2 Timothy 3:16,17.)

3. See the last two paragraphs of the BACKGROUND for further guidance. The Christian is assured of victory as he submits constantly to the Lordship of Christ, to the authority and the illumination of the Scriptures, to the discipline of overcoming prayer, and as he becomes involved with a dynamic group of believers in a local Bible-teaching church.

4. It may be that the inquirer is suffering severe guilt from actual sin in his life and is raising the issue of demonic influence in an attempt to transfer the blame instead of facing his personal responsibility for it. True repentance and confession of sin would remove the guilt and also the root causes of the "oppression."   Share "Restoration," page 11, emphasizing 1 John 1:9.

5. It may be that you are dealing with a legitimate case of one who is demonized. If so, follow the steps outlined below.

Dealing With One Demonized:

Be careful. You must be sure that you are dealing with a bona fide case of demon oppression and not a condition resulting from some physical, psychological or spiritual disorder. The inquirer could be greatly harmed if told that he is demonized when actually he isn't!

1. Note carefully the symptoms of the disturbed person, depending upon the Lord for wisdom and discernment. A demonized person is just that. He is either being influenced by or has been invaded by an evil spirit. Extremely bizarre behavior will be present. He may speak in a strange language or dialect. Sometimes blasphemous or foul and immoral language is used.

2. Dealing with such a person is not to be taken lightly. Resistance is often tenacious and much time is required to properly deal with the difficulties.

Obviously the telephone counselor can't spend this amount of time. Jesus once informed His disciples that they had no power in a particular instance because "this kind (demons) goeth not out but by prayer and fasting" (Matthew 17:21, KJV).

3. In cases where a demonized person was set free, those involved were unanimous in stating that much prayer, usually involving a group of Christians called together for the purpose, is a great necessity. As the Spirit of God leads, and at moments that He would indicate, a command should be given in the name of the Lord Jesus Christ and with His authority (Matthew 28:18), in order to expel the evil spirit. One person should assume a leadership role as the spokesman.

   On deliverance, immediately claim victory in the name of the Lord Jesus Christ, and praise God for it.

4. Counsel the inquirer immediately to seek strong friendships in the family of God. He can greatly fortify God's work in his life by reading and studying God's Word, praying, and beginning to witness to God's marvelous work in his life. (See Mark 9:19-22.)

Scripture

"Submit yourselves, then, to God. Resist the devil, and he will flee from you."
James 4:7, NIV

"Be self-controlled and alert. Your enemy the devil prowls around like a roaring lion looking for someone to devour. Resist him, standing firm in the faith, because you know that your brothers throughout the world are undergoing the same kind of sufferings."
1 Peter 5:8,9, NIV

"Then Jesus came to them and said, 'All authority in heaven and on earth has been given to me.'"
Matthew 28:18, NIV

"Dear friends, do not believe every spirit, but test the spirits to see whether they are from God, because many false prophets have gone out into the world. This is how you can recognize the Spirit of God: Every spirit that acknowledges that Jesus Christ has come in the flesh is from God, but every spirit that does not acknowledge Jesus is not from God. This is the spirit of antichrist, which you have heard is coming and even now is already in the world."
1 John 4:1-6, NIV

Revelation 12:11, NIV
1 John 3:8, NIV

DEPRESSION

Background

Depression is possibly responsible for more pain and distress than any other affliction of mankind. It is difficult to define, describe its symptoms, and treat. The dictionary defines it as an emotional condition, either neurotic or psychotic, characterized by feelings of hopelessness, inadequacy, gloominess, dejection, sadness, difficulty in thinking and concentration, and inactivity.

Depressed persons have a negative self-image which is often accompanied by feelings of guilt, shame, and self-criticism. Some neurotic depression is linked to wrong conduct or behavior and wrong reactions to such conduct. After a series of improper acts and subsequent faulty reactions, guilt and depression set in. If sin is at the heart of the problem, it should never be minimized. Neither should support be given to the idea that other things and other people are responsible for behaviorial problems. Either agreeing with him in this or not taking seriously his expression of sin and guilt could rob him of any real and lasting solutions. Both the Christian and the non-Christian may be victims of depression. Either is often concerned only with feeling better. But this is not first in order of priority. Rather, he must seek the causes which may have contributed to his depression. Putting his life in order spiritually will eventually make him feel better.

It is at this point where the Scriptures can be used. The release of the Holy Spirit's power must inevitably result in positive steps on a road to recovery and wholeness. The Christian witness must seek to be an encourager. Even if no spiritual decision is reached, try to leave your inquirer with a sense of hope and well-being. Be patient. Complex problems for which there are no quick and easy solutions are often involved in depression. The depressed will not "snap out of it" on command. Often months of professional help are needed.

Be a good listener. Don't probe too deeply, but do ask questions and then wait for something to emerge in the conversation which will provide the "handle" for offering spiritual solutions. Do not attempt to offer solutions before you are informed of the problem.

Counseling Strategy

For the Non-Christian:

1. Your inquirer may reveal symptoms of depression as a result of unresolved anger, resentment, real or imagined wrongs, self-pity, guilt, immorality, etc. Assure him of your interest and your desire to help him search for solutions.

2. Ask him if he has ever trusted in Jesus Christ as his personal Lord and Savior. If indicated, share "Steps to Peace with God," page 5. Remember that it would be a disservice to the inquirer to minimize in any way the seriousness of sin. In order for him to experience forgiveness, there must be recognition and confession of sin.

3. Share the section on "Assurance," page 9. Inform him that this experience with Christ offers real hope. It could result in new awareness and understanding in his desire and effort to cope with the problems related to his depressed state.

4. Encourage him to read and study God's Word. This will teach the will and ways of God. It will bring his thinking in line with God and result in inner peace (See Isaiah 26:3).

5. Encourage him to learn to pray and to do so daily. Through prayer we confess our sins and are renewed. We learn to experience God's constant presence and approval. We worship as we praise and thank Him. And we voice our requests for our own needs and those of others.

6. Suggest that he cultivate friendships with people who will provide the support and encouragement he needs. Such friends may be found in a Bible-teaching church, a Bible class, or a Christian singles' group. This fellowship may also provide opportunities for Christian service in which concerns are focused on the needs of others.

7. Encourage him to seek out a qualified pastor or a Christian psychologist for continued counseling in order that all the facets of his depression may be dealt with in the light of Scripture.

For The Christian:

1. A Christian also may suffer from depression in reaction to adverse situations, defeats, and set-backs; such as a death in the family, a rebellious son or daughter, or loss of employment.

    A. In such cases you should always offer a loving word of encouragement, such as:

    "You are not alone in your suffering."
    "God cares and will not leave you alone."
    "The Lord Jesus not only bore our sins, but also our sorrows and heartaches."

    B. Suggest that his present problem might be due to his inability to trust God fully in all circumstances of life. He may need to rededicate his life to Christ as he seeks to be responsive and obedient to God's will (See Romans 12:1,2).

    C. Suggest a recommitment to the disciplines of Bible study and prayer (See Proverbs 3:5,6 and Isaiah 26:3).

    D. Suggest that he be faithful in worship and service through the church.

Billy Graham has written: "Discouragement is the very opposite of faith. It is Satan's device to thwart the work of God in our lives. Discouragement blinds our eyes to the mercy of God and makes us perceive only the unfavorable circumstances. I have never met a person who spent time in daily prayer, in the study of the Word of God, and who was strong in faith, who was ever discouraged for very long."

2. A Christian may also be depressed because of spiritual disobedience and unresolved sin in such areas as anger and bitterness, jealousy, grudges, a divorce, immorality, etc.

   A. As the problem is revealed, encourage the inquirer by telling him that he is right to seek a solution. Reassure him that the first step back to wholeness is spiritual renewal.

   B. Share "Restoration," page 11, emphasizing Proverbs 28:13 and 1 John 1:9.

   C. As he responds to the Scriptures in Restoration, point out that other steps may be necessary beyond his act of recommitment. For example, he may have to mend fences broken down as a result of gossip, criticism, envy, immorality, etc. He should consider restitution in a case of theft or fraud.

   D. Suggest that he make serious commitment to Bible study. Learning to think God's thoughts is a valuable aid to spiritual recovery (See Philippians 4:8, NIV and Romans 12:2, NIV).

   E. Suggest that he become involved in a Bible-teaching church where worship, fellowship, and service are available.

   F. Suggest that he consider a serious commitment to professional counseling with a qualified pastor or Christian psychologist until all issues involved in the depression are resolved in the light of Scripture.

3. A Christian may also be depressed because of setting standards and goals for himself which are beyond his ability to attain. This may be true both for economic or spiritual goals; failure brings on depression.

   A. Patiently point out that goals which others may set for themselves and seem to attain may not be right for the inquirer. The fact that he has arrived at his present emotional state may indicate that he has not been on track in setting such goals.

   B. Point out that success or failure cannot be measured by any human standard, but by the following:
   Is what I desire in conformity with God's will and can it be supported by Scripture?
   Is what I desire for the glory of God or to satisfy some personal whim or selfish ambition? Have I been motivated by spiritual pride?
   Is what I desire in line with the guidance given by the Apostle Paul:
   (1) Be what I am — what God has made me; learn to live with my strengths and limitations. "But by the grace of God, I am what I am" (1 Corinthians 15:10, KJV).
   (2) Attempting to emulate someone else (keeping up with the Joneses)

is spiritually undesirable and counterproductive (see 2 Corinthians 10:12, NIV).

4. Suggest that the inquirer renew his spiritual commitment. "Seek ye first the kingdom of God, and his righteousness; and all these things shall be added unto you" (Matthew 6:33, KJV).

5. Suggest that he learn the disciplines of Bible study and prayer.

6. Suggest that he rearrange his priorities so that they are more in line with his abilities and that he take one day at a time in doing so.

7. Suggest that he make a serious commitment to professional counseling, if follow up is needed. A qualified pastor or Christian psychologist should be sought.

Scripture

"Surely he took up our infirmities and carried our sorrows, yet we considered him stricken by God, smitten by him, and afflicted. But he was pierced for transgressions, he was crushed for our iniquities; the punishment that brought us peace was upon him, and by his wounds we are healed."   Isaiah 53:4,5, NIV

"We are hard pressed on every side, but not crushed; perplexed, but not in despair; persecuted, but not abandoned; struck down, but not destroyed."   2 Corinthians 4:8,9, NIV

"I have been crucified with Christ and I no longer live, but Christ lives in me. The life I live in the body, I live by faith in the Son of God, who loved me and gave himself for me."   Galatians 2:20, NIV

"Trust in the Lord with all your heart and lean not on your own understanding; in all your ways acknowledge him, and he will make your paths straight."   Proverbs 3:5,6, NIV

"A man's spirit sustains him in sickness, but a crushed spirit who can bear?"   Proverbs 18:14, NIV

Psalm 38:1-4,21,22, NIV

DIVORCE

Background

Divorce could be described as a married couple deciding they no longer want to fulfill their commitment to marriage. Although usually only one person initiates the action, both may have contributed to the breakup to some degree.

Divorce is a shattering experience, and its wounds heal slowly. It takes time for the parties to get things sorted out so that they are able to deal objectively with themselves and their situation. It may be difficult for them to cut through all the feelings of alienation, rejection, bitterness and confusion. With a high percentage of our nation's marriages ending in divorce, it is probable that a counselor will be challenged with this problem.

Billy Graham comments: "I am opposed to divorce and regard the increase in divorces today as one of the most alarming problems in society. However, I know that the Lord can forgive and heal, even when great sin may have been involved. The church is made up of sinners. When Paul wrote to the Corinthians he gave a long list of evils and then added: 'And such were some of you' (1 Corinthians 6:11). They had been forgiven and had become a part of the Church, the Body of Christ."

Counseling Strategy

1. Encouragement is greatly needed.

    The inquirer may feel rejected, having lost the sense of personal worth. This is common for divorced persons. Tell him that you appreciate the call, that you want to talk with him. God loves and accepts us just as we are.

2. Question the inquirer about his relationship to Jesus Christ.

    Has he ever received Jesus as his Lord and Savior? If indicated, share "Steps to Peace with God," page 5. Although he may feel rejected, alienated, and devastated, emphasize that God can make all things new (2 Corinthians 5:17). What has been done — the divorce — perhaps cannot be undone. The inquirer must begin where he is to build life on a new foundation. That foundation is Jesus Christ.

3. Counsel about the importance of Bible reading and prayer as sources of strength.

    Does he have a Bible? If not, suggest going to a local Christian book store to obtain an easy-to-understand translation of the Bible: the New International Version, the Living Bible, or the New American Standard. Ask if we may send *Living In Christ* to encourage him in starting to study the Bible.

4. Suggest that the person seek a Bible-teaching church for fellowship, worship and service.

   He may need time to build understanding and new personal relationships. Often a Christian singles group will provide the needed encouragement.

5. Pray with him for healing of emotions, peace of mind, restored confidence, strength, and spiritual understanding.

6. Suggest that he seek special counseling if he feels the need for it. A pastor or a Christian psychologist may be helpful.

Points To Remember As You Counsel:

1. What has been done is past. Start where your inquirer is now and go on from there.

2. Try to guide the conversation so that he won't feel it necessary to engage in any "post mortems" of the experience. Attempt rather to direct his attention to God who will help him in reaching solutions.

3. Remain neutral. Do not assume that your inquirer is either guilty or innocent. A judgmental or "holier than thou" attitude will close doors to witnessing.

4. Christians are not immune to marriage breakups. If your inquirer is truly a Christian, proceed as follows:

   A. Ask him to confess any bitterness, anger or other sin. He may need to face realistically any wrong attitudes that contributed to the divorce. Share "Restoration," page 11. Emphasize 1 John 1:9.

   B. Encourage the person to develop a new interest in reading and studying the Bible. He should also be faithful in prayer. "Casting all your care upon him, for he careth for you" (1 Peter 5:7, KJV).

   C. Urge the inquirer to establish or renew a relationship with a church, in spite of feelings of guilt or fear of criticism. He needs the church now more than ever. Perhaps the church has a singles group which would be helpful.

   D. Pray with him for healing, peace of mind and the ability to make the necessary adjustments to a different life-style.

Scripture

Encouragement To Walk With The Lord:

"Trust in the Lord with all thine heart, and lean not unto thine own understanding; in all thy ways acknowledge him and he shall direct thy paths."
Proverbs 3:5,6, KJV

"Do not be anxious about anything, but in everything, by prayer and petition, with thanksgiving, present your requests to God."

Philippians 4:6, NIV

"Do your best to present yourself to God as one approved, a workman who does not need to be ashamed and who correctly handles the word of truth." 2 Timothy 2:15, NIV

"But grow in the grace and knowledge of our Lord and Savior Jesus Christ." 2 Peter 3:18, NIV

Healing The Wounds:

"Praise the Lord, O my soul; and forget not all his benefits. He forgives all my sins and heals all my diseases; he redeems my life from the pit and crowns me with love and compassion. He satisfies my desires with good things, so that my youth is renewed like the eagle's." Psalm 103:2-5, NIV

"Heal me, O Lord, and I will be healed; save me and I will be saved, for you are the one I praise." Jeremiah 17:14, NIV

2 Timothy 1:7, NIV
Psalm 23:3

DIVORCE, CONTEMPLATING
Background

Divorce, the legal dissolution of marriage, is a departure from what God intended and is not endorsed by Scripture except under limited conditions. Divorce is the result of sin in the lives of one or both of the partners. More often than not, both are to blame to some degree. Pride and selfishness often contribute to the conditions that lead to divorce.

Divorce is often the product of inflexible wills. "Jesus replied, Moses permitted you to divorce your wives because your hearts were hard. But it was not this way from the beginning" (Matthew 19:8, NIV). It was not God's original design for marriage.

No manipulation of Scripure or rationalization makes divorce right. Scripture states:

> "For this reason a man will leave his father and mother and be united to his wife, and they will become one flesh" (Genesis 2:24, NIV).

> The Apostle Paul wrote: "To the married I give this command (not I, but the Lord): a wife must not separate from her husband . . . And a husband must not divorce his wife" (1 Corinthians 7:10, NIV).

> "Has not the Lord made them one? In flesh and spirit they are his . . . So guard yourselves in your spirit, and do not break faith with the wife of your youth. 'I hate divorce,' says the Lord God of Israel" (Malachi 2:15,16, NIV).

Limited Conditions Under Which Divorce May be Permitted:

1. When a spouse is guilty of sexual immorality such as adultery or homosexuality and has no intention of repenting or seeking God's forgiveness, or forsaking his or her sin and living in faithfulness to his or her spouse. (See Matthew 19:9.)

2. When one partner deserts the other, especially when an unbelieving partner deserts a Christian spouse. (See 1 Corinthians 7:15.)

If someone is married and divorced before coming to Christ, he should continue on as he is. If the person has remarried, he should attempt to make a successful second marriage. Leaving the second spouse to return to the first would be wrong. Two wrongs never make a right!

Having an unbelieving spouse is not grounds for divorce. To the contrary, the Christian spouse is encouraged to "live in peace" with the unbelieving partner, with the goal of winning him to faith in Christ. (See 1 Corinthians 7:12-16.)

Count the Cost of Such Action:

1. Is it displeasing to God? (See Malachi 2:15,16.)

2. Will it disrupt the continuity of life and adversely affect other people: children, parents, extended families?

3. Will it really solve any problems, or will it rather create a whole range of new ones? Divorce is an emotionally traumatic experience.

Exhaust Every Option in Search for Solutions:

1. Attempt to work things out on a personal level in all humility and with a forgiving spirit. (See Matthew 18:21,22.)

2. Submit to serious counseling with a Christian marriage counselor or a qualified pastor.

3. If necessary, experiment with a trial separation while searching for a redemptive solution. In a case of physical or psychological abuse, homosexuality, drunkenness, drugs, etc., a separation might be advisable.

Counseling Strategy

1. Demonstrate a loving, caring attitude. Reassure the inquirer by telling him you are glad to talk with him in the search for a solution. You want to be a friend and share any insights you can.

2. Listen attentively, letting him tell the story and ventilate feelings until you feel you have a grasp of the situation.

3. Avoid playing judge or jury. Don't take sides. Your goal should be to present a scriptural point of view and challenge the inquirer to make his own decision, knowing that he will have to live with it for the rest of his life. Remember the example of Jesus. He dealt gently with the woman at the well, even though He knew that she had had five husbands and was then living with one who was not her husband. He revealed Himself as Savior, and offered her "living water." (See John 4:9-42.)

4. Tell the inquirer that to expect God's help he must commit his life to Christ, whatever the cost. This commitment must be permanent regardless of the outcome of the present dilemma. Ask if he has ever received Jesus Christ as personal Lord and Savior. If indicated, explain "Steps to Peace with God," page 5.

5. After receiving Christ, he can rightfully expect the Lord's help. The person will now have a new dimension to his life and a new perspective which should be helpful in reaching solutions. He may depend on the resources and insights found in God's Word, which he should begin to read and study. The inquirer may take his life and all his problems to God in prayer. Prayer and Bible Study will give him the disposition to make adjustments in his own personality and will help him in seeking restoration with the spouse through repentance and confession.

6. Encourage him to exhaust all of his options in the search for a scriptural solution.

7. Pray with him for God's intervention in putting his life and marriage together according to Scripture.

If he is a Christian, challenge him to put his life in order on the basis of "Restoration," page 11, emphasizing 1 John 1:9 and Romans 12:1,2.

Scripture

"When a woman marries, the law binds her to her husband as long as he is alive. But if he dies, she is no longer bound to him; the laws of marriage no longer apply to her. Then she can marry someone else if she wants to. That would be wrong while he was alive, but it is perfectly all right after he dies."
                                                                    Romans 7:2, TLB

"Whoso findeth a wife findeth a good thing, and obtaineth favor of the Lord."
                                                                    Proverbs 18:22, KJV

"The man should give his wife all that is her right as a married woman, and the wife should do the same for her husband: for a girl who marries no longer has full right to her own body, for her husband then has his rights to it, too; and in the same way the husband no longer has full right to his own body, for it belongs also to his wife."
                                                                    1 Corinthians 7:3,4, TLB

"Husbands, in the same way be considerate as you live with your wives, and treat them with respect as the weaker partner and as heirs with you of the gracious gift of life, so that nothing will hinder your prayers."
                                                                    1 Peter 3:7, NIV

"Do nothing out of selfish ambition or vain conceit, but in humility consider others better than yourselves. Each of you should look not only to your own interests, but also to the interests of others. Your attitude should be the same as that of Christ Jesus."
                                                                    Philippians 2:3-5, NIV

DIVORCE AFTER YEARS OF MARRIAGE

Background

It is difficult to describe the sense of shock, hurt, bewilderment, emptiness, anger, rejection, isolation, and loss of self-worth felt when someone has been deserted or divorced after many years of marriage. The person wonders:

Can this really be happening to me? How could he do this to me? Where did I fail? What could I have done differently? The most important question is what do I do now?

In spite of the trauma, the person must be helped to realize that life goes on. The fact of the divorce must be accepted; he is now single and must face the future as such. It is futile to continually dredge up the past, reliving it. Fact will not change by self-torturing questions. It is entirely possible that he couldn't have done anything differently to save the marriage.

An emotionally healthy person will go on and grow with the present. The Apostle Paul gives the example: "...this one thing I do, forgetting those things which are behind, and reaching forth unto (toward) those things which are before..." (Philippians 3:13, KJV). He must look at the experience as transitional, as a time to make adjustments, of expanding personality through reading, reflection and building or re-building friendships which will help him expand and grow.

If the person needs professional counseling during the transition he should look for a qualified pastor or a Christian psychiatrist or psychologist who can deal with the problems in the light of Scripture.

Counseling Strategy

1. Encourage the inquirer by projecting love and understanding. The hurts, emptiness, and sense of rejection may be very deep.

2. Be a good listener, attempting to get the whole picture before offering any comment. Sometimes we respond too quickly with advice, when a question to stimulate conversation would be more in order.

3. When you feel you have a proper understanding, reassure him with verses from SCRIPTURE at the end of this section. Emphasize that God loves him and cares about what is happening. Jesus knows what grief and sorrow is. "He (was) despised and rejected of men" (Isaiah 53:3, KJV). Ask the caller if he has ever received Jesus Christ as personal Lord and Savior. Explain "Steps to Peace With God," page 5.

4. Urge him to read and study the Bible. This will give the inquirer perspective and insight as he attempts to adjust to a new life-style and grow in the Lord.

5. Counsel the person to pray every day. "Do not be anxious about anything, but in everything, by prayer and petition, with thanksgiving, present your requests to God. And the peace of God, which transcends all understanding, will guard your hearts and minds in Christ Jesus" (Philippians 4:6,7, NIV)

6. Counsel him to become involved in a Bible-teaching church. Often a Christian singles group can be found which will provide opportunities to share experiences, to grow, and to serve.

7. Pray with the inquirer for the Lord's help in this difficult time of transition as he seeks to build a new life.

Scripture

"For I know the plans I have for you, declares the Lord, plans to prosper you and not to harm you, plans to give you hope and a future."

Jeremiah 29:11, NIV

"How precious to me are your thoughts, O God! How vast is the sum of them! Were I to count them, they would outnumber the grains of sand. When I awake, I am still with you." Psalm 139:17,18, NIV

"You have made known to me the path of life; you will fill me with joy in your presence, with eternal pleasures at your right hand."

Psalm 16:11, NIV

"Because the Sovereign Lord helps me, I will not be disgraced. Therefore have I set my face like flint, and I know I will not be put to shame."

Isaiah 50:7, NIV

Psalm 16:8, NIV
Psalm 18:2, NIV

DOUBT

Background

Doubt can be debilitating. Hesitation and uncertainty are characteristic of the doubter. James says the "double-minded" man is "unstable in all he does. That man should not think he will receive anything from the Lord" (James 1:7, NIV)

Yet, it is not unusual for even a Christian to experience doubt. He may question, "Is the Bible really true?" when he hears a critic attack God's Word. In confusion over unanswered prayer, he may question, "Is God real? Does He really answer prayer?" When confronted with the reality of his own sinful desires, he may question, "Has God really saved me?"

Billy Graham writes: "Probably everyone has had doubts and uncertainties at times in his religious experience. When Moses went up on Mt. Sinai to receive the tablets of the Law from the hand of God, and had been a long time out of the sight of the people who stood anxiously awaiting his return, they became doubtful of his return. 'And they erected a golden calf to worship' " (cf., Exodus 32:8). Their apostasy was the result of doubting and uncertainty.

In spite of the tendency to doubt, we can be encouraged because honest doubt often leads to solid faith and deeper commitment.

The opposite of doubt, of course, is faith. James encouraged those who were passing through trials to "ask of God" and "ask in faith" (James 1:5,6, KJV). We must remember that doubt can be an effective tool of Satan. He caused Eve to doubt by asking, "Yea, hath God said" (Genesis 3:1, KJV). He will afflict us with doubts where we are the most vulnerable. Spiritual disobedience, disappointment, depression, illness, and even the fears of old age can trigger doubt.

Counseling Strategy

Those Who May Doubt Their Salvation:

1. Congratulate the inquirer for being so concerned about his doubts. God's Word offers real encouragement for the doubter.

2. If you discern that he has been trusting in things other than a personal relationship with Jesus Christ, explain "Steps to Peace with God," page 5.

3. If convinced that he has previously made a genuine commitment to Jesus Christ, ask him:

   A. Is he being disobedient? If this is the case, guide him through the page on "Restoration," page 11. Emphasize 1 John 1:9.

B. Has he been indifferent to spiritual things, not faithful in attending church, not reading the Bible, or not praying? Take him through "Restoration," page 11. Emphasize 1 John 1:9 and Romans 12:1,2.

C. Encourage him to step out anew in faith, to believe God (Acts 27:25). Urge him to take a definite stand for Christ, to get into the Word of God, to learn the discipline of prayer, and to work for Christ in a local church. Offer to send him *Living In Christ*.

D. Pray with him for a stronger faith relationship to God.

Those Who May Be Disillusioned Through Disappointments:

They may doubt God because of a divorce, a death in the family, a wayward son or daughter, unanswered prayer, or betrayal by another Christian.

1. Encourage him. God does love and care for us. He wants the inquirer to learn to walk with Him by faith.

2. Help him to identify the source of his doubts, emphasizing that it is not wrong to ask, "Why?" in life.

3. Remind him that God has never promised freedom from adversity in life. It may be that he needs to get his eyes off himself and his problems and back on God! He may need to see beyond the circumstances of his life to what God is attempting to teach him through them.

    God is faithful. The encroachment of doubt into one's mind doesn't mean that God has ceased to care.

4. He needs to reflect on God's goodness that he has seen demonstrated in the past, to remember evidences of God's faithfulness in his own life and in the lives of others. This will help to reassure his mind.

    A renewal of faith is in order. Encourage him to begin to trust in God's promises again. He should saturate his life with the Scriptures and believe God. Jesus said, "Blessed are those who have not seen and yet have believed" (John 20:29, NIV).

5. Pray with him for renewal, asking that he confess his doubts to God and pray for a dynamic faith.

6. Encourage him to be faithful in worship with God's people. The cultivation of relationships with other Christians will be helpful. Getting involved in service for Christ through the local church will fortify resolves and strengthen his commitment.

Reassuring Older People of Salvation:

Due to a number of changes that accompany advancing age, older people sometimes need to be reassured about their salvation and eternal relationship to God. Help them to remember:

1. To trust unquestionably the Lord Jesus Christ as their Lord and Savior. "Jesus answered, 'I am the way and the truth and the life. No one comes to the Father except through me' " (John 14:6, NIV). "For I am convinced that neither death nor life, neither angels nor demons, neither the present nor the future, nor any powers, neither height nor depth, nor anything else in

all creation, will be able to separate us from the love of God that is in Christ Jesus our Lord" (Romans 8:38,39, NIV).

2. To trust unquestionably their relationship to their Heavenly Father. "Yet to all who received him, to those who believed in his name, he gave the right to become children of God" (John 1:12, NIV). "Beloved, now are we the sons of God, and it doth not yet appear what we shall be: but we know that, when he shall appear, we shall be like him; for we shall see him as he is" (1 John 3:2, KJV).

3. To trust unquestionably the Word of God. "Your word, O Lord, is eternal; it stands firm in the heavens. Your faithfulness continues through all generations" (Psalm 119:89,90, NIV). "We have also a more sure word of prophecy; whereunto ye do well that ye take heed, as unto a light that shineth in a dark place, until the day dawn, and the day star arise in your hearts" (2 Peter 1:19, KJV).

Scripture

"If any of you lack wisdom, let him ask of God, that giveth to all men liberally, and upbraideth not; and it shall be given him. But let him ask in faith, nothing wavering. For he that wavereth is like a wave of the sea driven with the wind and tossed. For let not that man think that he shall receive anything of the Lord. A double-minded man is unstable in all his ways."

James 1:5-8, KJV

"Jesus saith unto him, Thomas, because thou hast seen me, thou hast believed: blessed are they that have not seen, and yet have believed."

John 20:29, KJV

"But without faith it is impossible to please him: for he that cometh to God must believe that he is, and that he is a rewarder of them that diligently seek him."

Hebrews 11:6, KJV

"The fool hath said in his heart, There is no God."

Psalm 14:1, KJV

DRUG ABUSE

Background

A drug is any substance which produces physical, mental or psychological changes in the user. Since earliest times, man has experimented with drugs in an effort to escape reality. Today, hundreds of millions of persons are involved in drugs which range all the way from mildly addictive caffeine to illegal, deeply addictive drugs such as heroin and cocaine.

Anyone can become physically and psychologically addicted to any drug if exposed to high dosages for a sufficiently long period of time.

Drug users come from all walks of life. Many of the roots of dependency are to be found in insecurity, fear, guilt, disappointments, immorality and deviate sexual behavior, frustration, stress, peer pressures, and intense competition as exemplified in professional sports, etc. Add to these the great spiritual vacuum which has resulted in a breakdown of moral standards, the disintegration of the home, four major wars in 50 years, and the staggering availability of drugs of every kind to every age group, including grade school children.

Drug dependency is a problem of the whole person — spiritual, physical, emotional and social. Once addicted, the dependent lives in an illusory world characterized by paralyzed feelings and emotional responses, mental denials and delusions, social isolation, and spiritual limbo. For many it is a helpless state, a life of no return.

Withdrawal for those seeking deliverance can be very painful, both physically and psychologically. Unmonitored withdrawal can be dangerous! Getting free from dependency and the subsequent rehabilitation is usually a long-term process. A strong support system involving the spiritual, emotional, mental, and physical is needed.

In order to be helped spiritually, the drug dependent must desire to be helped and must take some initial step to seek such help. This is where the Christian counselor comes in. We should seek his/her commitment to Jesus Christ as Savior and Lord. This initial step of faith should lead to a new perspective and motivation for the drug user which will lead, hopefully, to rehabilitation and a life of wholeness.

Even after commitment to Christ, however, there is often a need to work on the personal issues that led to the addiction such as, a poor self image, insecurity, incest, homosexuality, immorality, fear, guilt, etc.

Counseling Strategy

We can contribute in three ways:
- Help the individual spiritually by seeking his commitment to Christ.
- Put him in touch with a group or a drug center in his area where he can commit himself to withdrawal and rehabilitation.
- Stay with him in order to offer support and encouragement until he has a deeper understanding of his commitment to Christ and its implications.

1. Do not moralize about the evils of drugs or his addiction. Use the Scriptures on sin only as it occurs naturally in your presentation of the Gospel.

2. Be cordial. Be compassionate. Encourage him by saying that you are sympathetic and willing to listen and offer counsel.

3. Hear him out, giving ample opportunity for his expression of feelings and opinions. Reassure him of God's love. God's grace is sufficient to meet any need in his life. (A definition of grace: God loves us with no strings attached.)

4. He will need to be faced with his responsibility in his addiction. He, at some point, made a conscious choice to take drugs. He has moral responsibility for his behavior which led him into drugs. If he attempts to lay the blame for his problem at the feet of circumstances, other people, society, etc., always bring him gently back to the issue of personal and moral responsibility. "But each one is tempted when, by his own evil desire, he is dragged away and enticed," (James 1:14, NIV).

5. At the opportune moment, share "Steps to Peace with God," page 5.

6. Continue to follow-up steps, if indicated: Start reading and studying God's Word. Learn to pray. Begin to fellowship with a Bible-teaching church.

7. The drug-dependent person must abandon the people and surroundings which have tied him to drugs. He must stop all use of drugs. This will probably mean treatment at a drug center where his withdrawal and early rehabilitation can be properly monitored. Around-the-clock supervision is often needed.

    NOTE: The counselor often must take the initiative to help the dependent find a center for treatment and help him check in, or perhaps assist the addict's family in doing this. The addict cannot be trusted to handle this alone. He may promise, but never follow through.

    Both during and following treatment, the counselor should be as supportive as possible. Visit frequently. Start him in the reading and study of God's Word and prayer. Help him find a support group of Christian ex-addicts, if such is available. Get him involved in the life of a caring, Bible oriented church. Get him in touch with a Christian professional counselor or group experienced in treatment of addicts. He will need on-going help with those personal problems which led him into the addiction in the first place.

8. The counselor may state that he will attempt to assist the counselee in reaching a drug treatment center and support people in the area where he lives. CAUTION: Do not promise help, only that he will do the best he can. The Billy Graham Evangelistic Association has contact with people who can assist the addict in some cities.

9. Pray with the drug dependent person for courage, commitment, and for the power of the Holy Spirit to be released in his life. All these are necessary in the redemptive process. "For God hath not given us the spirit

of fear; but of power, and of love, and of a sound mind," (2 Timothy 1:7, KJV).

Scripture

"If the Son therefore shall make you free, ye shall be free indeed."

John 8:36, KJV

"In the same way, count yourselves dead to sin but alive to God in Christ Jesus. Therefore do not let sin reign in your mortal body so that you obey its evil desires. Do not offer the parts of your body to sin, as instruments of wickedness, but rather offer yourselves to God, as those who have been brought from death to life; and offer the parts of your body to him as instruments of righteousness."

Romans 6:11-13, NIV

"The Spirit of the Lord is upon me, because he hath anointed me to preach the gospel to the poor; he hath sent me to heal the broken-hearted, to preach deliverance to the captives ... And he began to say unto them, This day is this scripture fulfilled in your ears ... And they were all amazed, and spake among themselves, saying, What a word is this! For with authority and power he commandeth the unclean spirits, and they come out."

Luke 4:18,21,36, KJV

"For you have spent enough time in the past doing what pagans choose to do — living in debauchery, lust, drunkenness, orgies, carousing and detestable idolatry."

1 Peter 4:3, NIV

"But every man is tempted, when he is drawn away of his own lust, and enticed. Then when lust hath conceived, it bringeth forth sin: and sin, when it is finished, bringeth forth death."

James 1:14,15, KJV

ENEMIES

Background

An enemy may show hostility or ill-will and seek to do harm because of an antagonistic or destructive attitude. None of us is entirely free from unhappiness caused by the wrongs of others. Our inclination may be to respond in kind, to retaliate, "get even" "give more than you get." (See 1 Corinthians 2:14.)

But the Word of God always speaks about these kinds of responses:

"Live at peace with everyone" (Romans 12:18, NIV).

"Do not repay anyone evil for evil" (Romans 12:17, NIV).

"Do not take revenge" (Romans 12:19, NIV).

"Love your enemies.   Bless them that curse you" (Matthew 5:44, KJV).

"Do good to them that hate you"

"Pray for them which despitefully use you"

There are certain attitudes and actions which tend to create enemies or widen differences:

1. Selfish actions or lack of sensitivity toward others.

2. An unwillingness because of pride to realize that we may be the "offender" rather than the "offended."

3. Talking about people rather than to them, "putting them down" or criticizing their attitudes and actions instead of humbly confronting them. Propagating our own version of a story serves to polarize a relationship; a story usually grows worse as it is repeated by others. Such actions are hypocritical.

4. Deliberately ignoring a tense situation rather than praying about it and acting to correct it. Ignoring someone will not reduce tensions.

5. Abdicating responsibilty by passively enduring a situation rather than taking initiative.

6. Taking refuge behind a facade of "righteous indignation."

7. Believing that we are morally superior because we found something to condemn in others.

8. Not realizing that it is often harder to forgive those we have wronged than those who have wronged us.

9. Refusing to "go the second mile" or to "turn the other cheek" as taught in the Scriptures. We are expected to forgive up to "seventy times seven" (Matthew 18:21,22, KJV). Forgiveness is the essence of a redeemed life. "Forgive, and ye shall be forgiven" (Luke 6:37, KJV).

10. Disobeying God's Word which specifically commands us to love our enemies, bless them, do good to them, and pray for them (Matthew 5:44).

Billy Graham writes: "God can and will give you a forgiving spirit when you accept His forgiveness through Jesus Christ. When you do, you will realize that He has forgiven you so much that you will desire to forgive any wrong done to you. In the world, the policy of getting even with the other fellow is generally accepted. Among Christians, it is the policy to endure wrongs for the sake of Christ, forgiving that others might discover through us the grace of God in forgiving the sinner."

Counseling Strategy

1. Reassure the inquirer that God is mindful of us in every situation. His Word has something to say about enemies.
2. Ask him if he has ever received Jesus Christ as his personal Lord and Savior. If not, share "Steps to Peace with God," page 5.
3. If the inquirer is a Christian, encourage him to renew his commitment to Christ. Use "Restoration," page 11, emphasizing 1 John 1:9 and Romans 12:1.

    A new or renewed relationship with Christ should help to bring a new perspective to feelings about enemies.

4. Proceed to use the following which may open some windows to understanding about reconciliation. Make an effort to understand. Request information about the persons and problems involved:
    A. What caused the break in the relationship?
    B. Does he feel that he may have contributed to the problem?
    C. As far as he can determine, what is the attitude of the other person? Is the inquirer being totally honest in his attempts to evaluate the situation?
    D. Ask him how he feels about the "enemy"? Is he resentful? Embittered? Is he harboring ill-will or resentment?
    E. Emphasize that he has the obligation to forgive with all that this implies. He is to take the first step toward reconciliation. The mature Christian will always assume the responsibility for being a peacemaker. Encourage him to assume the attitude of Christ, who never demanded His "rights." When He was reviled or spit upon, He didn't retaliate.
    F. It is in the inquirer's best interest to clear up the situation as early as possible. "Settle matters quickly with your adversary who is taking you to court ... or he may hand you over to the judge ... and you may be thrown into prison ... you will not get out until you have paid the last penny" (Matthew 5:25,26, NIV).
    G. Any approach must be made with humility. Remember, only Jesus

was totally righteous, without sin. "A soft answer turneth away wrath" (Proverbs 15:1). "Speak the truth in love" (Ephesians 4:15).

H. Prayer must be sincerely offered for the other person with one's own heart open to solutions.

I. As the counselor, remember to pray with the inquirer, asking God to intervene by working with both parties for a successful solution.

J. Ask him what he intends to do as the first step towards reconciliation. Remind him that delayed action will hinder reconciliation.

Scripture

"When a man's ways please the Lord, he maketh even his enemies to be at peace with him."
                                                          Proverbs 16:7, KJV

"If it be possible, as much as lieth in you, live peaceably with all men."
                                                          Romans 12:18, KJV

"He must turn from evil and do good; he must seek peace and pursue it."
                                                          1 Peter 3:11, NIV

"But I say unto you, Love your enemies, bless them that curse you, do good to them that hate you, and pray for them which despitefully use you, and persecute you; that ye may be the children of your Father which is in heaven: for he maketh his sun to rise on the evil and the good, and sendeth rain on the just and on the unjust. For if ye love them which love you, what reward have ye? Do not even the publicans do the same?"
                                                          Matthew 5:44-46, KJV

"Then said Jesus, Father, forgive them; for they know not what they do."
                                                          Luke 23:34, KJV

Psalm 34:14, KJV
Romans 14:17-19, KJV
2 Timothy 2:22, KJV

See also Forgiveness

ENVY, JEALOUSY AND COVETOUSNESS

Background

Envy, jealousy, and covetousness are interrelated evils. Discontent with our position and possessions often indicates a self-centered attitude which leads to intolerant, resentful, and even malicious feelings toward a real or imagined rival. We may covet the success, personality, material possessions, good looks, or position of another. Then, in order to compensate a frustrated ego, we make unkind and destructive remarks and submerge ourselves in self-pity, anger, bitterness, and depression.

Cain envied Abel because Abel's offering was accepted by God while Cain's was not. He became jealous, coveting what had been denied him. Anger, bitterness, depression, and murder followed. "For where you have envy and selfish ambition, there you find disorder and every evil practice" (James 3:16, NIV).

Envy and jealous ambition motivated Lucifer to rebel against God. "I will ascend to heaven. I will raise my throne above the stars of God . . . I will make myself like the Most High" (Isaiah 14:13,14, NIV).

Billy Graham writes: "You cannot have a full-orbed personality and harbor envy in your heart. We are told in Proverbs 14:30, 'A sound heart is the life of the flesh, but envy the rottenness of the bones.' Envy is not a defensive weapon; it is an offensive instrument used in spiritual ambush. It wounds for the sake of wounding and hurts for the sake of hurting."

The Apostle Paul gives the all-time antidote to the sins of envy, jealous, and covetousness. "I have learned the secret of being content in any and every situation, whether well-fed or hungry, whether living in plenty or in want. I can do everything through him who gives me strength" (Philippians 4:12,13, NIV).

Counseling Strategy

For The Non-Christian:

1. If you detect envy, jealousy, or covetousness in the inquirer, carefully but firmly point out that these attitudes are displeasing to God. Explain "Steps to Peace with God," page 5, and then share the pages on "The Results of Receiving Christ," page 7.

2. Counsel him to seek deliverance from envy, jealousy, and covetousness. Now that Christ has come into his life, the inquirer will be able to learn to redirect his thinking and actions in ways that reflect newness of his life in Christ. Envy, jealousy, and covetousness should be confessed as sin, and daily forgiveness and cleansing claimed.

3. Envy, jealousy and covetousness should be converted into "fruit in keeping with repentance" (Luke 3:8, NIV). (See also Philippians 2:3,4.)

   A. Pray for those once envied.

   B. Look for the good in others.

   C. Get to know those once envied; learn to express appreciation for their assets and qualities which formerly produced negative responses and sin in you.

4. Counsel him to start Bible reading, study, and memorization. As the Word of God begins to occupy our thinking, it crowds out the works of the flesh (Galatians 5:17-21).

5. Encourage him to learn and practice daily prayer.

6. Counsel him to become involved with a Bible-teaching church where he can worship, fellowship, and serve.

7. Pray with him for victory over envy, jealousy, and covetousness. Pray also that his commitment to Christ will transform his life.

For The Christian:

1. Counsel him to break his vicious line of thinking by openly recognizing the problem. He should focus on the real causes for his sin rather than on other people, circumstances, "bad luck," lack of acceptance, or failures to "get ahead." He should develop a mind-set which will enable him to face issues squarely.

2. Help him to repent and confess this sin. Share "Restoration," page 11, emphasizing 1 John 1:9 and 2:1. He should be open and specific with God.

3. Encourage him to get into the Word of God, reading and studying it. Dwight L. Moody said: "Sin will keep you from this Book. This Book will keep you from sin." Urge him to search faithfully for texts that speak to his problems and to pray over them. He should ask God to burn them into his heart. God's Word brings conviction, but also relief, as we learn to obey it.

4. Treat these sins as "bad habits" that need to be broken. Begin to practice the "Put-off," "Put-on" principle (Turn to BAD HABITS, page 43). This will be of great help. He should start with one aspect of the problem, focusing on it until he feels it is under control, and then tackle successively other aspects until he sees further progress. It is often helpful to enlist one's spouse or a Christian friend to help monitor progress. Praying with this person on specific issues is also helpful.

5. Encourage him to get involved in some form of Christian service through a Bible-teaching church. This could lead to more objective and constructive thinking which will aid in bringing his attitudes under control.

6. Encourage him to develop a thankful attitude toward life, towards the things that happen to him, and towards the people who cross his path. Substituting praise for criticism is a good practice that provides encouraging results.

7. Pray with him personally for victory and a new-found joy in his Christian experience.

Scripture

"Since, then, you have been raised with Christ, set your hearts on things above, where Christ is seated at the right hand of God. Set your minds on things above, not on earthly things. For you died, and your life is now hidden with Christ in God. When Christ, who is your life, appears, then you also will appear with him in glory."   Colossians 3:1-4, NIV

"A sound heart is the life of the flesh, but envy the rottenness of the bones."   Proverbs 14:30, KJV

"Let your conversation (manner of life) be without covetousness; and be content with such things as ye have: for he hath said, I will never leave thee nor forsake thee."   Hebrews 13:5, KJV

"And let us consider how we may spur one another on toward love and good deeds. Let us not give up meeting together, as some are in the habit of doing, but let us encourage one another — and all the more as you see the Day approaching."   Hebrews 10:24,25, NIV

Proverbs 27:4, NIV
1 Corinthians 3:3, KJV

FAITH, LACK OF
Background

Inquirers often express the need for more faith.

We could define faith as "a blind commitment to what God is, does, and says." It is staking our life on the reality of His trustworthiness. But unless faith becomes operative in our own life, it is only a word. The most well-known definition of faith in Scripture is a functional one; it does not tell us what faith actually is, but what it will do for us: "Now faith is being sure of what we hope for and certain of what we do not see" (Hebrews 11:1, NIV).

The Gospel is a way of faith. The Christian life is a walk of faith. Faith pleases God and He rewards it. "And without faith it is impossible to please God, because anyone who comes to him must believe that he exists and that he rewards those who earnestly seek him" (Hebrews 11:6, NIV).

Billy Graham has said, "Faith will manifest itself in three ways: in doctrine, worship, and fellowship. It will manifest itself in morality in the way we live and behave. The Bible also teaches that faith does not end with trust in Christ for our salvation. Faith continues! Faith grows! It may be weak at first, but it will become stronger as we begin to read the Bible, pray, go to Church, and experience God's faithfulness in your Christian life."

Counseling Strategy

For The Non-Christian:

If your inquirer speaks of faith in such a way as to reveal that he lacks understanding of saving faith, share "Steps to Peace with God," page 5. Emphasize that only by faith can we know God. Entering into right relationship to Him through Jesus Christ means a commitment by faith to His person and work as expressed in His death on the cross and His resurrection. "So then faith cometh by hearing, and hearing by the Word of God" (Romans 10:17, KJV). "For by grace are ye saved through faith; and that not of yourselves; it is the gift of God; not of works, lest any man should boast" (Ephesians 2:8,9, KJV). Share the contents of pages 9 and 37 on "Assurance."

For The Christian:

If your inquirer is a Christian who expresses concern for his lack of faith, or who desires to have more faith:

1. Question him:
     Why do you want more faith?
     What do you want faith to do for you?
     It may be that he lacks certainty in his relationship to Christ. If this sur-
   faces, share "Assurance," page 9, emphasizing also Ephesians 2:8,9.
2. If he stands firm in his commitment to salvation by faith in Christ, then
   share with him ideas on increasing his faith.
     A. A life of faith doesn't develop instantaneously through some
        mysterious process. It is spiritual discipline that leads to a deeper faith.
     B. Urge him to confess his lack of faith to God as sin. "...for whatsoever
        is not of faith is sin" (Romans 14:23, KJV). "Take heed, brethren, lest
        there be in any of you an evil heart of unbelief, in departing from the
        living God" (Hebrews 3:12, KJV).
     C. Urge him to go to the source book on faith, the Bible. There are ap-
        proximately 500 references to "faith," "belief," etc., in the New Testa-
        ment alone. He needs to read it and study it! Encourage him to write
        down every reference to faith, then study each one in its context to
        determine what God is saying about faith and how he can apply it to
        his life.
     D. Urge him to exercise faith through his prayer life. There are references
        relating faith to prayer: for example, Matthew 17:20 and James 5:15.
        Faith will grow as victories in prayer are experienced.
     E. Urge him to begin to use what he learns about faith, putting it to the
        test in his life and experiences. For example: in Proverbs 3:5,6, God
        promises His guidance if we meet certain conditions. If the inquirer
        desires the leading of the Lord for some decision he needs to make or
        action he needs to take, let him determine what God's conditions are
        in the reference given and meet them, in order to experience the prom-
        ised guidance.
     F. Urge him to begin to challenge faith by daring to believe God more
        and more and act on that belief. True faith is dynamic; it results in ac-
        tion! The great heroes of faith (Hebrews 11) were on the move for
        God! Get involved in Christian service. "Therefore, my beloved
        brethren, be ye steadfast, unmovable, always abounding in the work
        of the Lord, forasmuch as ye know that your labor is not in vain in the
        Lord" (1 Corinthians 15:58, KJV).

Scripture

"Therefore being justified by faith, we have peace with God through our
Lord Jesus Christ."   Romans 5:1, KJV

"Wherein ye greatly rejoice, through now for a season, if need be, ye are in
heaviness through manifold temptations: that the trial of your faith, being
much more precious than of gold that perisheth, though it be tried with
fire, might be found unto praise and honor and glory at the appearing of
Jesus Christ: whom having not seen, ye love; in whom, though now ye see

him not, yet believing, ye rejoice with joy unspeakable and full of glory: receiving the end of your faith, even the salvation of your souls."

1 Peter 1:6-9, KJV

". . .I tell you the truth, if you have faith as small as a mustard seed, you can say to this mountain, 'Move from here to there' and it will move. Nothing will be impossible for you."

Matthew 17:20, NIV

"And Jesus answering saith unto them, Have faith in God."

Mark 11:22, KJV

FALSE DOCTRINES

Background

The Apostle John wrote in his Second Epistle, "For if you wander beyond the teaching of Christ, you will leave God behind; while if you are loyal to Christ's teachings, you will have God too" (2 John 9, TLB).

Billy Graham has written, "All the way through the Bible we are warned against false prophets and false teachers 'which come to you in sheep's clothing, but inwardly they are ravening wolves' (Matthew 7:15). Sometimes it is extremely difficult for Christians to discern a false prophet ... Jesus spoke of '...false prophets, (who show) great signs and wonders; insomuch that, if it were possible, they shall deceive the very elect' " (Matthew 24:24, KJV).

The underlying principle of all Satan's tactics is deception. He is a crafty and clever disguiser. His deception began in the Garden of Eden and it continues until this day ... He invades the theological seminary and even the pulpit. Many times he even invades the church under cover of orthodox vocabulary, emptying sacred terms of their biblical sense.

What is a false doctrine? It is any teaching which is contrary to the basic doctrines of God's Word, such as the Trinity, the virgin birth of Christ, the atoning death of Christ, along with His bodily resurrection and second coming, salvation by grace through faith in Jesus Christ, the bodily resurrection of all believers and the reality of heaven, the eternal condemnation of those who reject Christ, etc.

Counseling Strategy

For the Non-Christian:

1. Commend the inquirer on his willingness to share his thoughts with the goal of getting at the truth. Tell him that God is not confused, the Bible is explicit, and you hope you can be of help as you talk together.

2. If the inquirer seems to have a difficult time in accepting correct biblical teaching, it may be that he has never received Jesus Christ as his personal Lord and Savior. Suggest to him that this step is crucial in understanding the Scripture. (See 1 Corinthians 2:14 and 2 Corinthians 4:4.)

   Share "Steps to Peace with God," page 5, with the individual, asking him to receive Christ.

3. Immediately share other follow-up steps:

   A. Urge him to start reading and studying the Word of God. To help him get started we will send him *Living In Christ* which contains the

Gospel of John. He should concentrate on reading John and completing the Bible studies in the book.

B. If he is influenced by or connected to a sect or cult, he should be encouraged to leave it immediately, severing all ties with the group. In its place, he should identify with a Bible-teaching church where he can fellowship with born-again believers, worship with them, and study the Word of God and pray with them.

4. Pray with him that he might know the mind of Christ in all things concerning God's Word.

For the Christian:

It is not uncommon for an apparently knowledgeable Christian to be influenced by false doctrine.

1. Take care not to offend the inquirer by telling him that he is in error or that he has been gullible. Remember that Satan often disguises himself as an "angel of light" (2 Corinthians 11:14, KJV).

   Do not suggest at the outset that he leave the cult or sect.

2. Trusting the Holy Spirit to lead you, look up additional information on the cult in other chapters of this handbook, such as CULTS, THE BIBLE, THE TRINITY, HEAVEN, HELL, JUDGMENT, and any other doctrinal section. Use your own knowledge of the Scriptures and your experience to counsel.

3. Ask your inquirer to write down the information, with accompanying Scriptures, which you share, for his future reflection and study. Offer to send him *Living In Christ* which will be a help in Bible study.

4. Finally, pray with him for an open mind and for a knowledge of God's will for his life as he seeks to know the Scriptures.

5. If, at this point, your inquirer asks for the recommendation of a church, you should feel free to suggest that he seek to identify with a group of believers where God's Word is preached and taught. Then trust the Holy Spirit to guide him to the right place. Do not suggest a specific denomination or church unless he requests this information.

Scripture

"Study to show thyself approved unto God, a workman that needeth not to be ashamed, rightly dividing the word of truth."   2 Timothy 2:15, KJV

"Beloved, believe not every spirit, but try the spirits whether they are of God: because many false prophets are gone out into the world. Hereby know ye the Spirit of God: every spirit that confesseth that Jesus Christ is come in the flesh is of God: and every spirit that confesseth not that Jesus Christ is come in the flesh is not of God: and this is that spirit of antichrist, whereof ye have heard that it should come; and even now already is it in the world."   1 John 4:1-3, KJV

"Beware lest any man spoil you through philosophy and vain deceit, after the tradition of men, after the rudiments of the world, and not after Christ. For in him dwelleth all the fulness of the Godhead bodily."

Colossians 2:8,9, KJV

"There is a way that seemeth right unto a man, but the end thereof are the ways of death."

Proverbs 16:25, KJV

"Now the Spirit speaketh expressly, that in the latter times some shall depart from the faith, giving heed to seducing spirits, and doctrines of devils; speaking lies in hypocrisy; having their conscience seared with a hot iron."

1 Timothy 4:1,2, KJV

See also Cults, The Bible, The Trinity, etc.

FEAR

Background

A moderate sense of fear may be considered normal, even healthy. It may be an emotion or an awareness of impending danger — a defense mechanism. It may be just the pounding heart, flushed face, and sweaty palms in anticipation of being called on in class or asked to make a speech at a meeting. Fears may be in reaction to imagined or real circumstances. They can be acute or chronic. Many fearful people tend to infect others with their anxieties and tensions.

The counselor must demonstrate love and attempt to discover causes for the fears, offering scriptural help. There may be no easy or instantaneous solutions to the total problem, but we can suggest a proper relationship to Jesus Christ, dependence upon the Holy Spirit, and the centering of his life in the Word of God as necessary steps to eventual solution.

The expressions "fear of God" or "fear God" in the Bible don't mean that God expects us to cringe in terror before Him in anticipation of punishment, but that we owe Him our reverential respect and trust. Solomon said, "The fear of the Lord is the beginning of wisdom" (Proverbs 9:10, KJV). The fear of God is the one fear (a trustful, worshipful attitude) which removes all other fears!

"I sought the Lord, and he heard me, and delivered me from all my fears (Psalm 34:4, KJV).

Billy Graham writes, "Jesus said we are not to fear; we are not to be anxious; we are not to fret; we are not to worry. The Bible teaches that this type of fear is sin. "Peace I leave with you, my peace I give unto you . . . Let not your heart be troubled, neither let it be afraid" (John 14:27, KJV).

Counseling Strategy

For the Non-Christian:

If the inquirer is a non-Christian expressing an unhealthy fear of God because of a guilty conscience or fear of punishment (future judgment), you are probably dealing with unresolved sin for which there is a remedy. Share "Steps to Peace with God, page 5. Emphasize:

1. God cleanses our conscience. "How much more, then, will the blood of Christ, who through the eternal Spirit offered himself unblemished to God, cleanse our consciences from acts that lead to death, so that we may serve the living God" (Hebrews 9:14, NIV).

2. God delivers from fears of future punishment. 'Therefore, there is now no condemnation for those who are in Christ Jesus, because through Christ

Jesus the law of the Spirit of life set me free from the law of sin and death" (Romans 8:1,2, NIV).

Share "Assurance," page 9.

For the Christian:

If the inquirer is a Christian whose greatest fear is personal inadequacy — not measuring up or failing — share the following:

1. God doesn't ask you to be successful, only to please Him! "Delight yourself in the Lord and he will give you the desires of your heart" (Psalm 37:4, NIV).

2. Learn to accept yourself as you are, not making excessive personal demands. Paul said: "But by the grace of God I am what I am, and his grace to me was not without effect" (1 Corinthians 15:10, NIV). "My grace is sufficient for you, for my power is made perfect in weakness" (2 Corinthians 12:9, NIV).

3. Don't compare yourself with others. Just be you. "We do not dare to classify or compare ourselves with some who commend themselves. When they measure themselves by themselves and compare themselves with themselves, they are not wise" (2 Corinthians 10:12, NIV).

4. God has given you all you need to be confident. "God hath not given us the spirit of fear; but of power (sufficiency), and of love, and of a sound mind" (2 Timothy 1:7, KJV).

5. Learn to trust God implicitly for what you want to be and do. "Trust in the Lord with all thine heart, and lean not unto thine own understanding. In all ways acknowledge him and he shall direct thy paths" (Proverbs 3:5,6, KJV).

6. Make your fears a definite matter for prayer. "Do not be anxious about anything, but in everything, by prayer and petition, with thanksgiving, present your requests to God. And the peace of God, which transcends all understanding, will guard your hearts and minds in Christ Jesus" (Philippians 4:6,7, NIV).

If the inquirer is a Christian with a sense of uneasiness or anxiety about the uncertainties of life and the future, encourage him with the following:

1. The Lord is mindful of us.

   "I am the good shepherd; I know my sheep and my sheep know me . . ." (John 10:14, NIV).

   "For I know the plans I have for you, declares the Lord, plans to prosper you and not to harm you, plans to give you hope and a future" (Jeremiah 29:11, NIV).

2. He has promised:

   - His presence. "Keep your lives free from the love of money and be content with what you have, because God has said, 'Never will I leave you; never will I forsake you' " (Hebrews 13:5, NIV).

- His provision. "I was young and now I am old, yet I have never seen the righteous forsaken or their children begging bread" (Psalm 37:25, NIV).
- His protection. "The Lord is my light and my salvation, whom shall I fear? The Lord is the stronghold of my life, of whom shall I be afraid?" (Psalm 27:1, NIV)

3. Point out that love is the antithesis of fear. "There is no fear in love. But perfect love drives out fear, because fear has to do with punishment. The man who fears is not made perfect in love" (1 John 4:18, NIV).

If the inquirer is a Christian with a fear of witnessing for Christ, encourage him to:

1. Be completely sure of his own relationship to Christ. "For I know whom I have believed, and am persuaded that he is able to keep that which I have committed to him against that day" (2 Timothy 1:12, KJV).

2. Make a conscious moral commitment of himself to God. "Present your bodies a living sacrifice . . . unto God which is your reasonable service" (Romans 12:1, KJV).

3. Trust God implicitly to be with him and to work through him. "My grace is sufficient for you, for my power is made perfect in weakness" (2 Corinthians 12:9, NIV). "Be not afraid of their faces; for I am with thee to deliver thee, saith the Lord" (Jeremiah 1:8, KJV).

4. Be faithful in witnessing in the small things. Live the Christian life through acts of kindness, watching one's attitudes, thanking God for a meal in a public place, etc.

5. Seek the companionship and strength of a stronger Christian so they may witness together. Confidence is gained as one becomes a part of evangelism. "Make plans by seeking advice; if you wage war, obtain guidance" (Proverbs 20:18, NIV).

6. Take a course in personal evangelism at a church or enroll in a correspondence course with the Navigators, Moody Correspondence School, Emmaus Bible School, etc.

7. Pray for a consuming compassion for the lost. "Yet when I preach the gospel, I cannot boast, for I am compelled to preach. Woe to me if I do not preach the gospel" (1 Corinthians 9:16, NIV).

If the inquirer is fearful of death, turn to the chapter on DEATH, page 64.

Scripture

"Fear not, for I have redeemed you; I have called you by name; you are mine. When you pass through the waters, I will be with you; and when you pass through the rivers, they will not sweep over you. When you walk through the fire, you will not be burned . . ."   Isaiah 43:1, 2, NIV

"I sought the Lord, and he answered me; he delivered me from all my fears."   Psalm 34:4, NIV

"So do not fear, for I am with you; do not be dismayed, for I am your God. I will strengthen you and help you; I will uphold you with my righteous right hand."
Isaiah 41:10, NIV

"For you did not receive a spirit that makes you a slave again to fear, but you received the Spirit of sonship. And by him we cry, 'Abba, Father.' The Spirit himself testifies with our spirit that we are God's children."
Romans 8:15,16, NIV

". . . whoever listens to me will live in safety and be at ease, without fear of harm."
Proverbs 1:33, NIV

See also Anxiety

FINANCIAL DIFFICULTIES

Background

Understanding and correctly handling finances should be a high priority for all persons. Much of our tension, family friction, strife and frustrations are caused, directly or indirectly, by money. High on the list for causes of divorce is financial disagreement. The Christian family is not immune. If a family cannot or does not pay its bills, or is beset by other problems related to money, it is a poor testimony. Too few churches offer training for their people in the area of financial accountability.

Chief Causes of Financial Problems:

1. Wrong attitudes toward money. Greed and covetousness quickly lead to all kinds of evil (see 1 Timothy 6:10, NIV). The "get rich quick" syndrome of speculative investment often leads to disaster.

2. Living beyond one's income. Failure to "count the cost" will result in chronic overspending. (See Luke 14:28-30). Some seem to have a great susceptibility to advertising, succumbing to attractive products and seemingly advantageous credit offers.

3. Credit buying. The best possible advice for those in financial trouble is to stay away from stores and showrooms and to destroy all their credit cards.

4. Self-indulgent living. Purchase of unnecessary things, consumption of alcoholic beverages, tobacco, and junk or gourmet foods are self-indulgent habits. By way of example, in a home where both husband and wife smoke heavily, upwards of $1,500 per year can be spent on cigarettes.

5. The fallacy that accumulating material things leads to contentment and happiness. "Then he (Jesus) said to them, 'Watch out! Be on your guard against all kinds of greed; a man's life does not consist in the abundance of his possessions' " (Luke 12:15, NIV).

6. Lack of a budget: projecting and monitoring expenses. Our income will go just so far. We list here some items to consider, along with suggested percentages, for governing expenditures. (Percentages vary slightly, depending on the one making them.)

Housing	30%	Recreation and vacations	5%
Food	14%	Clothing	5%
Transportation	13%	Medical and Dental	5%
Insurance	4%	Savings	5%
Debts	5%	Miscellaneous	4%
		Tithe	10%

Biblical Principles for Handling Money:

1. It is basically a spiritual matter, thus an understanding of the Lordship of

Jesus Christ is essential. Handling finances brings into perspective the totality of life as it relates to God's will and the issues of eternity.

"The earth is the Lord's, and everything in it" (1 Corinthians 10:26, NIV).

"You are not your own; you were bought at a price" (1 Corinthians 6:19-20, NIV).

"Offer your bodies as living sacrifices, holy and pleasing to God . . . Do not conform any longer to the pattern of this world, but be transformed by the renewing of your mind. Then you will be able to test and approve what God's will is—his good, pleasing and perfect will" (Romans 12:1,2, NIV).

2. An understanding of the principle that we are stewards (managers) of all that God has put under our care is also essential. We are not owners! Our lives, our time, and our assets are gifts from God. We are responsible to God for them, and He will hold us accountable. (See Matthew 25:14-30.)

3. God wants us to depend upon Him, not on material possessions. "Command those who are rich in this present world not to be arrogant, nor to put their hope in wealth, which is so uncertain, but to put their hope in God, who richly provides us with everything for our enjoyment" (1 Timothy 6:17, NIV). (See also Proverbs 3:5,6; Philippians 4:19; and Psalm 37:25.)

4. It is God's plan that stewards give a portion of their income to Him and to His work. "Bring ye all the tithes into the storehouse, that there may be meat in mine house, and prove me now herewith, saith the Lord of hosts, if I will not open you the windows of heaven and pour you out a blessing, that there shall not be room enough to receive it" (Malachi 3:10, KJV). (See also Luke 12:34; and Proverbs 3:9.)

Billy Graham says: "Although all our money actually belongs to God, the Bible suggests the tithe as a minimum response in gratitude to God . . . You cannot get around it; the Scriptures promise material and spiritual blessing to the person who gives to God. You cannot outgive God. I challenge you to try it and see."

Counseling Strategy

1. If the inquirer admits to financial difficulty, counsel him that a person needs the perspective which comes through an eternal relationship to Jesus Christ as Lord and Savior. We must know Him personally before we can expect to have His help. Share "Steps to Peace with God," page 5.

2. After the inquirer has explained his financial problem, counsel him to look upon it as basically a spiritual problem. He must not look just for a

temporary solution, but must bring God into the center of his life —
including the financial. Only this will bring lasting solutions. It wouldn't
be in the best interests of the inquirer for the counselor to accept explanations or excuses for the financial problems, such as, for example, the
problems of the economy. Many people are in trouble because they
mismanage.

3. How financial problems are dealt with in the future will be dependent
   upon one's attitude toward the principles of Scripture (see BACK-
   GROUND). Go over these, one by one. Then, question him about the
   cause of his financial problem. Is it:

   Wrong attitude about money?

   Living beyond his means?

   Credit purchases?

   Self-indulgent living?

   Lack of a budget — proper planning?

4. Counsel him to bring his finances and his life into line, making whatever
   adjustments or sacrifices that may be necessary. Perhaps his own future
   and that of his family depends upon his decisive action.

5. If the inquirer's financial solutions seem beyond his ability even after he
   has attempted to square away with the Lord on the principles, counsel him
   to consult frankly with a pastor for guidance as to recommending a
   professional counselor or financial planner who can work out steps to
   recovery. Or, he might go directly to a counselor, if he knows whom to
   contact. Avoid financial institutions which offer to consolidate one's debts.
   Many times such "consolidation" actually increases one's indebtedness.

Scripture

"But seek ye first the kingdom of God, and his righteousness; and all these
things shall be added unto you."   Matthew 6:33, KJV

"But my God shall supply all your need according to his riches in glory by
Christ Jesus."   Philippians 4:19, KJV

"Will a man rob God? Yet ye have robbed me. But ye say, Wherein have
we robbed thee? In tithes and offerings. Ye are cursed with a curse: for ye
have robbed me, even this whole nation. Bring ye all the tithes into the
storehouse, that there may be meat in mine house, and prove me now
herewith, saith the Lord of hosts, if I will not open you the windows of
heaven, and pour you out a blessing, that there shall not be room enough
to receive it."   Malachi 3:8-10, KJV

FORGIVENESS
Background

One of the most beautiful words in the human vocabulary is forgiveness. How much pain and unhappy consequences could be avoided if we all learned the meaning of this word. The Sweet Singer of Israel shared some of the emotion he personally experienced after he asked God to "wash away all my iniquity and cleanse me from my sin" (Psalm 51:2, NIV). "Blessed is he whose transgressions are forgiven, whose sins are covered. Blessed is the man whose sin the Lord does not count against him and in whose spirit is no deceit" (Psalm 32:1,2, NIV). In one bold stroke, forgiveness obliterates the past and permits us to enter the land of new beginnings.

> Billy Graham states: "God's forgiveness is not just a casual statement; it is the complete blotting out of all the dirt and degradation of our past, present, and future. The only reason our sins can be forgiven is that, on the Cross, Jesus Christ paid their full penalty. (But) only as we bow at the foot of the Cross, in contrition, confession, and repentance, can we find forgiveness."

The Basis for Forgiveness:

1. Own up to what we are and have done (repentance). "For I know my transgressions, and my sin is always before me. Against you, you only have I sinned and done what is evil in your sight..." (Psalm 51:3,4, NIV).
2. Ask for it (confession). "Cleanse me with hyssop, and I will be clean; wash me, and I will be whiter than snow. Hide your face from my sins and blot out all my iniquity" (Psalm 51:7,9, NIV).

The Results of Forgiveness:

1. Reconciliation. When God forgives, there is an immediate and complete change in relationship. Instead of hostility, there is love and acceptance. Instead of enmity, there is friendship. "God ... reconciling the world to himself in Christ, not counting men's sins against them" (2 Corinthians 5:19, NIV).
2. Purification. The very essence of forgiveness is being restored to our original standing before God. "Purge me ... and I shall be clean; wash me and I shall be whiter than snow" (Psalm 51:7, KJV). (See also 1 John 1:9, Romans 4:7.)

   Another aspect of purification is that God forgets our sin when He forgives it. "For I will forgive their wickedness and will remember their sins no more" (Hebrews 8:12, NIV). (See also Psalm 103:12; Isaiah 38:17.)

3. Remittance. Forgiveness results in God's dropping the charges against us. He will not enforce judgment because of our sins. Jesus said to the woman taken in adultery, ". . .Neither do I condemn thee: go, and sin no more" (John 8:11, KJV). (See also Romans 8:1.)

What a great privilege the counselor has in sharing the joy of God's forgiveness!

Counseling Strategy

We shall consider three areas: forgiveness from God, forgiving those who have wronged us, and forgiving ourselves by putting our past behind us.

For the Non-Christian:

1. Reassure him by saying that God understands sin and knows how to deal with it. He forgives sin. And the inquirer, too, can know the joy of pardon.

2. Explain "Steps to Peace with God," page 5. Emphasize the results of forgiveness from the BACKGROUND.

3. Share "Assurance," page 9.
   NOTE: If your inquirer insists that he can't be forgiven, that he has committed the unpardonable sin, turn to the chapter on that subject.

4. Encourage him to start reading and studying the Word of God. This will do much to reassure him of forgiveness. (See 1 John 3:19.) Ask him if he would like to receive *Living In Christ* which will help to get him started in Bible reading and study.

5. Encourage him to seek fellowship with a group of Bible-believing Christians. A good church will provide Bible teaching, worship, and opportunities for service and witnessing as well.

6. Encourage him to pray, practicing daily confession (1 John 1:9) as a requisite for daily forgiveness and renewal.

7. Pray with him for a full understanding of his new relationship and its consequences.

For the Christian Who is Bitter or Resentful:

1. Point out that his attitude is wrong. He needs first of all to put his own house in order, confessing his bitterness and resentment to God as sin.

2. Encourage him to forgive those who have offended or hurt him. This may be difficult, but God commands it! "Bear with each other and forgive whatever grievances you may have against one another. Forgive as the Lord forgave you" (Colossians 3:13, NIV). Sometimes those who deserve it least need forgiveness most! Forgiving as the Lord forgave you implies forgetting. This may be difficult and require time but God can change our attitudes. Jesus' answer of "seventy times seven" to Peter's question, "How oft shall my brother sin against me, and I forgive him?" implies that the Christian must be ready, even eager, to forgive (See Matthew 18:21-35).

3. Encourage the inquirer to seek to restore the broken relationship in the spirit of Colossians 3:13. In all probability, this will mean "going the second mile" (see Matthew 5:41), but may be necessary in order to renew the relationship. The Gospel always cuts across the grain of human reactions and conduct. Until one of the parties involved takes the initiative toward forgiveness and restoration, the broken relationship will continue.

For the Christian Who Cannot Forgive Himself:

1. Ask if he is truly repentant and has confessed, frankly and transparently, all sin to God. If so, share "Restoration," page 11 (1 John 1:9).

2. If he has done the above and the apprehension continues, point out that he, is guilty of unbelief. If God has forgiven him on his confession (1 John 1:9), then he is wrong to doubt God. He must take God at His word!

   Share David's testimony from Psalm 32:1,2 (KJV): "Blessed is he whose transgression is forgiven, whose sin is covered. Blessed is the man unto whom the Lord imputeth not iniquity, and in whose spirit there is no guile."

   False humility could be involved. Self-flagellation makes some people feel better, while others take pleasure in reviewing the past. This is like the Scribes and Pharisees: "Even so ye...appear righteous unto men, but within ye are full of hypocrisy and iniquity" (Matthew 23:28, KJV).

3. If he is truly repentant, urge him to see himself as God sees him, a new creature in Christ Jesus (2 Corinthians 5:17). God understands sin, and knows how to deal with it. He will forgive sin if we repent and confess. Paul's wisdom needs to be practiced: "Forgetting those things which are behind, and reaching forth unto those things which are before, I press toward the mark for the prize of the high calling of God in Christ Jesus" (Philippians 3:13,14, KJV).

Scripture

"If the Son therefore shall make you free, ye shall be free indeed."

John 8:36, KJV

"I, even I, am he that blotteth out thy transgressions for mine own sake, and will not remember thy sins."

Isaiah 43:25, KJV

"For if ye forgive men their trespasses, your heavenly Father will also forgive you: but if ye forgive not men their trespasses, neither will your Father forgive your trespasses."

Matthew 6:14,15, KJV

"Father, forgive them; for they know not what they do."

Luke 23:34, KJV

Psalm 51

GAMBLING

Background

Gambling may be practiced in many different ways. Some forms appear to be quite innocent, and sometimes a percentage of the profits are used for a good cause. God's Word, however, indicates that gambling in any form is contrary to His will for a Christian.

First, gambling or betting puts faith in chance or luck rather than in the care and provision of God. Second, one who gambles seeks to profit from another's loss. This borders on covetousness and stealing. Third, gambling promotes a greedy spirit. It emphasizes getting rather than giving, selfish interest rather than self-sacrifice, and erodes the moral fiber of society.

The Bible indicates that there are three ways by which to profit materially. First, work. "If any would not work, neither should he eat" (2 Thessalonians 3:10, KJV). Second, by wise investments (see the parable of the talents in Luke 19:1-27). Third, gift or inheritance. "Children ought not to lay up for the parents, but the parents for the children" (2 Corinthians 12:14, KJV).

Billy Graham writes, "The appeal of gambling is somewhat understandable. There is something alluring about getting something for nothing. I realize that, and that is where the sin lies. Gambling of any kind amounts to theft by permission. The coin is flipped, the dice are rolled, or the horses run, and somebody rakes in that which belongs to another. The Bible says, 'In the sweat of thy face shalt thou eat bread' (Genesis 3:19, KJV). It doesn't say, 'By the flip of a coin shalt thou eat thy lunch.' I realize that in most petty gambling no harm is intended, but the principle is the same as in big gambling. The difference is only in the amount of money involved."

The experience of the gambler is similar to that of the alcoholic. He deludes himself that he is master of his life which is actually out of control. He denies he has any problem, even though his family disintegrates. He ends up with enormous debts, and even steals to cover his losses.

The gambler may promises to quit, but rarely follows through unless he experiences a disaster which brings him face to face with the reality of his situation.

An encounter with Jesus Christ is the only solution for many, and some experience immediate freedom from the addiction. Complete victory and healing for many, however, is often a process. Many of the same emotional problems of the alcoholic are also present in the gambler, and the underlying causes must be dealt with in the light of the Word of God.

Gamblers Anonymous, the National Council on Compulsive Gambling, and others attempt to minister to those addicted. The former has chapters in many cities across the nation, and they usually have a listed telephone number.

Counseling Strategy

1. A compassionate but "tough" stance must be assumed by the counselor. The addiction is very real. The victim must be confronted with the fact that his life is out of control and that he must assume personal responsibility for his situation. Does he really want help? Then, he must stop gambling. Nothing short of this will solve his problem.

2. Has he ever committed his life to Christ, receiving Him as his Lord and Savior? Share "Steps to Peace with God," page 5. Christ can break the shackles of sin, making all things new. (See 2 Corinthians 5:17.)

3. Emphasize that now he must make a clean break, resolving never to return to the gambling table, purchase of lottery tickets, slot machines, etc. Living a day at a time, he must learn to trust God in regard to temptation. "But remember this — the wrong desires that come into your life aren't anything new and different. Many others have faced exactly the same problems before you. And no temptation is irresistible. You can trust God to keep the temptation from becoming so strong that you can't stand up against it, for he has promised this and will do what he says. He will show you how to escape temptation's power so that you can bear up patiently against it" (1 Corinthians 10:13, LB).

4. He must abandon the old haunts and sever all relationships related to gambling. He must establish new relationships. Attendance at Gamblers Anonymous could bring very positive results. (Look up in telephone book.) He should identify with a local Bible-teaching church where he can worship, study the Bible, learn to pray, and establish new friendships which will provide the support he needs to rebuild his life.

5. Pray with him for complete deliverance from bondage. Urge him to go to the Lord in prayer daily. The practice will provide increasing dependence upon God.

6. Urge him to start reading and studying the Bible on a personal basis. As one assimilates God's thoughts, a gradual transformation of the mind and life will be experienced. The counselor may offer "Living in Christ" at this point.

7. Urge him to counsel with a qualified pastor or Christian psychologist if further help is needed. Underlying causes that led to the addiction must often be dealt with in depth.

If the inquiry is about bingo, lotteries, or raffles, or attempts to justify them because they are sometimes sponsored by a church or are harmless and serve good causes, refer him to the BACKGROUND.

Following this, proceed as follows:

1. Ask if he has ever received Jesus Christ as Lord and Savior? Explain "Steps to Peace with God," page 5.

2. Emphasize that God's work is to be supported by the sacrificial giving of God's people, and not by such thing as raffles, bingo, or lotteries.

Scripture

"Whether therefore ye eat, or drink, or whatsoever ye do, do all to the glory of God."   1 Corinthians 10:31, KJV

"All things are lawful unto me, but all things are not expedient; all things are lawful for me, but I will not be brought under the power of any."
1 Corinthians 6:12, KJV

"Therefore, I urge you, dear brothers, in view of God's mercy, to offer your bodies as living sacrifices, holy and pleasing to God — which is your spiritual worship."   Romans 12:1, NIV

"Set your affection on things above, not on things on the earth. Mortify therefore your members which are upon the earth; fornication, uncleanness, inordinate affection, evil concupiscence and covetousness, which is idolatry. For which things' sake, the wrath of God cometh on the children of disobedience."   Colossians 3:2,5,6, KJV

"Thou shalt not steal. Thou shalt not covet thy neighbor's house . . . thou shalt not covet . . . any thing that is thy neighbor's." Exodus 20:15,17, KJV

GRIEF AND BEREAVEMENT
Background

Grief is an intense, emotional suffering caused by personal loss. There is acute sorrow, deep sadness, suffering, pain, and anguish. Bereavement is a sad and lonely state due to loss such as the death of a loved one.

It is a difficult time. The bereft will often feel that his experience is unique, that no one has ever endured such a loss or suffered as he is suffering. There are cycles of healing to the pattern of grief, which permit the sorrowing to recover in due time. Some individuals, however, continue grieving for long periods. In some ways, no one is ever completely delivered from the sense of loss.

The cycle of healing, mentioned above, usually proceeds as follows:

1. *The initial shock of death:* that intense emotional impact which sometimes leaves a person with a seeming paralysis.
2. *Emotional release:* a period of weeping.
3. *Loneliness and depression:* The sense of loss is often related to the degree of dependence on the deceased. There are many symptoms of depression.
4. *Guilt:* "I could have done more," or "I should have done something differently," etc.
5. *Anger, hostility:* "Why did God do this to me?"
6. *A stage of inertia:* Listlessness, "I can't get on with it"; "I couldn't care less."
7. *A gradual return to hope:* "Life will go on." "I will be able to cope." "God will help me get over this."
8. *The return to reality and normalcy:* admitting the loss and adjusting to it.

We must remember, however, that grief is not predictable nor can it be catalogued. Sometimes the stages of grief will seem to merge and overlap. The bereft may feel release from a certain "phase" of suffering, only to have it return.

Counseling grieving people calls for genuineness, special sensitivity and tenderness, sympathy, and empathy. We must depend upon the Holy Spirit for guidance. Convenient, glib, or pat answers have the ring of brass. Our words must be sincere and meaningful, "tailor made for the situation" because real comfort for the bereaving person depends upon where he actually is in the grieving process.

Don't pretend to have an answer for everything. Admit that you do not understand why or how God does what He does.

Don't be the "cheerleader" type, attempting to pump up the bereaved with cheer and good will.

Don't offer clichés or trite phrases about death and suffering.

Don't suggest that if the grieving one were more spiritual or closer to God, the pain might be less.

Remember that one short session will not meet all the needs of the inquirer. We do what we can, however, to share Jesus Christ, and the message of Scripture. We will trust God to do His work.

Counseling Strategy

1. Tell the inquirer you care and want to help. Encourage him to tell you about his loss and how he feels about it. Be a patient listener. It helps to ventilate feelings when one is grieving.
2. Tell him that it is healthy to mourn and grieve. This is a universal human experience through which we all must pass. Someone has said that grief is a "gift from God." It may be His way of helping us react to the tremendous shock of death and its emotional aftermath. Jesus said: "Blessed are they that mourn, for they shall be comforted" (Matthew 5:4, KJV). Jesus Himself wept at the grave of Lazarus (John 11:35, KJV).
3. Tell him that it is good to express feelings of guilt, anger, confusion, or despair. These feelings should not be repressed by the sorrower or rejected by the counselor. Encourage him to talk about the way he feels.
4. Tell him that the things he is feeling are often normal to the grieving process and that acceptance and healing will come, though perhaps slowly. God wants to bear our heartaches and loss and bring to us His comfort, hope and encouragement. Life may seem valueless at this point, but remember — Christ is permanent, the Solid Rock, the foundation on which to rebuild a life.
5. Ask him if he has ever received Jesus Christ as his personal Lord and Savior. If indicated, explain "Steps to Peace with God," page 5.

Billy Graham states: "Our confidence in the future is based firmly on the fact of what God has done for us in Christ. Because Christ is alive we need never despair, no matter what our situation may be. 'Now if we ... died with Christ, we believe that we shall also live with Him ... For the wages of sin is death; but the free gift of God is eternal life in Christ Jesus our Lord' " (Romans 6:8,23, NASB).

---

6. Tell him that, for the Christian, death is not the end of life. Through His death and resurrection, Christ has defeated sin and death, so that to believe in Him now means: we "shall never die" (John 11:25,26); we have eternal life (John 3:16); we have a place assured in heaven (John 14:1-6); we shall take part in the bodily resurrection (1 Corinthians 15:51,52). Also, "If we believe that Jesus died and rose again, even so God will bring with Him those who have fallen asleep in Jesus" (1 Thessalonians 4:14, NASB); thus, there will be a glorious reunion some day between us and all

those in the Lord whom we hold dear!

Encourage the inquirer to begin to read and study the Bible. It is a great source of comfort and strength.

7. Tell him that God sees our earthly life as preparation for the greater joys of heaven (Mark 8:36). Thus, He permits trials, sufferings and the death of loved ones to come into our lives so that we might see our need to trust Him. "Yet we believe now that we had this experience of coming to the end of our tether that we might learn to trust, not in ourselves, but in God who can raise the dead" (2 Corinthians 1:9, Phillips).

8. If he expresses guilt over some aspect of the death of his loved one (this is common in the case of suicides), counsel him not to "second guess" himself at this point. He should not carry guilt for something he should have done or not have done. This is past, and he needs to leave all his regrets with the Lord. If he has something to confess to God, do so, but accept the reality of His forgiveness in the light of 1 John 1:9.

9. If he seems overwhelmed with a sense of loss, of loneliness, of what to do in the future, etc., counsel him to confide in family and friends, and to trust them for emotional support and encouragement. The church can do a great deal to fill the areas left void. He should become involved in a local church. The pastor may be able to offer a great deal of emotional support. If he is not already a member, he should seek a Bible-teaching church and identify with it. Learning to accept God's will for what has happened, having a thankful heart for the years of love shared during the life of the loved one and for the promise of things to come, and reaching out in Christian love to help others who are hurting will all be great therapy and will serve as factors in learning to live fully again.

10. Pray with the inquirer for understanding, comfort, and blessing in his life.

The Death of Children:

The death of a child is especially difficult for surviving parents and families to handle. Death after such a short life-span often produces guilt, melancholy, and a lot of questions. In addition to the Counseling Strategy, we offer these points:

1. Though we cannot know why the child died, we do know that children are especially precious to God. Jesus said, "Of such is the kingdom of heaven" (Matthew 19:14, KJV). This implies that children who die are taken immediately into His presence.

2. When King David's child was taken from him in death, he said, "Can I bring him back again? I shall go to him, but he shall not return to me" (2 Samuel 12:23, KJV). Thus, if we believe that Jesus died and rose again, trusting in Him as our Lord and Savior, we have the blessed hope of seeing our loved one again.

Scripture

"And God shall wipe away all tears from their eyes; and there shall be no more death, neither sorrow, nor crying, neither shall there be any more pain: for the former things are passed away." Revelation 21:4, KJV

"For me to live is Christ, and to die is gain. For I am in a strait betwixt two, having a desire to depart, and to be with Christ, which is far better." Philippians 1:21,23, KJV

"Jesus said unto her, I am the resurrection, and the life: he that believeth in me, though he were dead, yet shall he live: and whosever liveth and believeth in me shall never die. Believest thou this?" John 11:25,26, KJV

"Let not your heart be troubled: ye believe in God, believe also in me. In my Father's house are many mansions: if it were not so, I would have told you. I go to prepare a place for you. And if I go and prepare a place for you, I will come again, and receive you unto myself; that where I am, there ye may be also." John 14:1-3, KJV

"Blessed be the God and Father of our Lord Jesus Christ, which according to his abundant mercy hath begotten us again unto a lively hope by the resurrection of Jesus Christ from the dead, to an inheritance incorruptible, and undefiled, and that fadeth not away, reserved in heaven for you, who are kept by the power of God through faith unto salvation ready to be revealed in the last time." 1 Peter 1:3-5, KJV

"For we know that if our earthly house of this tabernacle were dissolved, we have a building of God, an house not made with hands, eternal in the heavens." 2 Corinthians 5:1, KJV

Psalm 23:4-6, KJV

See also Death

GUILT

Background

Guilt has been defined as a feeling of sinfulness, wrongdoing, or a failure to measure up. God created in us a conscience, the moral discernment to evaluate our actions or conduct in terms of right or wrong. There are two kinds of guilt: real guilt and guilt feelings.

Real guilt comes as a result of breaking God's Law. This is sin. Because the sinner is seldom willing to face the issue squarely in God's way in order to experience relief, he suffers the consequences. Adam and Eve in the Garden of Eden are an excellent example of real guilt. Their sin (disobedience) resulted in guilt. Their relationship with God was broken; they knew it, so alienation and conviction followed. They ran from God, attempting to hide so that they would not have to face the consequences of their behavior. God found them, of course. They attempted to deny their own accountability, Adam blaming Eve ("The woman which thou gavest me!"), and Eve blaming the serpent ("The serpent beguiled me."). They had attempted to "cover up" by making fig-leaf aprons, but God further boxed them in with the question, "Who told you you were naked?" God forced them to deal with their problem of guilt. Atonement was then made for their sin, establishing the principle of sacrifice (Genesis 3:21).

Another illustration of dealing with real guilt is Nathan's openly confronting David with his adultery and murder, thus opening the way for repentance and confession. (See 2 Samuel 11 to 12:25 and Psalm 51.)

Guilt feelings are often associated with emotional illness stemming from negative experiences, many times in childhood. Even Christians who have the assurance that God has forgiven them and that they are His children continue to suffer from "false guilt." Such persons usually have a very low self-image, feelings of inadequacy (they can't do anything right or can't measure up), suffer from depression, etc. They cannot seem to find freedom from guilt even though they seek it, as in the case of Esau who "found no place of repentance, though he sought it carefully with tears" (Hebrews 12:17, KJV).

The guilt feelings of those who thus suffer will sometimes manifest themselves in different and complex ways:

- Deep depression from constantly blaming themselves.
- Chronic fatigue and headaches, or other illnesses.
- Extreme self-denial and self-punishment.
- A feeling of being constantly watched and criticized by others.
- Constant criticism of others for their own sins and shortcomings.
- Because of defeatist attitudes, actually sinking deeper into sin in order to feel more guilty.

Billy Graham has said of this complex problem: "The conscience of man is often beyond the grasp of a psychiatrist. With all his techniques, he cannot sound its depravity and depth. Man himself is helpless to detach himself from the gnawing guilt of a heart bowed down with the weight of sin. But where man has failed, God has succeeded."

Counseling Strategy

For the Non-Christian:

1. Offer hope to the inquirer by assuring him that God can take care of any problem he might have. God is able not only to forgive, but also to blot out any sin and guilt.

2. Do not excuse or minimize in any way the sins he shares. In all of us there is disobedience and sinful behavior which need to be dealt with in God's way; that is, confessed. We can never expect to find solutions to guilt if we attempt to cover up sin. "He that covereth his sins shall not prosper; but whoso confesseth and forsaketh them shall have mercy" (Proverbs 28:13, KJV).

3. Ask the inquirer if he has ever received Jesus Christ as his Lord and Savior. Share "Steps to Peace with God," page 5. Emphasize that freedom from guilt is included in Jesus' death on the Cross, but we must trust Him to cleanse us.

4. Encourage him to start reading and studying the Bible, beginning with the Gospels. Offer to send him *Living In Christ*, which will help him to get started.

5. Encourage him to cultivate the habit of daily prayer. At this time he can confess his sins, asking for forgiveness and cleansing. He should practice thanking God for taking away his sin and guilt, remembering that God takes away all our sins.

6. Counsel him to find a Bible-teaching church and identify with it. Here he can fellowship regularly with God's forgiven people, and hear and study God's Word.

7. Pray with him personally for deliverance and peace in his heart. "He is our peace" (Ephesians 2:14, KJV).

8. If your inquirer seems unable to respond immediately to your sharing Christ and if he continues to struggle with guilt, encourage him to find the pastor of a Bible-teaching church to help him further. It may be that in time he will be able to respond. Impress upon him that he should take the initiative in finding such a pastor.

For the Christian:

If the inquirer is a Christian who admits to re-occurring problems with guilt, proceed as follows:

1. Reassure him of God's love and forgiveness. He can cleanse guilt away! If

God has forgiven him, he must learn to forgive himself. A Christian has the right to claim with confidence the truth of 1 John 1:9. Christ, our Savior, removes all our sins — past, present and future — through His finished work on the Cross.

2. Counsel him to get into the Word of God, reading, studying, and reflecting at length on such passages as Psalm 103:1-6; Psalm 51; Isaiah 53, and John 18 and 19. Ask him to write the references of these passages down so that he can find them in his Bible. He can be confident that relief from guilt will come as he appropriates Christ's sacrifice and promised forgiveness and cleansing.

3. Counsel him to pray specifically and faithfully for a "conscience void of offense toward God and toward men" (Acts 24:16, KJV). He should continue praying until peace comes.

4. Recommend that he counsel with a pastor who could give him further help.

Scripture

"There is therefore now no condemnation to them which are in Christ Jesus . . ."
Romans 8:1, KJV

"If the Son therefore shall make you free, ye shall be free indeed."
John 8:36, KJV

"I know I am rotten through and through so far as my old sinful nature is concerned. No matter which way I turn I can't make myself do right. I want to, but I can't . . . So you see how it is: my new life tells me to do right, but the old nature that is still inside me loves to sin. Oh, what a terrible predicament I'm in! Who will free me from my slavery to this deadly lower nature? Thank God! It has been done by Jesus Christ our Lord. He has set me free."
Romans 7:18-25, TLB

"I have blotted out, as a thick cloud, thy transgressions, and, as a cloud, thy sins: return unto me, for I have redeemed thee."   Isaiah 44:22, KJV

"But this one thing I do, forgetting those things which are behind, and reaching forth unto those things which are before, I press toward the mark for the prize of the high calling of God in Christ Jesus."
Philippians 3:13,14, KJV

HEALING
Background

The biblical concept of healing means far more than relief from a set of physical symptoms. It means wholeness of body and spirit. The words healthy, whole, and holy all derive from the same old English root word.

Jesus questioned the man in John 5:6, "Wilt thou be made whole?"

Many sicknesses are the result of the individual's attitude and life-style.

- Many medical scientists maintain that much of our sickness is due to emotional causes: tensions, fear, sorrow, envy, resentment, hatred, etc. Physical pains and problems may be real enough, but their causes are rooted in the emotions.
- The lifelong smoker may develop a variety of illnesses such as emphysema, cancer, high blood pressure, etc., which affect the mouth, throat, esophagus, lungs, and heart.
- Alcoholic consumption may lead to devastating consequences, both emotional and physical. Many of these are irreversible because of an ulcerated digestive tract, a destroyed liver, or a damaged brain.
- Overeating or nutritional deficiency over a long period of time will also result in bad health.

However, many illnesses are not the result of abuses, dissipation, or emotional problems. Many people are just ill! Jesus, referring to the man born blind, said: "Neither hath this man sinned, nor his parents: but that the works of God should be made manifest in him" (John 9:3). Think of those with birth defects or genetic illnesses, accident victims, casualties of someone's carelessness or abuse, infectious and viral diseases, etc.

We point out the above in order to emphasize that there are various approaches to the problem of healing. Let us deal with three of these:

God heals through the new birth:

When a person becomes a "new creature" in Christ (2 Corinthians 5:17), he finds that Jesus can meet every need. Many testify that when they made things right spiritually, and began to live in proper perspective and relationship to God, their illnesses were taken away. The hymn writer, William B. Bradley, refers to this new perspective.

"Just as I am, poor, wretched, blind;
Sight, riches, healing of the mind,
Yea, all I need, in Thee I find,
O, Lamb of God, I come."

God heals through the confession of sin:

Many Christians live miserable, weakened and often sickly lives because of disobedience and unconfessed sin. Such persons can become completely well if they will deal with sin. The Psalmist said: "Who forgiveth all thine iniquities; who healeth all thy diseases; who redeemeth thy life from destruction; who crownest thee with loving kindness and tender mercies..." (Psalm 103:3,4).

God heals through miraculous intervention in keeping with His own sovereign will and purpose:

The Bible contains many such examples. There is present day evidence as well. However, God does not heal all who call on Him or who are prayed for by others. "God is no respecter of persons" (Acts 10:34), but He heals some and not others with a divine selectivity which reflects His own eternal wisdom and divine will. "His ways are higher than our ways" (cf., Isaiah 55:8). This divine selectivity may be seen in the example of Paul who prayed long for the removal of an affliction (2 Corinthians 12:8-10). God didn't heal Paul. He provided grace and strength — not that Paul might endure, but that he might learn the joy and glory of utter dependence! God is trying to teach His own that in all instances we must learn that "the excellency of the power [is] of God, and not of us" (2 Corinthians 4:7). The glorious will and ways of God came into focus in Paul's life when he learned "for when I am weak, then am I strong" (2 Corinthians 12:10).

None of this, however, should discourage or hinder us from praying in faith for the sick — or for anything else. God may answer our prayer of faith in ways that will amaze us. "Pray without ceasing" (1 Thessalonians 5:17) is His command. The counselor should be cautious, however, not to convey guaranteed physical healing as a result of his prayer.

Counseling Strategy

1. Reassure the inquirer that God loves him and is able to meet his needs. You are happy to share and pray with him.
   NOTE: In talking about their ailments, some individuals tend to go on and on. The counselor should be sympathetic and caring, but at an appropriate opportunity take command of the conversation.

2. After the inquirer has explained his problem, inform him that you would be glad to speak about the matter but you would first like to ask him a very important question directly related to the issue. Has he ever received Jesus Christ as his personal Savior and Lord? If indicated, explain "Steps to Peace with God," page 5, followed by pages 9 and 37 for "Assurance."

3. Now, redirect the conversation to the emotional or physical problem. Is it due, possibly, to habits or excesses such as those mentioned in the BACKGROUND? Some discussion may follow at this point. Help him to realize that these, if involved, might be directly related to his problems. Encourage him to trust God in order to bring his life-style under the control of the will of God.

4. Pray with him for victory over the contributing excesses, if any, as well as for his complete restoration to health.

5. If he is a Christian, try to determine if his illness is in any way related to a lack of harmony with God's will and plan for his life. Gently ask if there is

any anger, bitterness, resentment, or some other unconfessed sin. If so, share "Restoration," page 11. Emphasize 1 John 1:9 and 2:1.

Encourage the inquirer to live in fellowship with Christ, seeking always to glorify Him (1 Corinthians 10:31). Following this, pray earnestly and in faith for healing, according to Matthew 18:19.

6. If the inquirer is a Christian who feels that he has been walking in God's will, go immediately to prayer, claiming God's promise according to the prayer of faith.

7. Following your handling of any of the above cases, always speak of the peace and completeness which can be experienced as we learn to depend upon God's Word and prayer. These will provide the greatest encouragement in the face of illness or adversity. Offer to send him *Living in Christ,* the Bible study booklet which will help get him started in Bible reading and study.

8. Counsel him to get involved with a Bible-teaching church. The fellowship, care, and prayers of God's people are a great strength. Dependence upon the pastor for counsel and encouragement may be a definite asset.

Scripture

"Is any among you afflicted? Let him pray . . . Is any sick among you? Let him call for the elders of the church; and let them pray over him anointing him with oil in the name of the Lord: and the prayer of faith shall save the sick, and the Lord shall raise him up; and if he have committed sins, they shall be forgiven him. Confess your faults one to another, and pray for one another, that ye may be healed. The effectual fervent prayer of a righteous man availeth much." James 5:13-16, KJV

"But let him ask in faith, nothing wavering. For he that wavereth is like a wave of the sea driven with the wind and tossed." James 1:6, KJV

"If I regard iniquity in my heart, the Lord will not hear me." Psalm 66:18, KJV

"And lest I (Paul) should be exalted above measure through the abundance of the revelations, there was given to me a thorn in the flesh, the messenger of Satan to buffet me, lest I should be exalted above measure. For this thing I besought the Lord thrice, that it might depart from me. And he said unto me, My grace is sufficient for thee: for my strength is made perfect in weakness. Most gladly therefore will I rather glory in my infirmities, that the power of Christ may rest upon me." 2 Corinthians 12:7-9, KJV

HEAVEN

Background

Heaven is a prepared place for a redeemed people (John 14:1-6). As hell is the final abode of all who live and die in their sins, so heaven is the final abode of all who are redeemed by the blood of Christ and regenerated by the Holy Spirit. It is a known, permanent place, which is said to be:

The place where God dwells. "Hear from heaven, your dwelling place, and when you hear, forgive" (1 Kings 8:30, NIV).

The city of God. "But you have come to Mount Zion, to the heavenly Jerusalem, the city of the living God" (Hebrews 12:22, NIV).

My Father's house. "In my Father's house are many mansions" (John 14:2, KJV).

Where Christ is in God's presence. "For Christ did not enter a man-made sanctuary that was only a copy of the true one; he entered heaven itself, now to appear for us in God's presence" (Hebrews 9:24, NIV).

The dwelling place of angels and saints. "See that you do not look down on one of these little ones. For I tell you that their angels in heaven always see the face of my Father in heaven" (Matthew 18:10, NIV). "In the same way, I tell you, there is rejoicing in the presence of the angels of God over one sinner who repents" (Luke 15:10, NIV).

The eternal home of all believers. "We are confident, I say, and willing rather to be absent from the body, and to be present with the Lord" (2 Corinthians 5:8, KJV). "Then we which are alive and remain shall be caught up together with them in the clouds, to meet the Lord in the air: and so shall we ever be with the Lord" (1 Thessalonians 4:17, KJV).

A "state" of perfect love and perfect rest. It is entirely separated from earth's impurities and imperfections, its deceptions and alterations. Heaven is a place of worship, praise, and service where the redeemed will be forever relieved of sinfulness by Him who will be our unending joy.

"And there shall in no wise enter into it anything that defileth, neither whatsoever worketh abomination, or maketh a lie: but they which are written in the Lamb's book of life" (Revelation 21:27; see also Revelation 5:9-13, KJV).

"Beloved, now are we the sons of God, and it doth not yet appear what we shall be: but we know that, when he shall appear, we shall be like him; for we shall see him as he is" (1 John 3:2, KJV).

We will recognize our loved ones who died in Christ, and also fellowship with the great Bible saints. "And, behold, there appeared unto them Moses and (Elijah) talking with him. Then answered Peter, and said unto Jesus, Lord, it is good for us to be here: if thou wilt, let us make here three tabernacles; one for thee, and one for Moses, and one for (Elijah)" (Matthew 17:3,4, KJV).

Heaven's completeness and glories are indescribable. "But we speak the wisdom of God in a mystery, even the hidden wisdom, which God ordained before the world unto our glory: . . . as it is written, Eye hath not seen, nor ear heard, neither have entered into the heart of man, the things which God hath prepared for them that love him" (1 Corinthians 2:7,9).

Billy Graham comments: "Heaven will be a place in which its inhabitants will be freed from the fears and insecurities that plague and haunt us in the present life. No energy crisis there . . . We will be free from the economic and financial pressures that burden us down here, free from the fear of personal and physical harm . . . There will be no fear of personal failure . . . Our relationship with Him will be intimate and direct. I'm looking forward to that glorious day of going to heaven."

Counseling Strategy

1. For the Christian who wants to be reassured about heaven and the future life, share the material in the BACKGROUND. Perhaps he has lost a loved one; be sympathetic and sensitive to the Holy Spirit as you attempt to encourage and comfort. "Wherefore comfort one another with these words" (1 Thessalonians 4:18). Make sure your inquirer is a Christian, and is ready for heaven. Use "Steps to Peace with God," page 5.

2. For the non-Christian with questions about future events and heaven, share the material in the BACKGROUND, turning, if indicated, to the chapter on the Second Coming for additional truth. Share "Steps to Peace with God," page 5.

Scripture

"And God shall wipe away all tears from their eyes; and there shall be no more death, neither sorrow, nor crying, neither shall there be any more pain: for the former things are passed away."   Revelation 21:4, KJV

"For to me to live is Christ, and to die is gain. But if I live in the flesh, this is the fruit of my labor: yet what I shall choose I wot not. For I am in a strait betwixt two, having a desire to depart, and to be with Christ; which is far better."   Philippians 1:21-23, KJV

John 14:1-6

HELL

Background

Hell is not the kingdom of Satan where he will reign over demons and all who are bad. There is nothing in Scripture to indicate that hell will be some sort of fellowship of sinners, where life will continue pretty much as it was on earth. The pathetic jokes about plans for "living it up" in hell demonstrate ignorance of its purpose and nature.

There are three Greek words translated hell in our English Bible:

Tartaros is found only once in the Bible. "God spared not the angels that sinned, but cast them down to hell, and delivered them into chains of darkness to be reserved for judgment" (2 Peter 2:4, KJV). The angels mentioned here refer to those "which kept not their first estate, but left their own habitation" (in rebellion) (Jude 6). Tartaros, then, is a place of confinement for the rebellious angels until the time of their judgment.

Hades is found ten times in the New Testament. (Matthew 11:23; 16:18; Luke 10:15; 16:23; Acts 2:17,31; Revelation 1:18; 6:8; 20:13,14)

It is not the final destiny of those who die having rejected Christ, but a place of torment until they are resurrected to stand before the great white throne judgment (see Revelation 20:13-15). The suffering, though real, is not physical. *Hades* is also a place of separation from God and of no escape. ". . . between us and you there is a great gulf fixed: so that they which would pass from hence to you cannot; neither can they pass to us, that would come from thence" (Luke 16:26, KJV). NOTE: The imagined place of remedial suffering (purgatory) has absolutely no scriptural foundation.

Geena or *Gehenna* is translated hell twelve times: (Matthew 5:22, 29, 30; 10:28; 18:9; Mark 9:43,45,47; Luke 12:5; James 3:6) Eleven of the twelve references are from the lips of Jesus Himself.

Geena refers to the valley of Hinnom, once a place where children were sacrificed to the god Molech (2 Chronicles 33:1-6). Located outside the south wall of Jerusalem, it was a convenient place for the residents to throw their rubbish. Even dead bodies of animals and criminals were thus disposed. This "city dump" was a place of decomposition and continuous fire (Mark 9:44), and was used by Jesus to teach about the eventual abode of them who reject Him as Savior.

Geena is also mentioned as the lake of fire. "Whosoever was not found written in the book of life was cast into the lake of fire" (Revelation 20:15, KJV). There will be no appeal after passing of sentence at the great white throne judgment. All who have rejected Christ will be present. "The sea gave up the dead which were in it; and death and hell (*Hades*) delivered up the dead which were in them . . . And death and hell (*Hades*) were cast into the lake of fire. This is the second death" (Revelation 20:13-15, KJV).

Billy Graham writes: "No matter how excruciating or how literal the fire of hell may or may not be, the thirst of a lost soul for the Living

Water will be more painful than the fires of perdition. Hell, essentially and basically, is banishment from the presence of God for deliberately rejecting Jesus Christ as Lord and Savior."

Counseling Strategy

1. If the inquirer is fearful of hell and the possibility of going there, encourage him to make sure of his eternal salvation. Explain "Steps to Peace with God," page 5. In Christ, he need not fear hell. "Therefore, there is now no condemnation for those who are in Christ Jesus." (Romans 8:1, NIV).

2. If the inquirer denies the existence of hell, share material in the BACK-GROUND.

3. If the inquirer accuses God of being unjust in condemning people to hell, point out that "the everlasting fire," according to Matthew 25:41, was prepared for the Devil and his angels, not for mankind. If a person goes to hell it will be because of his willful sin in rejecting Jesus Christ as Lord and Savior. (See John 3:16-18 and John 5:24.)

    Point out that God will forgive him and save him if he will receive Jesus Christ. Share "Steps to Peace with God," page 5.

4. If the inquirer accuses God of being unjust for condemning those who have never had an opportunity to hear the Gospel, remind him that God has condemned no one to hell (see above).

    In the case of those who have never heard, trust God to do the right thing! We can be assured that He will be fair and merciful. There are degrees of rewards to be given at the judgment seat of Christ. One may logically conclude that there will also be degrees of reckoning for those deprived of the Gospel.

Scripture

Matthew 11:23
Matthew 16:18
Luke 10:15
Acts 2:17,31
Luke 12:5

THE HOLY SPIRIT

Background

A Christian can never be "complete," or mature, without a comprehensive knowledge of the Person and work of the Holy Spirit. It is always a sense of need and insufficiency that motivates us to seek this knowledge.

The Holy Spirit is one of the three Persons of the Holy Trinity. He is equal in position and power, possessing all the essential aspects of deity. He shares all the attributes of the Godhead: He is eternal, having neither beginning nor end (Hebrews 9:14); omnipotent, having all power (Luke 1:35); omnipresent, everywhere present at the same time (Psalm 139:7); and omniscient, all knowing (1 Corinthians 2:10,11).

He possesses all the characteristics of personality. The Holy Spirit is not an "it" (see Romans 8:16 and 26, NIV).

The Holy Spirit has intellect, emotions, and will. He speaks (Acts 13:2), intercedes (Romans 8:26), testifies (John 15:26), guides (John 16:13), commands (Acts 16:6,7), appoints (Acts 20:28), leads (Romans 8:14), and reproves and convicts of sin (John 16:8). He can be lied to and tested (Acts 5:3,4,9), resisted (Acts 7:51), grieved (Ephesians 4:30) and blasphemed (Matthew 12:31).

Each Christian must understand his own relationship to the Holy Spirit.

- That which has been realized:

  We are born of the Holy Spirit (John 3:6,8).

  God has given us the Holy Spirit (John 14:16; 16:7).

  We are baptized by the Spirit (1 Corinthians 12:13).

  We are the temple of the Holy Spirit (1 Corinthians 6:19,20).

  We are sealed by the Holy Spirit (Ephesians 1:13).

- That which is potential reality:

  Each Christian has the Holy Spirit, but not every Christian is filled with the Holy Spirit. We ought to desire this fullness because God commands it. "Be filled with the Spirit" (Ephesians 5:18, KJV).

Billy Graham writes: "I believe the Bible teaches that there is one baptism in the Spirit — when we come to faith in Christ. The Bible teaches that there are many fillings — in fact, we are to be continually filled by the Holy Spirit. One baptism, many fillings. When we are filled with the Spirit, it is not a question of there being more of Him, as though His work in us is quantitative. It is not how much of the Spirit we have, but how much the Spirit has of us . . . As we come to understand more and more of Christ's leadership, we surrender and yield more to Him. So, in seeking the fullness of the Spirit, we receive and enjoy His filling and His fullness more and more."

Counseling Strategy

1. If a question is asked about the Holy Spirit, attempt to answer it from material in the BACKGROUND.

2. If a question is asked or desire expressed about the fullness of the Holy Spirit, share the following points:

   A. Understand that God has given us His Holy Spirit and that He dwells within. See Scriptures in the BACKGROUND.

   B. Understand that God commands us to be filled with the Holy Spirit. (Ephesians 5:18).

   C. Understand that before we can receive His fullness we must deal honestly with every known sin in our life. This involves repentance and confession to God.

   D. We clearly and completely turn over the control of our life to the Lord in a definite act of commitment. We renounce our own way and seek above all else to continuously submit to Christ as Lord so that we may be ruled by Him in every area of life. This obedience demands a daily yielding of ourselves to God so that we may learn the secrets of walking in faith.

   When we are yielded to God and His will, we are filled with the Holy Spirit. The Holy Spirit controls and dominates us. Now we are to act on this truth, and walk or live with full assurance that God has already filled us, and that we are under His control.

3. Pray with the inquirer about the application of these truths to his life and that he may be filled with the Spirit.

Scripture:

"And I will pray the Father, and he shall give you another Comforter, that he may abide with you for ever; even the Spirit of truth; whom the world cannot receive, because it seeth him not, neither knoweth him: but ye know him; for he dwelleth with you, and shall be in you."

John 14:16,17, KJV

"But ye shall receive power, after that the Holy Ghost is come upon you: and ye shall be witnesses unto me both in Jerusalem, and in all Judea, and in Samaria, and unto the uttermost part of the earth."   Acts 1:8, KJV

"Nevertheless I tell you the truth; It is expedient for you that I go away; for if I go not away, the Comforter will not come unto you; but if I depart, I will send him unto you. And when he is come, he will reprove the world of sin, and of righteousness, and of judgment: of sin, because they believe not on me; of righteousness, because I go to my Father, and ye see me no more; of judgment, because the prince of this world is judged."

John 16:7-11, KJV

John 3:6-8
1 Corinthians 12:13
John 16:13,14
1 Corinthians 6:19,20
Ephesians 1:13
Romans 8:14-16

See also Fruit of and Gifts of the Holy Spirit

HOLY SPIRIT, FRUIT OF
Background

The filling of the Holy Spirit (previous chapter) includes two areas: evidence of the fruit of the Holy Spirit (this chapter) and the gifts of the Spirit (following chapter).

To be filled with the Spirit means that the believer will demonstrate the fruit of the Spirit in his life. The New Testament pattern for living is set in Matthew 7:16, "Ye shall know them by their fruits" (KJV). The first evidence of being filled with the Spirit is godly living. God wants mature Christians, those who manifest the fruit of the Spirit according to Galatians 5:22,23: "love, joy, peace, patience, kindness, goodness, faithfulness, gentleness and self-control" (NIV).

"The fruit of the Spirit is God's expectation in our lives," states Billy Graham. "Unlike the gifts of the Spirit, the fruit of the Spirit is not divided among believers. Instead, ALL Christians should be marked by all the fruit of the Spirit. Put in the simplest terms, the Bible tells us we need the Spirit to bring fruit into our lives because we cannot produce godliness apart from the Spirit. In our own selves we are filled with all kinds of self-centered and self-seeking desires which are opposed to God's will for our lives."

Practically, how do we begin to work this fruit of the Spirit into our lives?

We must consciously surrender ourselves to the Holy Spirit in the light of 1 Corinthians 6:19,20 and Romans 12:1,2. Ask yourself, have you ever realized that you belong to God, that your body is the actual residence of the Holy Spirit? Have you ever offered your body (life) to God as Romans 12:1 demands?

Next, we must see ourselves as having died to sin but having become alive to Christ (Romans 6:11). Paul said in Galatians 2:20 (KJV), "I am crucified with Christ (I died when He died), nevertheless I live, and the life which I now live in the flesh I live by the faith of the Son of God who loved me and gave himself for me." You are dead to sin in the sense that it no longer has control over you (see Romans 6:12,13).

Then, we determine by faith to bring ourselves under the Lordship of Christ. This happens progressively as we bring our minds under control. Our actions respond to the Spirit's control over our thoughts. "And be not conformed to this world, but be ye transformed by the renewing of your mind, that ye may prove what is that ... acceptable, and perfect, will of God" (Romans 12:2, KJV).

We work on one "fruit" at a time, praying in faith and trusting God that the love, joy, peace, patience spoken of in Galatians 5:22 and 23 might become a reality in our lives.

Counseling Strategy

1. If the inquirer expresses concern about having the fruit of the Spirit in his life, you may review from the BACKGROUND the appropriate information.

2. Sometimes questions reveal where the focus is needed. Ask:

   "Is there any unconfessed sin in your life which is keeping you from a close walk with God?"

   "Do you know of any lack of personal discipline?"

   "Is there a broken relationship with another person that needs healing?"

   "Are you consciously abiding in Christ?"

   "Are you reading and studying the Word daily?"

   "Are you praying about your relationship to Christ, asking Him to develop the fruit of the Spirit in you?"

3. Pray with the inquirer that his desires for the fullness of the Spirit and the fruit of the Spirit may be fulfilled.

Scripture

"I beseech you therefore, brethren, by the mercies of God that ye present your bodies a living sacrifice, holy, acceptable unto God, which is your reasonable service. And be not conformed to this world: but be ye transformed by the renewing of your mind, that ye may prove what is that good, and acceptable, and perfect, will of God."   Romans 12:1,2, KJV

"What? know ye not that your body is the temple of the Holy Ghost which is in you, which ye have of God, and ye are not your own? For ye are bought with a price: therefore glorify God in your body, and in your spirit, which are God's."   1 Corinthians 6:19,20, KJV

"Likewise reckon ye also yourselves to be dead indeed unto sin, but alive unto God through Jesus Christ our Lord. Let not sin therefore reign in your mortal body, that ye should obey it in the lusts thereof. Neither yield ye your members as instruments of unrighteousness unto sin; but yield yourselves unto God, as those that are alive from the dead, and your members as instruments of righteousness unto God."
                                                    Romans 6:11-13, KJV

Galatians 5:22,23

HOLY SPIRIT, GIFTS OF
Background

The truly committed Christian will want to appropriate all that God has in reserve for his life. We have received God's grace through the Person and work of the Lord Jesus Christ. Now we should be open to receive the gifts of the Holy Spirit. "But eagerly desire the greater gifts" (1 Corinthians 12:31, NIV).

We need to be careful, however, not to be presumptuous in claiming any gifts, but rather trust the sovereign Holy Spirit to give "to each man, just as He determines" (1 Corinthians 12:11, NIV). Many persons claim to be possessors of certain gifts, but their lives and ministry do not give evidence of such possession. Spiritual gifts are not to be thought of as making any one believer or group of belivers any more holy or more spiritually advanced than others.

Spiritual pride can nullify the effectiveness of any gift.

Some Christians obviously possess the more overt gifts, such as preaching, teaching, or evangelizing. This does not mean that they are "super-Christians." They are merely exercising the gifts God has given them. The Christian who exercises the quiet gift of faith is just as important to God and to the building up of the Body. Nowhere in the Scripture is it indicated that we are to seek the same gifts. All gifts are not the same, but they all have the same goal: they are all to work toward the unification and building up of the body, the Church (Ephesians 4:12-16).

Two Scripture portions enumerate the gifts of the Holy Spirit:

"To one there is given through the Spirit the message of wisdom, to another the message of knowledge by means of the same Spirit, to another faith by the same Spirit, to another gifts of healing by that one Spirit, to another miraculous powers, to another prophecy, to another the ability to distinguish between spirits, to another the ability to speak in different kinds of tongues, and to still another the interpretation of tongues. All these are the work of one and the same Spirit, and he gives them to each man, just as he determines" (1 Corinthians 12:8-11, NIV).

"It was he who gave some to be apostles, some to be prophets, some to be evangelists, and some to be pastors and teachers, to prepare God's people for works of service, so that the body of Christ may be built up" (Ephesians 4:11,12, NIV).

Billy Graham's comments on this important subject are helpful. "These gifts come to us from the Holy Spirit. He chooses who gets which gifts, and He dispenses them at His good pleasure. While we are held accountable for the use of any gifts He gives us, we have no responsibility for gifts we have not been given. Nor are we to covet what someone else has or be envious of that person. We may wish to have certain gifts and even ask for them, but if it is not the will of the

Holy Spirit, we will not get what we ask for. And if we are dissatisfied because the Holy Spirit does not give us the gifts we want, we sin."

Counseling Strategy

1. Stay within the guidelines of the above BACKGROUND when counseling in the area of the gifts of the Spirit. It is possible to be diverted by some who would make the gifts something they were never meant to be.

2. Make it clear that one must be a born-again Christian in order to appropriate the gifts of the Spirit. Contrary to the insistence of some, this order cannot be reversed. Ask the inquirer if he has received the Lord Jesus Christ as Lord and Savior. If not, share "Steps to Peace with God," page 5.

3. If your inquirer is a believer who is sincerely seeking the fullness of the Holy Spirit and identification of a gift, counsel him to give time to a prolonged and careful study of the Scriptures that deal with the gifts, including the book of Acts and the epistles of Paul, where we see the gifts being exercised. Careful and thoughtful prayer should accompany such study, as spiritual discernment and wisdom will come to guide the seeker away from excesses.

4. Counsel him not to be unduly influenced by persons or groups who insist on a kind of standardized approach for the receiving and exercising of any gift or gifts, or who insist that all believers must possess certain gifts. Each one must trust the Holy Spirit to distribute as He wills (see John 3:8 and 1 Corinthians 12:11).

A comment by Billy Graham helps put this into perspective: "I believe that a person who is Spirit-filled — constantly submitting to the Lordship of Christ — will come to discover his gifts with some degree of ease. He wants God to guide him in his life, and that is the kind of person God stands ready to bless, showing him the gifts that the Holy Spirit has bestowed on him."

5. Counsel him that along with the gifts of the Spirit we should constantly seek to demonstrate the fruit of the Spirit. "But the fruit of the Spirit is love, joy, peace, patience, kindness, goodness, faithfulness, gentleness and self-control. Against such things there is no law" (Galatians 5:22,23, NIV). Fruit and gifts must go hand in hand. We are known by our fruit (Matthew 7:16,20).

6. Pray with the inquirer for a demonstration of the fruit of the Spirit in his life and for increased and effective service to the Body of Christ and to the world using some gift according to the will of the Sovereign Spirit of God.

Scripture

Study 1 Corinthians 13 in relation to other portions for perspective on the gifts of the Holy Spirit.

"As every man hath received the gift, even so minister the same one to another, as good stewards of the manifold grace of God."1 Peter 4:10, KJV

THE HOME
(Conflicts Between Parents and Teenagers)
Background

In our fast-moving electronic age, kids grow up quicker and want to be free earlier in life than their parents did. Parents often find it difficult to keep pace with the lightning changes in their children, and as a result, conflicts come.

It seems that one day, a child is in his parent's arms and the next day he is beginning school, bringing home friends, helping around the house, starting Little League or Brownies — in general, a pretty good kid! Then, suddenly, the roof caves in! He begins to talk back, questions rules and breaks them, sometimes is sullen and non-communicative. The teen years have arrived, catching the parents completely off-guard.

There can be many areas of conflict: their friends (many of whom we don't approve), make-up, dating, chores around the home, an allowance, the family car, school and homework, and discipline, to name a few.

A communication barrier develops. Parents find it difficult to talk things over with their children. They delay explanations of crucial physical and mental changes, especially in the areas of sex and reproduction. Controls are tightened by the parents and the teenager fights even harder for independence. The gap widens, they become antagonists — and the battle goes on.

Billy Graham writes: "Rebellion, waywardness, lack of discipline, confusion, and conflict prevent happy relationships within the home. (But) God is interested in your family, your marriage, your children. He shows us the ideals and the goals for the family. He's willing to help us . . . Have you sought God's will? Have you gotten on your knees and committed your children to the Lord? Do you gather them for family devotions? The answer is in surrendering your heart and life to Jesus Christ so that every member of the home knows Jesus Christ and loves the Word of God."

Counseling Strategy

In counseling parents in conflict with their children, urge them to put their house in order, spiritually. Read Billy Graham's paragraph in the BACK-GROUND, then:

1. Advise them that in order to have the peace of God in the home, they must have the peace of God in their hearts. This comes through a personal relationship with Jesus Christ. Explain "Steps to Peace with God," page 5.

2. Encourage parents to take a firm stand for Christ in the spirit of Joshua, who said, "Choose ye this day whom ye will serve ... but as for me and my house, we will serve the Lord" (Joshua 24:15, KJV). They must determine to have a home that exalts Christ.

3. Counsel them to learn to rely on God's resources, available through prayer. They should covenant with God for the wisdom He offers (James 1:5) and claim His help for the proper spiritual development for their children. (See Philippians 4:6.) They must learn to pray with their children as well as for them.

4. Urge parents to build the life of the family around the Word of God, helping each member to understand the issues of life from its viewpoint. Encourage them to:

   A. Seek each one's conversion to Christ.

   B. Center the family activities largely around a Bible-teaching church.

   C. Be willing to deal patiently with the children's spiritual doubts.

5. Parents must establish rules governing the home which are equitable, reasonable, and "keepable." Respect is learned as a response to authority. Be as flexible as you can where their identity, independence and self-esteem are concerned. Teenagers need a lot of support and encouragement. Conflicts are never resolved by argument or fighting.

6. Parental example and stability influence children greatly. A good, happy marriage will do more to prepare young people for life than rules and surveillance. A consistant demonstration of Christian virtues such as love, patience, understanding, encouragement, and trust will provide the anchor the teenager needs in stressful and changing times. The beliefs of the parents should never be divorced from experience and practice, especially in the home.

7. Close communication with the teenager will do much to avoid conflict. This means not only meaningful conversation, but spending quality time with him. This personal attention will help create a positive self-image and fortify family solidarity. Don't be afraid to show physical affection. A fatherly hug or a motherly kiss will aid in making the child feel accepted and loved.

Scripture:

"Train a child in the way he should go, and when he is old he will not turn from it."   Proverbs 22:6, NIV

"Fathers, do not embitter your children, or they will become discouraged."   Colossians 3:21, NIV

"Be careful to obey all these regulations I am giving you, so that it may always go well with you and your children after you, because you will be doing what is good and right in the eyes of the Lord your God."
                                                 Deuteronomy 12:28, NIV

"Children, obey your parents in the Lord, for this is right. Honor your father and mother — which is the first commandment with a promise — that it may go well with you and that you may enjoy long life on the earth. Fathers, do not exasperate your children; instead, bring them up in the training and instruction of the Lord."   Ephesians 6:1-4, NIV

"The righteous man leads a blameless life; blessed are his children after him."   Proverbs 20:7, NIV

THE HOME
(Raising and Disciplining Children)
Background

A recurrent theme in the Bible is the training of children through teaching and example. The book of Deuteronomy is explicit in stating that children be taught the ways of God. "And these words, which I command thee this day, shall be in thine heart: and thou shalt teach them diligently unto thy children, and shalt talk of them when thou sittest in thine house, and when thou walkest by the way, and when thou liest down, and when thou risest up" (Deuteronomy 6:6,7, KJV).

The book of Proverbs is a compendium of the wisdom of God's people. The family and the nurturing of children in the faith is one of its strong emphases. "Train up a child in the way he should go; and when he is old, he will not depart from it" (Proverbs 22:6, KJV).

Timothy had been taught the Scriptures from infancy, according to God's command and Jewish custom. "And that from a child thou hast known the holy scriptures, which are able to make thee wise unto salvation through faith which is in Christ Jesus" (2 Timothy 3:15, KJV).

Paul speaks of the necessity for continuity in training and disciplining our children: "When I call to remembrance the unfeigned faith that is in thee, which dwelt first in thy grandmother Lois, and thy mother Eunice; and I am persuaded that in thee also" (2 Timothy 1:5, KJV).

The Bible teaches that parents have the responsibilty of training and disciplining their children so that they might be brought up knowing the Scriptures and honoring the Lord.

Billy Graham cautions: "The basic reason for unhappiness in the home is that we have disregarded God and the principles He has given us. We have refused to acknowledge His plan for the family. The members of the home have refused to accept their particular responsibilities as given in the Bible. It is well known that obedience doesn't come naturally. It must be taught and learned. Children must be taught obedience just as much as they need to be taught to read and write."

Counseling Strategy

1. Encourage parents to provide the kind of home which is conducive to solid spiritual and mental development.

   A. A stable, peaceful, and loving home.

   B. A family-centered home where there is a sense of solidarity, mutual respect, and encouragement. A home where the family does things together, especially when children are younger.

C. A God-centered home where each member has the right to respond to God's love in Christ, and to be taught how to live from a spiritual perspective. See Proverbs 22:6. (This would be an appropriate time to ask the parent if he has ever received Jesus Christ as Lord and Savior.) As indicated, share "Steps to Peace with God," page 5.

D. A church-oriented home. It is much easier to raise children when their lives and those of their families and friends are centered in the church.

E. Parents should introduce their children to the world of the mind by example and practice. If parents are readers, children are likely to read also. Good books and magazines on the child's level should be introduced into the home. Music lessons, hobbies, and sports should be introduced while children are at grade school level. This will be a safeguard against conflicts as the teen years come.

2. Encourage parents to recognize that their child has certain rights, but that these rights integrate with those affecting all members of the family.

A. The child has the right to be loved and accepted.

B. The child has the right to receive that kind of reinforcement which leads to self-respect and a sense of security and significance.

C. The child has the right to see parents demonstrate genuine affection and respect for each other. Examples of mature, Christian behavior are needed in order that children may see how the parents handle problems and stress.

D. The child has the right to be disciplined and punished with fairness and consistency.

(1) Do not expect more from a child than he can deliver.

(2) Be fair and just in administering punishment. Excessive demands and harsh, physical punishment lead quickly to resentment and rebellion. Parents should be flexible and not demand the "letter of the law."

(3) Never punish in anger or on the spur of the moment.

(4) Always give an explanation to the child so that he knows why he is being punished.

3. Encourage the parent to keep the lines of communication open at all costs.

A. The parent must take time to be an attentive listener and take the initiative in encouraging dialogue. There must be frank discussion in regard to sex, drugs, alcohol, dating, etc.

B. The parent should share experiences from his childhood and teen years, including the mistakes and failures.

C. The parent must be honest, permitting a child to question his standards and beliefs. This gives the opportunity to explain and defend them. Through this, your child will formulate his own standards of beliefs and values. You can challenge them and help them in setting goals for the moment and for life.

Scripture

"The just man walketh in his integrity: his children are blessed after him."
Proverbs 20:7, KJV

"Fathers, provoke not your children to anger, lest they be discouraged."
Colossians 3:21, KJV

"My son, do not despise the Lord's discipline and do not resent his rebuke, because the Lord disciplines those he loves, as a father the son he delights in."
Proverbs 3:11,12, NIV

"Children, obey your parents in the Lord, for this is right. Honor your father and mother — which is the first commandment with a promise — that it may go well with you and that you may enjoy long life on the earth. Fathers, do not exasperate your children; instead, bring them up in the training and instruction of the Lord."
Ephesians 6:1-4, NIV

Proverbs 31:10,26,27,28, KJV
Proverbs 30:11, KJV
Deuteronomy 12:28, NIV

THE HOME
(Winning Parents to Christ)

Background

Paul, in writing to Timothy, counseled him as follows:

"Don't let anyone look down on you because you are young, but set an example for the believers in speech, in life, in love, in faith and in purity ... Watch your life and doctrine closely. Persevere in them, because if you do, you will save both yourself and your hearers" (1 Timothy 4:12,16, NIV).

Though this advice was given nearly 2,000 years ago, it is still timely for the young person who has received Christ and is deeply concerned for his parents' spiritual welfare.

Recently a pastor said that when a teenager is converted and wants to know how to witness, he tells him to go home, straighten up his room, make his bed, mind his parents, smile, listen to other people, and wait until his parents ask him what has happened before telling them that Christ has changed his life.

NOTE: Christian teenagers are not the only ones with unsaved parents. Some Christian adults also have non-Christian parents — and some of them are getting on in years!

In *Billy Graham Answers Your Questions*, he offers this advice: "First of all, I suggest patience with your parents. They will want to be sure that your experience with Christ is not just a passing fancy. Second, let Christ so possess you that they see a difference in you. Third, pray for them. They may seem to be turning a deaf ear to you, but they are hearing more than you think. This won't happen in a week, in a month, or perhaps even in a year, but God's Spirit is always at work. Remember, the Bible says, 'Be not weary in well doing; for in due season we shall reap if we faint not' (Galatians 6:9, KJV)."

Counseling Strategy

1. Congratulate the young person seeking advice about witnessing. It is an indication of a more-than-average spiritual concern.

2. Read Billy Graham's counsel from the BACKGROUND, then emphasize the following:

   A. In the Scripture (1 Timothy 4:12,16), the key word is example. In the home, this would be best demonstrated by respect, obedience, and acts of love and kindness. Remember the old saying, "What you do speaks so loudly I cannot hear what you are saying."

B. Make sure of consistency in Christian living, not being up one day and down the next.

3. Urge him to give much attention to the development of his own spiritual life by reading and studying God's Word, by prayer (he can put his parents' names at the top of his prayer list), by being a good student at school, and by becoming involved in Christian activities with other young people.

4. Counsel him to pray patiently for opportunities to witness. This may be done personally or by inviting his family to a special Christian function or to church.

5. Pray with the young person that Paul's advice to Timothy might be a reality in his life. The above may not sound too exciting to him, but experience has indicated that it is the best, if not the only, way to go.

Scripture

"Don't let anyone look down on you because you are young, but set an example for the believers in speech, in life, in love, in faith and in purity . . . Be diligent in these matters; give yourself wholly to them, so that everyone may see your progress. Watch your life and doctrine closely. Persevere in them, because if you do, you will save both yourself and your hearers."   1 Timothy 4:12-16, NIV

"Do not be anxious about anything, but in everything, by prayer and petition, with thanksgiving, present your requests to God. And the peace of God, which transcends all understanding, will guard your hearts and your minds in Christ Jesus."   Philippians 4:6,7, NIV

"But you will receive power when the Holy Spirit comes on you; and you will be my witnesses in Jerusalem, and in all Judea and Samaria, and to the ends of the earth."   Acts 1:8, NIV

"Therefore put on the full armor of God, so that when the day of evil comes, you may be able to stand your ground, and after you have done everything, to stand."   Ephesians 6:13, NIV

HOMOSEXUALITY
Background

A homosexual is a person who is sexually attracted to those of his own sex. A lesbian is the term used for a female homosexual.

This is a very complex problem and greatly misunderstood by a large segment of society. The complexity defies stereotyping, such as the effeminate man and the masculine woman, although some do manifest such characteristics. Unfortunately, it is a life-style practiced by millions which has invaded all levels of society. In fact, a significant number is found among the well educated, the urbane and sophisticated who hold responsible positions in business and industry, the professions, and in government.

Although there is an increasing militancy among homosexuals, resulting in an open defense of their life-style and the formation of gay organizations and fights for rights, millions among them live a double life due to societal pressures and intolerance. Many become devious as they attempt to cover up their behavior and associations. Fear of discovery becomes an obsession and a heavy load of guilt is carried by many as they realize the moral implications of the practice.

Such behavior cannot be dismissed simply as an alternate life-style or a different sexual orientation. Neither can it be argued that any were "born this way." Attempts to explain such behavior as sickness avoid the real issue.

God doesn't love the homosexual any less than He does anyone else. Such behavior, however, is a departure from God's expressed order. Though many homosexuals may feel that they have not chosen their sexual orientation, the fact remains that they have responded improperly to this orientation; it is this "response" which must be dealt with in the light of Scripture.

No doubts are left as to what is a proper sexual relationship:

"For this reason a man will leave his father and mother and be united to his wife, and they will become one flesh" (Genesis 2:24, NIV).

"As for you, be fruitful and increase in number; multiply on the earth and increase upon it" (Genesis 9:7, NIV).

"Sons are a heritage from the Lord, children a reward from him" (Psalm 127:3, NIV).

"The husband should fulfill his marital duty to his wife, and likewise the wife to her husband. The wife's body does not belong to her alone, but also to her husband. In the same way, the husband's body does not belong to him alone but also to his wife" (1 Corinthians 7:3,4, NIV).

According to these Scriptures, it should be obvious that God has ordained the establishment and perpetuation of the human race through the sexual union of a man and a woman. Of great importance in God's established order is that the family — consisting of father, mother and children—is the basis for society, and families are the greatest strength of any society. There is a preponderance of evidence in the Scriptures to substantiate this order. One should not assume, however, that all are going to marry and reproduce. Celebacy and singleness are also a part of God's order.

There are also many Scriptures which do not approve the practice of homosexuality. The Bible includes homosexuality in the list of carnal immorality along with adultery, fornication, prostitution, lust, etc. It is not to be singled out as a "special sin" especially offensive to God beyond any other sin. God deals with all sin through the Cross. It is only as any of us is willing to confess sin that God is able to deal with our rebellious, proud and guilt-laden hearts.

Billy Graham comments: "No matter how we may rationalize the practice (of homosexuality) as a viable alternative to heterosexual relationships, the reference in Romans 1 makes it clearly the product of a reprobate mind. By making this statement, I am not exonerating all heterosexual activity. As Dr. Harold Lindsell has put it, 'The immoral heterosexual is neither better nor worse than the practicing homosexual. Both come under divine judgment.' . . . When we come to Christ, we are called upon to repent of our sins and no longer to practice the ungodly patterns of living we may have enjoyed before."

The church needs to take a hard look at her attitudes and treatment of gays and lesbians in the past. She cannot, of course, condone the homosexual life-style nor encourage their involvement as unrepentant sinners in the life of the church. However, she should begin to address the problem honestly and realistically, in love and understanding. It is not God's will that anyone should be bound by homosexuality. His grace is sufficient to bring victory to those who are willing to submit this area to Him. The church needs to take the initiative in encouraging the homosexual with this message.

It is a source of encouragement that homosexuals are beginning to testify to deliverance through the power of the Gospel, even though some of them may never be completely free from homosexual tendencies or even temptation. St. Paul, in writing to people who had been involved in homosexuality and many other types of sin, says, "There was a time when some of you were just like that but now your sins are washed away, and you are set apart for God, and He has accepted you because of what the Lord Jesus Christ and the Spirit of our God have done for you" (1 Corinthians 6:11, TLB).

This gives us confidence to witness to the transformation which the person and work of Jesus Christ can effect in a life. The only real antidote to this problem, as in fact to any type of sinful behavior, is a personal, intimate, continuous relationship to Jesus Christ. This relationship is an ongoing process of growth and change. Sometimes it can be a painful process, punctuated by relapses and discouragement. Such set-backs should not lead to a sense of despair or to the thought that it is not worth the effort because all is so easily lost. The Christian's fellowship with Christ is maintained on the basis of 1 John

1:9, with such confession resulting in immediate renewal of our on-going relationship to Him.

Counseling Strategy

In anticipation of witnessing in this delicate area, the counselor should examine his attitudes towards the problem. If one is not objectively and genuinely able to offer God's love and grace to the homosexual, he should refer the inquirer to another Christian.

Three situations are likely to arise:

- The family member who has just learned that a loved one is a practicing homosexual and asks, "How can I live with this? What should I do?"
- An individual who admits to being a practicing homosexual and seeks counsel. Frequently a homosexual will want to talk without revealing the problem, or will attempt to cover up. Sometimes the subject will be obliquely approached, such as, "I have this friend..."
- A Christian who admits to having this problem.

If the Family Is Facing this Problem:

1. Counsel him not to panic, asking God to give him the grace to accept the situation, however difficult.
2. Urge him to keep the love lines open. We must love as God loves us all — in spite of what we are.
3. He must avoid condemning or putting down. This only results in antagonism and loss of communication.
4. On the other hand, advise him not to condone the homosexual practice or rationalize it. Don't re-interpret the Scriptures in accommodation.
5. He must take a firm but loving stand with the Scriptures as he firmly and gently witnesses to the person involved, using the Bible as a sword, not a club.
6. Urge him to commit the loved one to God in faith (see Proverbs 3:5,6), seeking to deepen his prayer life as those "shut up to faith." God sometimes permits us to live through a crisis situation in order to sharpen our dependence on Him.
7. Counsel him not to attempt to live with bottled-up emotions. He might want to take a Christian friend into his confidence and learn to share concerns and disappointments. A Christian prayer partner is a great resource.
8. Advise him to be prepared to live with disappointment if the situation doesn't change.

If Inquirer is a Practicing Homosexual:

1. The attitude of the witness must be tempered by love and understanding. Often you will be speaking to one who feels lonely, guiltridden, and rejected. Demonstrate a sympathetic, caring attitude without being

patronizing. Be prepared to dispel the "smoke screens" the inquirer may throw up in order to hide the real reason for making contact. Do not be intimidated by accusations that "you don't know what it's like." Do not begin your conversation by confronting the individual with his sinful life-style. This will emerge more naturally as you share "Steps to Peace with God."

2. Attempt to win confidence by encouraging the inquirer. "I am glad to talk with you and will share anything I can to help."

3. At some convenient point in the conversation, even if you must suggest that other things be temporarily set aside, ask the inquirer if he has ever received Jesus Christ as his personal Lord and Savior. Proceed with "Steps to Peace with God," page 5. Reassure the individual that, as in the case of anyone without Christ, the transforming experience of the new birth is the first step to spiritual health. "He restoreth my soul" (Psalm 23:3).

4. If he responds affirmatively, pray with the inquirer for deliverance and for the renewing of his mind through the Gospel. Tell him he must be willing to let God change some things in his life, whatever the inconvenience and discomfort.

5. Tell him it is important to start reading and studying God's Word. It is the source of our knowledge of God and His ways with us. No one can learn to think God's thoughts apart from the Scriptures.

6. Encourage the inquirer to establish new relationships after breaking with former associations. This can best be done by becoming a part of a Bible-teaching church where friendships can be established with committed Christians for fellowship and strength. Sometimes a singles group is available.

7. For on-going help, encourage the inquirer to seek professional counseling with a Christian psychologist or a qualified pastor.

NOTE: The Counseling Department of the Billy Graham Association has a limited number of contacts for referrals of homosexuals in some cities. The counselor may ask permission of the counselee to put him in contact with a Christian support group, should such be available in his area. Please do not promise. Suggest only that he will do the best he can.

If Inquirer Confesses to Being a Christian:

We must realize that many Christians struggle with homosexuality and homosexual temptation.

1. An attitude of love and compassion is needed. Determine to be a patient listener until you have the inquirer's story.

2. At a convenient time, share "Steps to Peace with God" in order to determine if he has ever received Christ as personal Savior and Lord.

3. If you encounter resistance, or if there is an attempt to justify the inquirer's life-style, patiently but firmly confront him with the message of Scripture on the subject. Ask him how he can reconcile his behavior with Bible

teaching. No amount of rationalization will change the fact that Scripture condemns homosexual behavior. He must recognize it as wrong and as sin. Confessing it as such before God and turning from its practice offers the only real hope for rehabilitation.

4. Encourage him to read and study the Bible. Assimilating God's Word will result in a "renewing of the mind." As thought patterns change, behavior and life-style will follow suit.

5. Encourage him to identify with a Bible-teaching church for the purposes of developing Christian fellowship, studying the Word of God, learning to pray, and worshiping and witnessing.

6. Encourage him to seek additional help from a Christian professional or a pastor.

Scripture

Homosexuality Is Sin:

"Therefore, God gave them over in the sinful desires of their hearts to sexual impurity for the degrading of their bodies with one another. They exchanged the truth of God for a lie, and worshiped ... created things rather than the Creator — who is forever praised. Amen. Because of this, God gave them over to shameful lusts. Even their women exchanged natural relations for unnatural ones. In the same way the men also abandoned natural relations with women and were inflamed with lust for one another. Men committed indecent acts with other men, and received in themselves the due penalty for their perversion."

Romans 1:24-27, NIV

"Yes, these laws are made to identify as sinners all who are immoral and impure; homosexuals, kidnappers, liars, and all others who do things that contradict the glorious Good News of our blessed God, whose messenger I am."

1 Timothy 1:10, 11, TLB

Homosexuality Will Be Judged By God:

"Do you not know that the wicked will not inherit the kingdom of God? Do not be deceived: Neither the sexually immoral nor idolaters nor adulterers nor male prostitutes nor homosexual offenders nor thieves nor the greedy nor drunkards nor slanderers nor swindlers will inherit the kingdom of God."

1 Corinthians 6:9, NIV

Genesis 18 and 19 (Please read)

The Power of the Gospel to Deliver:

"When someone becomes a Christian he becomes a brand-new person inside. He is not the same any more. A new life has begun!"

2 Corinthians 5:17, TLB

"For I am not ashamed of the gospel of Christ: for it is the power of God unto salvation to everyone that believeth ..."

Romans 1:16, KJV

"The Spirit of the Lord is upon me, because he hath anointed me to preach the gospel to the poor; he hath sent me to heal the brokenhearted, to preach deliverance to the captives, and recovering of sight to the blind, to set at liberty them that are bruised, to preach the acceptable year of the Lord."

Luke 4:18, 19, KJV

"But as many as received him, to them gave he power to become the sons of God, even to them that believe on his name."   John 1:12, KJV

"There was a time when some of you were just like that but now your sins are washed away, and you are set apart for God, and he has accepted you because of what the Lord Jesus Christ and the Spirit of our God have done for you."   1 Corinthians 6:11, TLB

Temptation Can Be Overcome:

"But remember this — the wrong desires that come into your life aren't anything new and different. Many others have faced exactly the same problems before you. And no temptation is irresistible. You can trust God to keep the temptation from becoming so strong that you can't stand up against it, for he has promised this and will do what he says. He will show you how to escape temptation's power so that you can bear up patiently against it."   1 Corinthians 10:13, TLB

"For since he himself has now been through suffering and temptation, he knows what it is like when we suffer and are tempted, and he is wonderfully able to help us."   Hebrews 2:18, TLB

"But Jesus the Son of God is our great High Priest who has gone to heaven itself to help us; therefore let us never stop trusting him. This High Priest of ours understands our weaknesses, since he had the same temptations we do, though he never once gave way to them and sinned. So let us come boldly to the very throne of God and stay there to receive his mercy and to find grace to help us in our times of need."   Hebrews 4:14-16, TLB

A Renewed Mind:

"Therefore, I urge you, brothers, in view of God's mercy, to offer your bodies as living sacrifices, holy and pleasing to God — which is your spiritual worship. Do not conform any longer to the pattern of this world, but be transformed by the renewing of your mind. Then you will be able to test and approve what God's will is — his good, pleasing and perfect will."   Romans 12:1,2, NIV

"Put off your old nature which belongs to your former manner of life and is corrupt through deceitful lusts, and be renewed in the spirit of your minds, and put on the new nature, created after the likeness of God in true righteousness and holiness."   Ephesians 4:22-24, RSV

"These weapons can break down every proud argument against God and every wall that can be built to keep men from finding him. With these weapons I can capture rebels and bring them back to God, and change them into men whose hearts' desire is obedience to Christ."

2 Corinthians 10:5, TLB

"Thou wilt keep him in perfect peace, whose mind is stayed on thee: because he trusteth in thee."

Isaiah 26:3, KJV

INCEST

Background

Incest is sexual contact between persons of the same family. We are most likely to deal with a young female who reports sexual contact (not always intercourse) with her father, step-father, etc. Young boys are also likely victims of incest.

A recent news telecast called this problem the "hidden shame," and the "least reported devastating crime in America, having doubled each year for the last five years." It is feared that from 100,000 to 1,000,000 youngsters are sexually abused each year.

Incest is very destructive to a child, and often the damage cannot be undone. A U.S. District Judge recently observed: "Abused children have suffered unspeakable injuries to body and soul." Because of shame, fright, or a feeling that they have done something terribly wrong or that they are being punished, the victims of incest rarely report their involvement. Being trapped in such a situation leads to confusion and a "learned helplessness."

Sexually abused children have a low self-image, are depressed, and often harbor thoughts of self-destruction. Many run away from home and frequently get involved in drugs, alcohol, and further deviant sexual behavior such as prostitution and homosexuality. Unable to concentrate on learning, they may do poorly in school. Chances of a successful adulthood are poor, because many do not recover from the effects of the relationship and many commit suicide.

There is little hope of freeing the victim from her helpless situation unless the offender is stopped. The person guilty of incest is unlikely to change unless faced with the legal implications of his crime. Once called to the attention of the courts, authorities will intervene, removing the victim from her surroundings. Eventually, both the parents and the victim will need counseling, separately and together, if any solutions are to be found. It is hoped that these services exist in her community.

Often the victim will be intimidated by family members not to press charges or testify against the offender because of the shame if the "family secret" becomes known. A pastor will be of inestimable help. In fact, he may be the only one available to intervene.

Counseling Strategy

1. Such individuals demand a special sympathy and tenderness. Attempt to project all the love you can.

2. Assure the inquirer that she has done the right thing in sharing the problem. We are her friends and we want to help.

3. Assure her that though she may feel defiled, she is not bad or vile. She has been forced or tricked into something degrading, and may be confused but is not crazy. What has happened is very wrong, but she is not responsible for it. Though abused, she no longer needs to feel intimidated and

drowned by feelings of helplessness, self-pity, and self-doubt. We want to help solve the terrible problem.

4. Assure her that God loves her. To Him she is special, just as worthy as anyone. God loved her so much that He sent His Son, Jesus Christ, to die for her sins. Explain "Steps to Peace with God," page 5.

5. Counsel her to begin to read the Bible. Offer to send *Living in Christ,* which has recommended Bible readings and studies.

6. Does she know a pastor she can contact? Urge her to plan to see him immediately in order to relate what has been happening. He will help. She should also go to her guidance counselor or the school nurse. This will be difficult and embarrassing, but must be done.

7. Pray with her, committing the problem to the Lord. After praying, reassure her of your loving concern and prayers.

Scripture

"Trust in the Lord with all your heart and lean not on your own understanding; in all your ways acknowledge him, and he will make your paths straight."   Proverbs 3:5,6, NIV

"Do not be anxious about anything, but in everything, by prayer and petition, with thanksgiving, present your requests to God. And the peace of God, which transcends all understanding, will guard your hearts and your minds in Christ Jesus."   Philippians 4:6,7, NIV

"Let him have all your worries and cares, for he is always thinking about you and watching everything that concerns you."   1 Peter 5:7, TLB

"Come to me, all you who are weary and burdened, and I will give you rest. Take my yoke upon you and learn from me, for I am gentle and humble in heart, and you will find rest for your souls."
                                                    Matthew 11:28,29, NIV

"Jesus said, Let the little children come to me, and do not hinder them, for the kingdom of heaven belongs to such as these."   Matthew 19:14, NIV

"You will keep in perfect peace him whose mind is steadfast, because he trusts in you. Trust in the Lord forever, for the Lord, the Lord, is the Rock eternal."   Isaiah 26:3,4, NIV

JESUS CHRIST

Background

Jesus has been acclaimed as the greatest religious leader who ever lived, as being the most influential person to have lived on our planet, and as being unique to the degree that no one can be compared to Him.

But considering Jesus Christ merely on the basis of an exemplary life and His superior moral teaching will not remove the stumbling blocks to Christianity raised by an unbelieving world. The real test of what one thinks of Him must revolve around who He claimed to be and what He accomplished during His brief mission to our planet. Our conclusion must be that there is no Christianity without Christ; all centers in Him.

The predominant theme of the Scriptures is the Person and the work of Jesus Christ. He is God. He became a human being, died by crucifixion, and was buried. He rose again from the dead. He is the only, all-sufficient Savior of the world. He will come again to this earth. Removing this from the Scriptures robs them of all coherent meaning and continuity.

Jesus Christ is God:

Deity is the only explanation for all that He was and all that He did.

1. He was pre-existent with the Father. "The same was in the beginning with God. All things were made by him; and without him was not anything made that was made" (John 1:2,3, KJV). (Also see John 17:5 and Colossians 1:17.)

2. He is the Son of God.
   A. His enemies admitted: "He ... said also that God was his Father, making himself equal with God" (John 5:18, KJV).
   B. Peter confessed: "And we believe and are sure that thou art the Christ, the Son of the living God" (John 6:69, KJV).
   C. Jesus affirmed: "I and my Father are one" (John 10:30, NIV).

3. He was sinless, as only God can be.
   A. Jesus challenged His enemies:"Which of you convinceth me of sin?" (John 8:46, KJV).
   B. Peter testified: "'. . .Christ also suffered for us, leaving us an example, that ye should follow his steps: who did no sin, neither was guile found in his mouth" (1 Peter 2:21,22, KJV).
   C. Paul stated: "For he ... made him to be sin for us, who knew no sin; that we might be made the righteousness of God in him" (2 Corinthians 5:21, KJV).

4. He forgives sin, as only God can.
   A. The Scribes said: "Who can forgive sins but God only?" (Mark 2:7, KJV).

B. Jesus said: "But that ye may know that the Son of man hath power on earth to forgive sins . . ." (Matthew 9:6, KJV). (Also see John 8:11.)

C. Peter wrote: "Who his own self bare our sins in his own body on the tree, that we, being dead to sins, should live unto righteousness: by whose stripes ye were healed" (1 Peter 2:24, KJV).

5. He performed miraculous works.

A. He healed the sick: Matthew 8:9-13; Luke 4:31-44; 5:12-15; John 4:43 to 5:16; and other references.

B. He fed the hungry: John 6; Mark 8, etc.

C. He raised the dead: Luke 7:11-18; John 11:1-46.

Jesus Christ Became Man:

"And the Word was made flesh and dwelt among us . . . full of grace and truth" (John 1:14, KJV). (See also Philippians 2:7,8.)

1. His miraculous birth was prophesied 800 years before His coming: "Behold a virgin shall conceive, and bear a son, and shall call his name Emmanuel" (Isaiah 7:14, KJV).

2. The prophecy was fulfilled to the letter. "Fear not, Mary: for thou hast found favor with God. And, behold, thou shalt conceive in thy womb, and bring forth a son, and shalt call his name Jesus" (Luke 1:30,31, KJV).

3. Jesus demonstrated human characteristics: He became tired (John 4:6). He thirsted (John 19:28), He ate food (Luke 24:40-43), He showed feelings (Mark 6:34), He wept (John 11:35), He knew temptation (Hebrews 4:15), and He died (John 19:30).

Jesus Christ Accomplished the Works of His Father:

1. He died on the Cross. This is the fundamental theme of the Gospel.

A. The fact of His death — One-fourth of the Gospels are dedicated to His Passion and Resurrection.

(1) For this purpose He came into the world (John 12:27).

(2) His death was prophesied hundreds of years before He came (Isaiah 53:3-8).

B. The meaning of His death.

(1) It was a ransom for sin (Matthew 20:28; Romans 3:24; 1 Peter 1:18).

(2) It was to pay the penalty for sin (Romans 3:24; 1 John 2:2; 4:10). Man is the object of God's wrath because of rebellion and sin, but God took the initiative in satisfying His wrath by sending His own Son to Calvary.

(3) It is a reconciliation. The enmity between us and God has ended (Romans 5:10), and we are restored to God (2 Corinthians 5:18,19).

       (4) It is a substitution: He died in our place (1 Peter 3:18, 2 Corinthians 5:21).

       (5) In summary, the matter of sin has been completely dealt with (1 Peter 2:24; Hebrews 9:26; Hebrews 10:12).

2. He was resurrected from the dead: This is unique and fundamental to Christianity.

   A. The reality of the Resurrection (John 20:1-10; 1 Corinthians 15:4).

   B. The credibility of the Resurrection:

       (1) Jesus predicted it: Matthew 13:39-41; Luke 24:1-7.

       (2) The tomb was empty: John 20:11-13.

       (3) Many witnesses saw Him alive: the women (Luke 23:55,56); Mary Magdalene (John 20:1,2, 11-18); Peter and the other disciples (John 20:3-9,19,20,24-31; 21:1-14).

The Results of His Work:

1. He ascended to His Father (Luke 24:49-53; Acts 1:6-11).

2. He is our eternal Mediator (1 Timothy 2:5; Hebrews 8:6; 1 John 2:1).

3. He is our Savior: "Thou shalt call his name Jesus: for he shall save his people from their sins" (Matthew 1:21, KJV). "Him hath God exalted with his right hand to be a Prince and a Savior, for to give repentance to Israel, and forgiveness of sins" (Acts 5:31, KJV).

   A. He is the only Savior. "Salvation is found in no one else, for there is no other name under heaven given to men by which we must be saved" (Acts 4:12, NIV).

   B. He is a complete Savior. "Wherefore he is able also to save them to the uttermost that come unto God by him, seeing he ever liveth to make intercession for them" (Hebrews 7:25, KJV).

   C. He is a personal Savior. "That if thou shalt confess with thy mouth the Lord Jesus, and shalt believe in thine heart that God hath raised him from the dead, thou shalt be saved. For with the heart man believeth unto righteousness: and with the mouth confession is made unto salvation" (Romans 10:9,10, KJV).

The Consummation of His Work:

1. He shall return again to this earth (Acts 1:11; Hebrews 10:37; John 14:3).

2. Believers in Christ shall be bodily resurrected to begin a new, undying life (1 Thessalonians 4:17-18; 1 Corinthians 15:51-58).

3. He will reign as King of kings and Lord of lords over His new creation (2 Peter 3:10-13; Revelation 22:3-5).

Counseling Strategy

The greatest response we can make to Jesus Christ and His claims is to:

1. Receive Him as Lord and Savior ... Ask the inquirer if he has done this. Share "Steps to Peace with God," page 5.
2. Enthrone Him as Lord of our life. "These people honor me with their lips, but their hearts are far from me" (Matthew 15:8, NIV). "I beseech you therefore, brethren, by the mercies of God, that ye present your bodies a living sacrifice, holy, acceptable unto God, which is your reasonable service. And be not conformed to this world: but be ye transformed by the renewing of your mind, that ye may prove what is that good, acceptable, and perfect, will of God" (Romans 12:1,2, KJV).
3. Witness for Him as He commands. "That which we have seen and heard declare we unto you, that ye also may have fellowship with us: and truly our fellowship is with the Father, and with his Son, Jesus Christ" (1 John 1:3, KJV). "But ye shall receive power, after that the Holy Ghost is come upon you: and ye shall be witnesses unto me both in Jerusalem, and in all Judea, and in Samaria, and unto the uttermost part of the earth" (Acts 1:8, KJV).

Scripture

His Deity:
John 1:1-3; John 17:5; John 8:56-59; John 10:30-33; Colossians 1:15-19; Colossians 2:8,9; Philippians 2:6-11; Revelation 5:12-14.

His Humanity:
John 1:14; Philippians 2:5-8; John 10:30; 1 John 1:1-4; Luke 1:30-33; Matthew 1:18; Hebrews 4:15; Mark 6:34; John 11:35; John 19:28; Luke 24:40-43.

His Death:
Matthew 27:32-56; Mark 15:20-47; Luke 23:26-49; John 19:1-42; 2 Corinthians 5:21; 1 Peter 1:18,19; 2:22-24; Isaiah 53; 1 John 3:5-8; 1 Corinthians 15:2-4.

His Resurrection:
Matthew 28; Mark 16; Luke 24; John 20 and 21; Acts 2:24-36; 1 Corinthians 15; Galatians 2:20; Romans 10:9,10; 1 Peter 1:19-21; 1 Thessalonians 1:10.

His Second Coming:
1 Thessalonians 4:13-18; 2 Thessolonians 2:1-11; 1 Corinthians 15:51-57; John 14:1-6; Acts 1:11; Matthew 24:30; Revelation 1:7; John 21:23; Matthew 24:42-44; 1 John 3:2,3.

JUDGMENT

Background

God's righteousness and justice are the basis of His judgments. Biblical judgment is one of the most misunderstood subjects among Christians. The idea of a general judgment, when all the people of all ages will stand before the Maker of heaven and earth, has always been erroneously prevalent: The "sheep" will be separated from the "goats," and each will go to his respective place.

All people — saints and sinners — will be judged, but not at the same time. The judgments differ as to subjects, times, places, and results. For our purposes in this handbook, we shall touch on the aspects of judgment with which we are more likely to deal.

- There are to be three judgments for the believer in Christ:
  1. He has already been judged for his sins at Calvary.

     "For he hath made him to be sin for us, who knew no sin; that we might be made the righteousness of God in him" (2 Corinthians 5:21, KJV).

     "Who his own self bore our sins in his own body on the tree, that we, being dead to sins, should live unto righteousness: by whose stripes ye were healed" (1 Peter 2:24, KJV).

     Jesus bore the full thrust of God's righteous judgment against sin. The believer receives Christ as his sin-bearer, meaning that he trusts fully in the redemption accomplished at Calvary, and is freed from sin and guilt. The believer will never again be judged for his sins.

  2. He will someday stand before the judgment seat of Christ (Greek, Bema) to be judged for his works or performance as a Christian. "For we must all appear before the judgment seat of Christ; that every one may receive the things done in his body, according to that he hath done, whether it be good or bad" (2 Corinthians 5:10, KJV).

     This judgment will bring rewards to some, but loss to others. Some will have no profitable works to lay at the Master's feet while others will be called "good and profitable servants" and asked to enter into the joy of their Lord. This judgment follows immediately the Rapture of believers, both alive and dead, as recorded in 1 Thessalonians 4:15-17. (See SCRIPTURE.)

  3. There is also the daily self-judgment of the believer.

     "Search me, O God, and know my heart; try me and know my thoughts; and see if there be any wicked way in me, and lead me in the way everlasting" (Psalm 139:23,24, KJV).

     "Keeping short accounts" with God is the only way to spiritual maturity. This judgment of self results in confession and forgiveness. "He that covereth his sins shall not prosper: but whoso confesseth and forsaketh them shall have mercy" (Proverbs 28:13, KJV). "If we confess our sins, he is faithful and just to forgive us our sins, and to cleanse us from all unrighteousness" (1 John 1:9, KJV).

- There will be a judgment of the lost, or unbelievers, known as the great white throne judgment. (Revelation 20:11-15 — see SCRIPTURES.)

All persons who find themselves in hell will be there because they have rejected God's salvation and have chosen instead to serve Satan. The Scripture indicates clearly that all such persons must appear before the Great White Throne Judgment and that they will be judged on the basis of the light they had and rejected while on earth.

This judgment follows God's final judgment of the devil (Revelation 20:10) and the rebellious angels (Jude 6), and comes after the millennial reign. The lost of all ages will stand before God for this most terrible of all judgments (Matthew 12:36). God's justice will weigh each one in the balance in order to ratify the condemnation of those who have rejected His Son's work of redemption.

- There are also judgments in the future for the living nations and for Israel. See Matthew 25:31-46 and Ezekiel 20:33-44. (Because of the length of passages, please look these up in your Bible.)

Counseling Strategy
If Fearful of Coming Judgment and Consequences:

1. Assure him that God is reaching out in love and is "not willing that any should perish, but that all should come to repentance" (2 Peter 3:9, KJV). "For God sent not his Son into the world to condemn the world; but that the world through him might be saved" (John 3:17, KJV).

2. Invite him to receive Jesus Christ as Savior and Lord, sharing "Steps to Peace with God," page 5.

3. Challenge him to take a firm stand for Jesus Christ, to stand up and be counted. He should get into the Word of God by reading and studying it on a daily basis. (Offer to send Living in Christ.")

4. Advise him to seek fellowship, worship and service in a local Bible-teaching church.

5. Pray with him that he might know the reality of Christ in his life.

If Ignorant of Bible Teaching on Judgments:

1. Explain the material in the BACKGROUND. Note: Most cults are in error in regard to this subject.

2. Invite him to receive Christ, if this is indicated in the conversation.

3. Follow the counsel above in numbers 3, 4 and 5.

Scripture

"There is therefore now no condemnation to them which are in Christ Jesus, who walk not after the flesh, but after the Spirit."

Romans 8:1, KJV

"For other foundation can no man lay than that is laid, which is Jesus Christ. Now if any man build upon this foundation gold, silver, precious stones, wood, hay, stubble; every man's work shall be made manifest: for the day shall declare it, because it shall be revealed by fire; and the fire shall try every man's work of what sort it is. If any man's work abide which he hath built thereupon, he shall receive a reward. If any man's work shall be burned, he shall suffer loss; but he himself shall be saved; yet so as by fire."   1 Corinthians 3:11-15, KJV

"And I saw a great white throne, and him that sat on it, from whose face the earth and the heaven fled away; and there was found no place for them (to hide). And I saw the dead, small and great, stand before God; and the books were opened: and another book was opened, which is the book of life: and the dead were judged out of those things which were written in the books, according to their works. And the sea gave up the dead which were in it; and death and hell delivered up the dead which were in them: and they were judged every man according to their works."   Revelation 20:11-14, KJV

LONELINESS
Background

Loneliness is the painful realization that we lack meaningful and close relationships with others. This lack leads to emptiness, melancholy, isolation, and even to despair. A sense of rejection and a low self-image are present because we can't relate, or we feel left out and unwanted, no matter how hard we try to belong.

The kind of society we live in contributes to loneliness. It is difficult for some to maintain identity and meaningful relationships in the jungle of bureaucracy, specialization, regimentation and competition. Mobility and constant change tend to make some individuals feel rootless and fragmented.

Loneliness can be self-inflicted. Some persons find it difficult to communicate with others or lack confidence because they have a poor self-image. Others yearn for togetherness, yet their demand for privacy and independence inhibits the development of meaningful ties with others. The fear of exposure of their inner selves results in a kind of social paralysis.

In many of his messages, Billy Graham has referred to that "cosmic loneliness" of the person who is separated from God and feels that life has little meaning. He says, "There are thousands of lonely people who carry heavy and difficult burdens of grief, anxiety, pain and disappointment; but the loneliest of all is one whose life is steeped in sin."

One of the results of the Fall is that man became alienated from God. Alienation caused Adam and Eve to hide from God and to attempt to cover up. (Perhaps these three conditions help describe the lonely person.) Our spiritual condition can be summarized as follows: "Man was created with a God-sized vacuum in his breast which only God can fill."

It is only as we find Christ that we transcend self and develop that perspective on life which can mitigate the pain of our loneliness. The Psalmist exulted in God's work in his life by writing, "He restoreth my soul." This restoration removes the causes of our alienation. "Once you were alienated from God and were enemies in your minds because of your evil behavior. But now he has reconciled you by Christ's physical body through death to present you holy in his sight, without blemish and free from accusation..." (Colossians 1:21,22, NIV). It also results in our lives becoming the abode of God's Holy Spirit. "Do you not know that your body is a temple of the Holy Spirit, who is in you, whom you have received from God?" (1 Corinthians 6:19, NIV). Thus, we are complete in Him. "And ye are complete in him, which is the head of all principality and power" (Colossians 2:10, KJV).

Counseling Strategy

We will approach loneliness from the perspective of the spiritual as well as the practical, both for the non-Christian and the believer. We reach out for fellowship with God and we reach for fellowship with other human beings.

For the Lonely Non-Christian:

1. Offer a word of encouragement. In sharing his problem of loneliness, the inquirer is admitting his need. This is important in solving any problem in life. Assure him that this first important step can be followed by others which can lead to solutions.

2. Attempt to determine causes for his loneliness. If not enough information is forthcoming, ask questions about himself personally: where does he live, who are his neighbors, where does he work, does he like his job? What about hobbies, friendships, church, etc.?

3. Ask if he has ever received Jesus Christ as his Savior. Explain "Steps to Peace with God," page 5. The first step in God's plan for his life will be realized in the inquirer's receiving Christ, but he can also be assured that the feeling of alienation will be taken care of. He will be at peace with God (Romans 5:1), and Christ will be his constant friend. "There is a friend that sticketh closer than a brother" (Proverbs 18:24, KJV).

4. Counsel him to seek spiritual growth by reading and studying the Word of God and learning to pray. Offer to send him *Living In Christ* to help him get started in the Word.

   The daily exercise of prayer will do much to ameliorate his feelings of aloneness, providing an immediate access to God who is "a very present help in trouble" (Psalm 46:1, KJV).

5. Counsel him to seek a relationship with a Bible-teaching church where he may be able to find the warmth of fellowship, worship and service. Advise that he must not expect too much, too quickly. Meaningful relationships do not develop overnight. They need to be cultivated, and this does take some time. The more he will give of himself as he gets involved in church life, the more he will receive from others. "A man that hath friends must show himself friendly" (Proverbs 18:24, KJV). Inform him that some churches have a singles fellowship, if this should be of interest.

6. Advise him to strengthen any home ties that may not be all they should be. Communication with other members of the family will do much to develop mutual respect and caring. Now that he knows Christ he should seek to win family members to the Savior.

7. Pray with him for his spiritual growth and the development of meaningful relationships with both Christian and non-Christian friends.

For the Lonely Christian:

1. Counsel him to develop a daily quiet time. A sense of God's never-failing presence will help diminish feelings of loneliness.

Billy Graham offers his own experience for encouragement. "I will give you a little recipe I have found for conquering loneliness. First, I am never lonely when I am praying, for this brings me into companionship with the greatest friend of all — Jesus Christ. He said, 'I call you not servants, but friends' (John 15:15). Then, I am never lonely when I am reading the Bible. I read it every day — whole chapters of it. Nothing dissolves loneliness like a session with God's Word."

As we grow in this devotional relationship to God, we begin to change. The attitudes of loving and caring which gradually develop become the basis for contacts with others and the deepening of friendships.

2. Encourage him to seek a meaningful place of service in an active Bible-teaching church. Focusing on the needs of others will put our problems into perspective and make them seem a little less important. Service helps us cultivate relationsips with other Christians who serve and tends to increase our self-esteem as we become a part of the group.

Billy Graham says about service, "I am never lonely when I am sharing Him with others. There is a great exhilaration in talking to others about Christ. This is something we can all do."

3. Counsel him to strengthen bonds within his family. Lonely people often have some "loose ends" in regard to family relationships. Constant efforts to communicate with our own family — learning to share, to respect and care, to become a part of each other — will do much to prevent loneliness. Improved relationships at home will always mean improvement elsewhere.
4. Encourage the inquirer to seek counsel from a local pastor, preferably his own. A pastor can help to develop relationships and recommend areas of service through the church.

Scripture

"Come unto me, all ye that labor and are heavy laden, and I will give you rest. Take my yoke upon you, and learn of me; for I am meek and lowly in

heart: and ye shall find rest unto your souls. For my yoke is easy, and my
burden is light."   Matthew 11:28-30, KJV

"I will never leave thee, nor forsake thee. So that we may boldly say, The
Lord is my helper, and I will not fear what man shall do unto me."
                                                         Hebrews 13:5,6, KJV

"Lo, I am with you always, to the close end of the age."
                                                         Matthew 28:20, RSV

"I waited patiently for the Lord; and he inclined unto me, and heard my
cry. He brought me up also out of an horrible pit, out of the miry clay, and
set my feet upon a rock, and established my goings. And he hath put a
new song in my mouth, even praise unto our God: many shall see it, and
fear, and shall trust in the Lord. Blessed is that man that maketh the Lord
his trust, and respecteth not the proud, nor such as turn aside to lies.
Many, O Lord my God, are thy wonderful works which thou hast done,
and thy thoughts which are to us-ward: they cannot be reckoned up in
order unto thee: if I would declare and speak of them, they are more than
can be numbered."   Psalm 40:1-5, KJV

"God is faithful, by whom ye were called unto the fellowship of his Son
Jesus Christ our Lord."   1 Corinthians 1:9, KJV

Proverbs 3:5,6

LOSS OF EMPLOYMENT
Background

We need to be sensitive to the trauma confronting an individual who has lost a job, who can't find another, whose bills continue to mount, whose mortgage payments may be in default. Such people feel a loss of personal worth, discouragement, frustration, and even depression. A recent report from a reliable source quotes the following:

With every 1% rise in unemployment:

- 4.3% more men and 2.3% more women are admitted to mental hospitals for the first time;
- 4.1% more people commit suicide;
- 4.7% more people are murdered;
- 4% more people end up in prisons;
- 1.9% more people die of heart disease, cirrhosis of the liver, and other stress-related ailments;
- Child abuse increases.

Counseling Strategy

1. Offer encouragement by telling the individual you are glad he called, that we care, and that you are happy to spend time with him to talk about the problem.
2. Remind him that he is not alone, that many others are going through the same difficulty. Employment loss is not unusual. In the light of this, he shouldn't feel "singled out" or take personally his loss of employment.
3. Tell the inquirer he shouldn't feel any less worthy. There is no reason to lose self-respect or to feel inadequate.
4. Tell him to remain confident and not to panic because God knows, loves, and cares. He must learn to trust Him.
5. Encourage him to pray that God will help him to weather the financial strain, provide for the needs of his family, and open a new door of employment.
6. Suggest that he share the problem with Christian friends who may also pray, and with a sympathetic pastor who may be able to offer help in seeking employment opportunities.
7. Counsel the individual not to take out his frustrations on his spouse or children. They will stand by him in the emergency. All are in it together, and the crisis can actually serve to strengthen family solidarity. They should find it helpful to pray together as a family.
8. Introduce the inquirer to Jesus Christ as Lord and Savior, if the conversa-

tion reveals that he does not know Him. Share "Steps to Peace with God," page 5.

Scripture

"I was young and now I am old, yet I have never seen the righteous forsaken or their children begging bread."   Psalm 37:25, NIV

"I can do everything through him who gives me strength. ... And my God will meet all your needs according to his glorious riches in Christ Jesus."   Philippians 4:13 and 19, NIV

"Do not be anxious about anything, but in everything, by prayer and petition, with thanksgiving, present your requests to God. And the peace of God, which transcends all understanding, will guard your hearts and minds in Christ Jesus."   Philippians 4:6,7, NIV

LOVE

Background

Until the Good News of Jesus Christ burst on the human scene, the word love was understood mostly in terms of seeking its own advantage. Loving the unlovely was incomprehensible. A loving God reaching down to sinful man was unthinkable in the pagan world.

The New Testament writers had to coin a new word for love, *agapē*, to express what God wanted to reveal about Himself in Christ and how He wanted Christians to relate to each other. "Hereby perceive we the love of God, because he (Christ) laid down his life for us; and we ought to lay down our lives for the brethren" (1 John 3:16, KJV).

This new love bond was revealed at Calvary. The redeemed, henceforth, would reach out to God and towards each other in a dimension never before understood or experienced. *Agapē* would now be the "more excellent way" (1 Corinthians 12:31, KJV). Immediately it became an identifying characteristic of the early Church. Jesus had said: "A new commandment I give unto you . . . as I have loved you, that ye also love one another" (John 13:34) and, "By this shall all men know that ye are my disciples, if ye have love one to another" (John 13:35, KJV).

But as the years passed, much of the true force of *agapē* faded. The Church of today is in the position of having to rediscover its meaning. *Agapē* is not mere sentiment; love that is dormant is powerless. It is dynamic only when it actively loves God, even as He loved us; dynamic only when it is surging, unconstrained —loving brothers, sisters, neighbors, and the world for which Christ died. (See 1 John 4:10-12 and 2 Corinthians 5:14.)

On the human plane, as on the divine, love says: "I respect you. I care for you. I am responsible for you."

> *I respect you:*
> I see you as you are, a unique individual — as we are all unique. I accept you as you are and will permit you to develop as God purposes for you. I will not exploit you for my own benefit. I will attempt to know you as well as I can because I know that increased communication and knowledge will enhance my respect for you.
>
> *I care for you:*
> It matters to me what happens to you. I am concerned for your life and growth. My desire is to promote your interests, even if it means sacrificing my own.
>
> *I am responsible for you:*
> I will respond to you, not out of a sense of duty which obligates me, but voluntarily. Your spiritual needs will motivate me to pray for you. I will protect you, but will guard against overprotection. I will correct you in love, but will attempt not to overcorrect. I will find no pleasure in your

weaknesses or failures, and will keep no records of either. By God's grace, I will be patient and will not fail you. (See 1 Corinthians 13.)

We understand God's love only as we respond to it in Christ. The most important point in the life of any individual is the moment of decision to receive this unmerited, unearned love through which we learn to love Him and to pass this love on to others.

"...God is love. This is how God showed his love among us: He sent his one and only Son into the world that we might live through him. This is love: not that we loved God, but that he loved us..." (1 John 4:8-10, NIV).

Counseling Strategy
For the Non-Christian:

If the inquirer has never experienced God's forgiving love, share "Steps to Peace with God," page 5, emphasizing John 3:16.

For the Christian:

1. If the inquirer is a Christian expressing the desire to love God more, encourage him. This is also God's highest will for us. "Jesus said unto him, Thou shalt love the Lord thy God with all thy heart, and with all thy soul, and with all thy mind" (Matthew 22:37, KJV).

   A. We are to love Him because He first loved us. (See 1 John 4:10, KJV.)

   B. We are to love Him "because God has poured out his love into our hearts by the Holy Spirit, whom he has given us" (Romans 5:5, NIV). "But the fruit of the Spirit is love" (Galatians 5:22, KJV).

   C. We are to love Him through obedience. "Jesus replied, 'If anyone loves me, he will obey my teaching. My Father will love him, and we will come to him and make our home with him. He who does not love me will not obey my teaching' " (John 14:23,24, NIV).

   D. We demonstrate our love through devotion to Him. "I delight to do thy will, O my God; yea, thy law is within my heart" (Psalm 40:8, KJV).

   (1) We seek Him through his Word: "But his delight is in the law of the Lord, and on his law he meditates day and night" (Psalm 1:2, NIV).

   (2) We seek Him through prayer: "Then you will call upon me and come and pray to me, and I will listen to you. You will seek me and find me when you seek me with all your heart. I will be found by you, declares the Lord..." (Jeremiah 29:12-14, NIV).

   (3) We seek to serve Him: "Always give yourselves fully to the work of the Lord, because you know that your labor in the Lord is not in vain" (1 Corinthians 15:58, NIV). "He will not forget your work

and the love you have shown him as you have helped his people and continue to help them" (Hebrews 6:10, NIV).

Agapē love is the greatest motivation to become involved in evangelism and missions. We share His love with a lost world.

2. If the inquirer is a Christian who has problems in loving a brother in the Lord, point out that we only begin to understand God's love as we reach out in love to each other.

A. It is a command of God to love our brother in Christ. "Be devoted to one another in brotherly love. Honor one another above yourselves" (Romans 12:10, NIV).

B. God has made it possible for us to demonstrate love without consideration of the object. "...Because God has poured out his love into our hearts by the Holy Spirit whom he has given us" (Romans 5:5, NIV). Share the outline in the BACKGROUND on the dimensions of agapē love: respect, care, and responsibility.

Billy Graham says: "The fruit of the Spirit is love. I cannot love on my own, I cannot have joy, peace, long suffering, gentleness, goodness, faith, meekness and temperance by myself. There is no one who has the ability to really love...until he really comes to Christ. Until the Holy Spirit has control of one's life, he doesn't have the power to love."

C. Point out that love doesn't demonstrate itself automatically; it is a learned, practiced behavior. The more we love, and the more deeply we love, the more love is perfected in us.

(1) Prayer for others stimulates a deeper love for them.

(2) Acts of kindness, service, and sacrifice add the dynamic dimension to love. "Be kindly affectioned one to another with brotherly love; in honor preferring one another" (Romans 12:10, KJV). "Love is patient, love is kind. It does not envy, it does not boast, it is not proud. It is not rude, it is not self-seeking, it is not easily angered, it keeps no record of wrongs. Love does not delight in evil but rejoices with the truth. It always protects, always trusts, always hopes, always perseveres. Love never fails" (1 Corinthians 13:4-8, NIV).

Scripture

"For God so loved the world that he gave his one and only Son, that whoever believes in him shall not perish but have eternal life."

John 3:16, NIV

"But because of his great love for us, God, who is rich in mercy, made us alive with Christ even when we were dead in transgressions — it is by grace you have been saved."   Ephesians 2:4,5, NIV

"How great is the love the Father has lavished on us, that we should be called children of God! And that is what we are! The reason the world does not know us is that it did not know him."   1 John 3:1, NIV

"No one has ever seen God; but if we love each other, God lives in us and his love is made complete in us."   1 John 4:12, NIV

"Let us have no imitation Christian love. Let us have a genuine break with evil and a real devotion to good. Let us have real warm affection for one another as between brothers, and a willingness to let the other man have the credit."   Romans 12:9,10, Phillips

"Greater love has no one than this, that one lay down his life for his friends."   John 15:13, NIV

Matthew 22:37, NIV

MARRIAGE, ANTICIPATING
Background

Marriage is the most serious long-term contract a couple will make in their lifetime, but many enter into it with a lack of maturity and knowledge. The growing number of divorces shows how imperative it is that young people be adequately prepared for marriage.

Here are a few helpful marriage principles for all who anticipate repeating their wedding vows:

- A good marriage is not made in heaven, but on earth. Love is a fragile commodity which needs to be cultivated and nourished constantly. Of course, those intending to marry should look to God for His guidance, but the success of their marriage will be largely dependent on the couple and their efforts in response to God's leading.

- A good marriage is not based on idealism, but on reality. The Cinderella syndrome where every girl finds a prince and "lives happily ever after" is usually a fairy tale. Far too many marry with unrealistically high expectations, and then spend years suffering and adjusting — if they stay together at all.

- A good marriage is based on respect for one's self and for the partner.

    A poor self-image, inherited from a stressful home background or immaturity, can lead to stormy seas. A solid relationship with Jesus Christ and an understanding of one's self in the light of that relationship are very important.

    A poor understanding of each other can also lead to misunderstanding and conflict. It doesn't take too much discernment to realize that male and female are different physically, but how many anticipate that their partner-to-be is just as different emotionally and mentally? Each partner must realize this and be prepared to make the necessary allowances and adjustments. "Male and female created He them; and blessed them . . ." (Genesis 5:2, KJV).

- A marriage where there are similarities in the partners has a better chance to succeed. This means:

    The same religious background.

    Similar cultural and social backgrounds.

    Comparable economic levels.

    Equal educational advantages.

    A stable home situation.

- Marriage was never intended to be a "reform school"! One who marries another with the hope of "correcting" problem behavior is courting a disastrous future. What could not be changed before marriage is not likely to change at all. This should be taken seriously in those instances where alcohol, drugs, or immorality are involved.

- Couples who "marry in the Lord" (1 Corinthians 7:39) have the potential for a much better relationship than those outside of Christ.

Billy Graham advises: "The home only fulfills its true purpose when it is God controlled. Leave Jesus Christ out of your home and it loses its meaning. But take Christ into your heart and the life of your family, and He will transform your home."

Counseling Strategy

1. Congratulate the inquirer on his or her initiative in seeking counsel about a forthcoming marriage. Share the following Scriptures:

   "And the Lord God said, It is not good that the man should be alone; I will make him an help meet for him" (Genesis 2:18, KJV).

   "Whoso findeth a wife (husband) findeth a good thing, and obtaineth favor of the Lord" (Proverbs 18:22, KJV).

2. Advise him that in order to have God's presence and guidance in life and marriage, he or she would do well to commit his or her heart and life to Jesus Christ. Share "Steps to Peace with God," page 5.

3. Counsel the inquirer to take a firm stand for Jesus Christ whether previously a Christian, or having just received Christ. He or she should also begin to read and study God's Word, to pray about all matters, and to become involved in a Bible-teaching church. All these things will deeply enrich life, enabling him or her to offer much more to the marriage.

4. When the individual marries, be sure that it is "in the Lord" (1 Corinthians 7:39). "Be ye not unequally yoked together with unbelievers: for what fellowship hath righteousness with unrighteousness? And what communion hath light with darkness?" (2 Corinthians 6:14, KJV).

5. Before marriage, the inquirer should improve the chances for making it a success by:

   A. Seeking God's blessing and control over his or her own life and that of the partner through prayer.

   B. Assimilating all the knowledge possible about a Christ-centered home and marriage.

      Search the Scriptures for passages on marriage and the home.

      Read books by Christian counselors and pastors. Such materials are available at a local Christian bookstore. Many church libraries are well stocked with books on marriage and the home.

      Take advantage of seminars, courses, and films prepared for this purpose.

      Seek counseling from a qualified pastor, marriage counselor, or

Christian psychologist. Such counseling should include a comprehensive approach to marriage, including personal, spiritual, financial and sexual matters.

6. After marriage, practice the following:

Become grounded in a local Bible-teaching church where the marriage will be able to flourish spiritually, and where the future family can be received and nurtured in eternal things.

Resolve to communicate freely and honestly with the partner on all levels of life: mental, emotional, and physical. Such a practice will help greatly in problem solving as issues arise in the marriage.

7. Pray with the inquirer for God's blessing, presence and leading in his or her life and coming marriage.

Scripture

"Submit to one another out of reverence for Christ. Wives, submit to your husbands as to the Lord."   Ephesians 5:21,22, NIV

"Husbands, in the same way be considerate as you live with your wives, and treat them with respect as the weaker partner and as heirs with you of the gracious gift of life, so that nothing will hinder your prayers."
1 Peter 3:7, NIV

"By wisdom a house is built, and through understanding it is established; through knowledge its rooms are filled with rare and beautiful treasures."
Proverbs 24:3,4, NIV

"Do two walk together unless they have agreed to do so?"   Amos 3:3, NIV

2 Corinthians 6:14,15, NIV

MARRIAGE
(Pressure to do Wrong in Matters of Conscience)

Background

When a person is converted to Christ, his body becomes the dwelling place of the Holy Spirit (1 Corinthians 6:19,20), and his conscience is subject to the Word and will of God.

The Christian's conscience is cleansed from the sins and disobedience of the past in order that he may serve the living God (Hebrews 9:14).

The Christian's conscience is made holy and sincere, according to the Word of God, so that he may walk with integrity in this world. "Now this is our boast: our conscience testifies that we have conducted ourselves in the world, and especially in our relations with you, in the holiness and sincerity that are from God. We have done so not according to worldly wisdom but according to God's grace" (2 Corinthians 1:12, NIV).

If a Christian has a weak conscience, he is apt to submit to evil and thereby become defiled. (See 1 Corinthians 8:7.)

Our goal as Christians should be that of the Apostle Paul: "And herein do I exercise (exert) myself, to have always a conscience void of offense toward God, and toward men" (Acts 24:16, KJV).

Many Christians have problems in the area of conscience. For example, one may be married to a nonbeliever or have become converted to Christ after marriage and find that he or she is pressured to submit or to act contrary to the Scriptures in conduct, worldly involvements and even sexual practices. This can lead to unhappy conflicts in marriage.

The Bible teaches that the role of a wife is to be submissive, but it also enjoins a husband to love his wife as his own body (see Ephesians 5:22,28). Thus, neither mate has the right to order his or her partner to do something contrary to the Scriptures that would offend conscience.

Counseling Strategy

1. If this problem is presented, commend the inquirer for being sensitive to the leading of the Holy Spirit in his or her life, and for wanting to do right.

2. Encourage a firm stand for Christ, in the light of Romans 12:1,2.

3. Urge the individual to keep the lines of communication open with his or her mate in order to discuss freely and fully the problems involved and the reasons why it is not possible to agree to such requests.

   Make an effort not to be critical or judgmental. "We catch more flies with honey than with vinegar." If one is not careful at this point, the point of no-return could quickly be reached, bringing conflict and hostility.

4. Love covers a multitude of sins. Counsel the caller to love sincerely, demonstrating it through word and action. The Christian partner should

express appreciation, admiration, and praise as much as possible in those areas where it is due.

5. Encourage the inquirer to pray, first for wisdom and guidance in both the discussion and suggested action (see James 1:5), and then for the partner's obedience to the Word of God and commitment to personal faith in Christ. Caution: One should not be too aggressive in attempting to win a husband or wife to Christ. Please see chapter on MARRIAGE (Winning One's Mate To Christ).

6. Pray with the inquirer in order to encourage and fortify his or her resolve.

Billy Graham comments: "Complete fulfillment in marriage can never be realized outside the life in Christ. It is written in the Scriptures that Christ came into the world to destroy the works of the devil. Christ's power over the devil is available to the Christian, and the destroyer of the ideal home can only be routed (put to flight) through the power of Christ."

Scripture

"How much more, then, will the blood of Christ, who through the eternal Spirit offered himself unblemished to God, cleanse our consciences from acts that lead to death, so that we may serve the living God!"
Hebrews 9:14, NIV

"We must obey God rather than men."   Acts 5:29, NIV

"Wives, in the same way be submissive to your husbands so that, if any of them do not believe the word, they may be won over without talk by the behavior of their wives, when they see the purity and reverence of your lives... For this is the way the holy women of the past who put their hope in God used to make themselves beautiful... Husbands, in the same way be considerate as you live with your wives, and treat them with respect as the weaker partner and as heirs with you of the gracious gift of life, so that nothing will hinder your prayers. Finally, all of you, live in harmony with one another; be sympathetic, love as brothers, be compassionate and humble... But in your hearts set apart Christ as Lord. Always be prepared to give an answer to everyone who asks you to give the reason for the hope that you have. But do this with gentleness and respect, keeping a clear conscience, so that those who speak maliciously against your good behavior in Christ may be ashamed of their slander."
1 Peter 3:1,2,5,7,8,15,16, NIV

MARRIAGE PROBLEMS

Background

When two lives are bonded together in a long-term intimate relationship, there is bound to be an occasional problem. Many couples go into marriage with very little preparation for it. Sometimes they lack sufficient emotional maturity, stability, or flexibility which a successful union must have.

What are the components of a good marriage?

- *Mutual Respect.*

  Respect means that each accepts the partner as he or she is, not attempting to manipulate, and unselfishly nourishing the partner in such a way that he or she may become the person God intended. Respect distinguishes between the ideal and the real, and does not demand too much. "Each one of you also must love his wife as he loves himself, and the wife must respect her husband" (Ephesians 5:33, NIV).

- *Genuine Commitment.*

  The marriage vow says, "Forsaking all others." The Scriptures state, "For this cause shall a man leave his father and mother, and shall cleave to his wife and they twain shall be one flesh" (Matthew 19:5, KJV). Time and experience in marriage reveal that being "one flesh" does not mean an abdication of personality or personal rights. Rather, it is a fulfillment.

- *Good Communication.*

  In order to communicate, there must be understanding of the emotional, mental and physical differences between men and women. There must be companionship. "I'd rather be with my spouse than with anyone else." There must be conversation, not only a discussion of differences when such arise, but a meaningful exchange on the intellectual and emotional levels.

- *Time and Effort.*

  Love must be given the opportunity to mature. The climate for this is set in God's Word. When the going gets rough, a couple just doesn't "fall out of love"; they stay together and work things out. They do not consider themselves as martyrs of a "bad bargain," but "heirs together of the grace of life" (1 Peter 3:7, KJV). "Each one of you also must love his wife as he loves himself, and the wife must respect her husband" (Ephesians 5:33, NIV).

  Problems and differences are resolved through forgiveness. "Be kind and compassionate to one another, forgiving each other, just as in Christ God forgave you" (Ephesians 4:32, NIV).

  Cliff Barrows often gives a message to Christian couples, entitled, "Ten Words that Will Safeguard a Marriage." They are:

I was wrong.	Forgive me.
I'm sorry.	I love you.

This same formula will work to safeguard one's spiritual life as well. Couples need to learn to clean up issues as soon as they develop and to erase the slate every day. See Ephesians 4:26.

- *Spiritual Unity.*

    Understanding the spiritual dimension in marriage has profound implications. Paul compared marriage — the union of husband and wife — to the eternal relationship between Christ and the Church. (See Ephesians 5:22-33.)

Billy Graham writes: "The perfect marriage is a uniting of three persons — a man, a woman and God! That is what makes marriage holy. Faith in Christ is the most important of all principles in the building of a happy marriage and a happy home."

Counseling Strategy

1. Be supportive and encouraging. Listen carefully with understanding. Don't judge. Don't take sides. Sometimes the inquirer is at fault.

2. Attempt to discover reasons for disagreements and problems. Ask questions, if necessary. Does the inquirer feel that he or she has any responsibility in any of the negative developments?

    Ask how the inquirer would rate the marriage in the light of "What Constitutes a Good Marriage" found in the BACKGROUND. How has he or she fallen short? What might be done to improve the relationship? In humility he or she could ask forgiveness for insensitivities, hurts and offenses. It may take time, but it is worth the effort.

3. Ask if God has ever been brought into their life and marriage. Share "Steps to Peace with God," page 5.

4. Where does the individual go from here? Share follow-up steps.

    A. Get into the Word of God, reading, studying and applying it to his or her life and marriage.

    B. Learn to pray daily. Pray for each other. Pray about existing or potential problem areas. "Cast all your anxiety on him because he cares for you" (1 Peter 5:7, NIV). Better attitudes lead to a deeper sensitivity as to the needs of one's mate, producing better relationships. This is one of the values of Bible study and prayer: it will help us to anticipate problems as it makes us more spiritually sensitive.

    C. Become involved with spouse and family in a Bible-teaching church. Active participation in a dynamic church can revolutionize a marriage and family. Spiritual resources and support can be found in fellowship with committed Christians and in consultation with a committed pastor.

D. Should further counseling be needed, and it often is in troubled marriages, help could be found through contacting a qualified pastor or a Christian psychologist or marriage counselor.

If the inquirer is a Christian, encourage him to start serious counseling with a Christian marriage service or qualified pastor. Often many concessions and adjustments have to be made on the part of each partner, requiring prolonged professional sessions. The important thing is for them to honestly and sincerely face their situation in the light of the Word of God. A good place to start might be an application of the Cliff Barrows formula from the BACKGROUND.

Scripture

"Let nothing be done through strife or vainglory; but in lowliness of mind let each esteem (the) other better than themselves. Look not every man on his own things, but every man also on the things of others. Let this mind be in you, which was also in Christ Jesus."   Philippians 2:3-5, KJV

"Let the husband render unto the wife due benevolence: and likewise also the wife unto the husband. The wife hath not power of her own body, but the husband: and likewise also the husband hath not power of his own body, but the wife."   1 Corinthians 7:3,4, KJV

"Likewise, ye husbands, dwell with them according to knowledge, giving honor unto the wife, as unto the weaker vessel, and as being heirs together of the grace of life; that your prayers be not hindered."
1 Peter 3:7, KJV

Ephesians 5:22-33

MARRIAGE
(Winning One's Mate to Christ)

Background

On a certain occasion, Jesus startled His disciples with a paradox. "Do not suppose that I have come to bring peace to the earth. I did not come to bring peace, but a sword. For I have come to turn a man against his father, a daughter against her mother, a daughter-in-law against her mother-in-law — a man's enemies will be the members of his own household" (Matthew 10:34-36, NIV).

In no situation is the cost of discipleship more evident than in a marriage where one partner is a Christian and the other is not. Life sometimes becomes complicated because the interests, activities, and goals are at variance. The conversion to Christ of one's mate should receive the highest priority, but extreme caution should be exercised as to methods followed in pursuit of this goal. Many marriages end in divorce because of the insensitivity and over-zealousness of the Christian partner in attempting to witness.

Counseling Strategy:

1. Congratulate the inquirer for the concern in wanting to share this most wonderful of life's experience with someone so dear. The caller must be aware, however, of the "sword" in the above quotation.

2. Counsel the individual not to attempt to play God. He or she cannot force the mate to accept Christ, nor can one do it for the other. Those who attempt to take things into their own hands may be headed for disaster.

3. Counsel him not to come on too strong but to maintain a humble attitude rather than a judgmental one. Attitude is extremely important.

4. Counsel the Christian to devote himself or herself to personal spiritual maturity through the reading and studying of God's Word, to learn to pray, and to practice it faithfully. Prayer is of great value. Commit the mate to the Lord and by faith claim conversion. It would be wise not even to reveal the prayer concern. Trust God. He has a wonderful way of working things out.

5. Example is powerful! Let the mate see Jesus in the other's attitudes and actions.
    Let love overflow. True love cannot be counterfeited. Paul says: "Love is patient, love is kind. Love never fails" (1 Corinthians 13:4,8, NIV). Make an attempt to demonstrate that "God has poured out his love into our hearts..." (Romans 5:5, NIV).

6. Never try to win the day through argument or sermonizing. This will usually produce antagonism and deepen resistance. Peaceful co-existence is a method suggested by the Apostle Paul. See 1 Corinthians 7:12-15.

Billy Graham touches on this: "The Apostle Peter had something to say about this. He said: 'Ye wives, be in subjection to your own husbands; that, if any obey not the word, they may without the word be won by the (behavior) of the wives' (1 Peter 3:1). This is no easy assignment, but the responsibility is upon you, not on your husband, to live a life that will challenge him to make his own decision. This cannot be done by nagging or lecturing, but by the manifestation of a spirit of meekness and submission that he had not discovered in you before. Whether it is the husband or the wife who is the Christian, as a Christian he must always accept and expect some ridicule and even mistreatment for the faith. Just bear this in mind: no one is in a better relationship to win the other to Christ than a life partner."

7. Do not insist that the mate attend church or special Christian services unless there seems to be a disposition to do so. An alternative to church would be introducing Christian friends into the home on social occasions. The husband or wife is bound to see the difference in their lives. The opportune moment for sharing Christ will come.

8. Pray with the inquirer for perception, wisdom, and patience to await the right moment, putting into practice all the above as indicated.

Scripture

"Wives, in the same way be submissive to your husbands so that, if any of them do not believe the word, they may be won over without talk by the behavior of their wives, when they see the purity and reverence of your lives. Your beauty should not come from outward adornment, such as braided hair and the wearing of gold jewelry and fine clothes. Instead, it should be that of your inner self, the unfading beauty of a gentle and quiet spirit, which is of great worth in God's sight."   1 Peter 3:1-4, NIV

"If any of you lack wisdom, let him ask of God, that giveth to all men liberally, and upbraideth not; and it shall be given him."   James 1:5, KJV

"But the wisdom that is from above is first pure, then peaceable, gentle, and easy to be intreated, full of mercy and good fruits, without partiality, and without hypocrisy. And the fruit of righteousness is sown in peace of them that make peace."   James 3:17, KJV

"Do not be anxious about anything, but in everything, by prayer and petition, with thanksgiving, present your requests to God. And the peace of God, which transcends all understanding, will guard your hearts and your minds in Christ Jesus."   Philippians 4:6,7, NIV

MENTAL ILLNESS
Background

"Mental illness" is a generalization commonly used to cover the whole range of psycho-neurological disorders. There are those who are truly ill, suffering some type of malfunction due to a brain injury, an inherited illness, glandular or chemical imbalance, etc. These must be treated by medical science through the means available.

There is, however, a wide area often classified as mental illness which is the result of unresolved carnal attitudes and sinful conduct. Those affected may display the symptoms of illness, but many times these symptoms are stress-related and due to spiritual problems. At times such people will feign illness rather than face the reality of their situation. They will blame other people and circumstances for their problems in order to divert attention from themselves. "Then the man and his wife heard the sound of the Lord God as he was walking in the garden in the cool of the day, and they hid from the Lord God...The man said, 'The woman you put here with me — she gave me some fruit from the tree, and I ate it.' The woman said, 'The serpent deceived me, and I ate' " (Genesis 3:8,12,13, NIV).

It would be a disservice merely to treat the symptoms or excuse such a person just "because of the way he is." The fact is that he will never feel good until he corrects the problem. The first step in recovery is to assume personal responsibility for his attitudes and actions. "Everything is uncovered and laid bare before the eyes of him to whom we must give account" (Hebrews 4:13, NIV). "So then, each of us will give an account of himself to God" (Romans 14:12, NIV).

Change is possible, if such an individual will face reality: lay bare his life before God, repent of what is wrong in attitudes and actions, and confess it to God with the intention of abandoning it in favor of newness of life in Christ Jesus.

Many lives have been re-directed through receiving Jesus Christ as personal Lord and Savior. The power of the Word of God and the ministry of the Holy Spirit, unleashed in a life, have positive effects.

In his "My Answer" column, Billy Graham calls attention to the "multitudes of people who, through God's Word, have become thoroughly integrated persons. Writing to Timothy, the Apostle Paul once said: 'For God hath not given us the spirit of fear; but of power, and of love, and of a sound mind' " (2 Timothy 1:7).

Counseling Strategy

1. Encourage the inquirer by telling him he has called the right place and that you are glad to talk with him and help if you can.

2. Be prepared to listen if the inquirer is willing to talk. Ask questions as needed to stimulate the conversation, hoping that something will emerge to give you the opportunity to suggest a spiritual solution.

3. When you feel the time is opportune, ask him if he has ever received Christ as his Lord and Savior. Share "Steps to Peace with God," page 5. His commitment may initiate a new awareness and a new perception which will provide the desire and the motivation for facing his "mental illness" with reality and determination.

4. Encourage him to start Bible reading and study. Offer him *Living in Christ*, to help him start his study. This discipline will help direct his thoughts toward the Lord, which will bring an inner peace. (See Isaiah 26:3.)

5. Encourage him to learn to pray daily.

6. Counsel him to become involved in a Bible-teaching church where he can learn to worship, fellowship, and serve Christ. A good church relationship will be most helpful in teaching him the basics of the Bible and the "how to" of prayer, and in offering him opportunities of service.

7. Pray with him personally that his commitment to Christ might redirect his attitudes and actions so that he might live in a manner pleasing to God. Share Romans 12:1,2, pointing out that if he follows these principles, he can become a whole person.

8. Encourage him to seek further counseling with a Christian pastor or psychologist so that there may be a continuity in the treatment of his problems in the light of Scripture.

If the inquirer is a Christian with unresolved personal problems, share "Restoration," page 11, and then the follow-up steps above.

Scripture

"Thou wilt keep him in perfect peace, whose mind is stayed on thee, because he trusteth in thee."   Isaiah 26:3, KJV

"The Spirit of the Lord is upon me, because he hath anointed me to preach the gospel to the poor; he hath sent me to heal the broken-hearted, to preach deliverance to the captives, and recovering of sight to the blind, to set at liberty them that are bruised, to preach the acceptable year of the Lord."   Luke 4:18,19, KJV

"Therefore, I urge you, brothers, in view of God's mercy, to offer your bodies as living sacrifices, holy and pleasing to God — which is your spiritual worship. Do not conform any longer to the pattern of this world, but be transformed by the renewing of your mind. Then you will be able to test and approve what God's will is — his good, pleasing and perfect will."   Romans 12:1,2, NIV

"Let this mind be in you, which was also in Christ Jesus."
                                    Philippians 2:5, KJV

"Make every effort to live in peace with all men and to be holy; without holiness no one will see the Lord. See to it that no one misses the grace of God and that no bitter root grows up to cause trouble and defile many."
                                    Hebrews 12:14,15, NIV

"So get rid of your feelings of hatred. Don't just pretend to be good! Be done with dishonesty and jealousy and talking about others behind their backs. Now that you realize how kind the Lord has been to you, put away all evil, deception, envy, and fraud. Long to grow up into the fullness of your salvation; cry for this as a baby cries for his milk."
                                    1 Peter 2:1,2, TLB

"Oh, the joys of those who do not follow evil men's advice, who do not hang around with sinners, scoffing at the things of God: but they delight in doing everything God wants them to, and day and night are always meditating on his laws and thinking about ways to follow him more closely. For the Lord watches over all the plans and paths of godly men, but the paths of the godless lead to doom."   Psalm 1:1,2,6, TLB

OBEDIENCE, DESIRE FOR

Background

Each Christian is responsible to determine the will of God for his life and then to do it. It is often easier for us to do anything other than what we know to be the will of God, thus deviating from essentials and substituting frenetic activity. But "to obey is better than sacrifice" (1 Samuel 15:22). "My food," said Jesus, "is to do the will of him who sent me, and to finish his work" (John 4:34, NIV).

> Billy Graham says: "Only by a life of obedience to the voice of the Spirit, by a daily denying of self, by full dedication to Christ, and by constant fellowship with Him, are we enabled to live a godly life and an influential life in this present ungodly world."

The first step towards obedience is to commit ourselves to obeying God. Joshua said: "Now fear the Lord and serve him with all faithfulness . . . as for me and my household, we will serve the Lord" (Joshua 24:14,15, NIV). A conscious decision to obey leads to submission to the principle of obedience. "Present your bodies a living sacrifice . . . unto God, which is your reasonable service" (Romans 12:1, KJV).

The second step is discipline because obedience is progressive. Obedience leads to growth as we live up to the light we have received. It is a learning process. Jesus learned "obedience by the things which he suffered" (Hebrews 5:8, KJV).

As we mature in Christ and in the knowledge of His Word, God expects from us an ever-deepening obedience. As we understand new demands, we must respond immediately and irrevocably so that He may reveal yet deeper levels of His will for our lives. He desires that we bring "into captivity every thought to the obedience of Christ" (2 Corinthians 10:5, KJV).

Counseling Strategy

1. A person who asks questions about the will of God for his life and about obedience to the will of God is a maturing Christian, one who is interested in a deeper walk with God. Congratulate him for this desire and assure him that God wants to take him just as far as his willingness to obey allows.

2. Take time to listen to concerns and desires. It may be helpful to refer to some aspect of the BACKGROUND to encourage and guide him further.

3. Encourage the inquirer to repent of any disobedience or vacillation. Only as we confess all known sin can we aspire to a deeper commitment.

4. Encourage him to get into the Word. There are no shortcuts in the life of obedience. Our minds must be set always to seek the will of the Lord. Following the progressive discipline revealed through the Word will result in a walk of obedience to God. We must "hunger and thirst for righteousness" (Matthew 5:6, NIV).

5. Pray with him that his desire for obedience to God's will be realized.

6. Encourage him to cultivate fellowship with spiritually minded Christians in a Bible-teaching church where he can learn more of the will and ways of God.

Scripture

"If you love me, you will obey what I command ... "Whoever has my commands and obeys them, he is the one who loves me. He who loves me will be loved by my Father, and I too will love him and show myself to him."   John 14:15,21, NIV

"But if anyone obeys his word, God's love is truly made complete in him. This is how we know we are in him."   1 John 2:5, NIV

"But Samuel replied: 'Does the Lord delight in burnt offerings and sacrifices as much as in obeying the voice of the Lord? To obey is better than sacrifice, and to heed is better than the fat of rams.' "
1 Samuel 15:22, NIV

"See, I am setting before you today a blessing and a curse — the blessing if you obey the commands of the Lord your God that I am giving you today; the curse if you disobey the commands of the Lord your God and turn from the way that I command you today by following other gods, which you have not known."   Deuteronomy 11:26-28, NIV

"Why do you call me, Lord, Lord, and do not do what I say?"
Luke 6:46, NIV

1 Peter 2:13-16, NIV

THE OCCULT
Background

A writer for a national newspaper reported recently that occultism is the most rapidly growing religion in our country. When a spiritual vacuum exists, the empty, curious, and gullible are going to fill it with something. Occultism is a disturbing sign of the accelerating disintegration of our culture.

The term "occult" is somewhat ambiguous, covering a wide range of that which is thought of as secret or concealed, mystical and metaphysical, often touching the supersensory realms. In general, the following are identified as occult:

Spiritism: The belief that people can make contact with the dead through a medium in order to receive revelations from the beyond.

Clairvoyance: The belief that certain people possess extra-sensory ability to perceive what cannot be clearly seen.

Fortune telling: The claim of foretelling the future by reading tea leaves, palms, tarot cards, etc.

Astrology: The belief that the future can be foretold by studying the relative positions of the sun, moon, stars, and planets.

Horoscopes: An outgrowth of astrology using predictions based on a chart with the signs of the zodiac. Advice is offered (often in the news-paper) on the basis of predictions of future events.

Witchcraft: This false religious system has its roots in ancient pagan prac-tices. Using priests and priestesses, rituals and chants, and teaching from the Book of Shadows, witches claim that they are able to contact and utilize powers from the unseen world.

Some persons who identify with and practice the above beliefs have been involved in drugs and sexual promiscuity.

The Bible Forbids Involvement in the Occult:

"Let no one be found among you ... who practices divination or sorcery, interprets omens, engages in witchcraft, or casts spells, or who is a medium or spiritist or who consults the dead. Anyone who does these things is detestable to the Lord" (Deuteronomy 18:10-12, NIV).

"The acts of the sinful nature are obvious: sexual immorality, impurity and debauchery; idolatry and *witchcraft;* hatred, discord, jealousy, fits of rage, selfish ambition, dissensions, factions and envy; drunkenness, orgies, and the like. I warn you, as I did before, that those who live like this will not inherit the kingdom of God" (Galatians 5:19, NIV).

God was displeased when Saul sought the help of the Witch of Endor. "Saul died because he was unfaithful to the Lord; he did not keep the word of the Lord and even consulted a medium for guidance, and did not inquire of the Lord. So the Lord put him to death and turned the kingdom over to David son of Jesse" (1 Chronicles 10:13, 14, NIV).

Revelation 21:8 condemns those who practice magic arts. In pronouncing judgment against Babylon in Isaiah 47:11-15, the Lord enumerates a long list of the occult practices of that nation.

From the scriptural evidence available, we deduce that anything which seeks to detract from an all-knowing, all-powerful, and all-loving God and His purposes for human life is to be rejected.

Counseling Strategy

For the Christian:

1. Inform him that any involvement in the occult displeases God (see BACKGROUND).
2. If he is anxious because of the uncertainties of life, wanting to know the future, assure him that God has promised to "never leave us nor forsake us" (Hebrews 13:5). We are to "seek first his kingdom and his righteousness, and all these things will be given to [us] as well" (Matthew 6:33, NIV). The Bible tells us that "no good thing will he withhold from them that walk uprightly" (Psalm 84:11, KJV).

   We can leave it all with Him! (Also see Philippians 4:6.)
3. Counsel the Christian to seek God's forgiveness for his involvement. Go over "Restoration," page 11. Also share "Assurance," page 9.
4. Counsel him to pray especially about his involvement in the occult so that he never becomes entangled with it again. He should begin to read and study the Word of God. This is a way of redeeming misspent hours involved with the occult. "Redeeming the time, because the days are evil" (Ephesians 5:16, KJV). Offer to send him *Living In Christ* which will help him get started in Bible study.
5. Encourage the inquirer to seek fellowship with committed Christians and to get involved with a Bible-teaching church for worship, Bible study, prayer, and witnessing. As he seeks this new identity, he should sever all relationships with any former friends and destroy any books on the occult in his possession.
6. Pray with him for complete deliverance and restoration to the Lord.

For the Non-Christian Involved With the Occult:

1. Congratulate him for his evident desire to know the truth. God's Word has an answer to the occult.
2. Tell him that any involvement with the occult is displeasing to God. (See BACKGROUND.)
3. Invite him to receive Jesus Christ as his personal Lord and Savior. Share "Steps To Peace with God," page 5.
4. Counsel the inquirer to sever all ties with persons involved in the occult

and to get rid of any literature and paraphernalia on magic and the occult, including horoscopes and Ouija boards.

5. Urge him to read and study the Word of God. Offer him *Living In Christ*, explaining its purpose.

6. Counsel him to seek fellowship with committed Christians in a Bible-teaching church so that he may worship, study the Bible, pray and serve with them. Development of new relationships will be a big help in erasing the past.

7. Pray with him for complete deliverance from his former interest in occult practices and for his full commitment to Christ.

Scripture

This Scripture text gives understanding about the "spirit of the age" in which we live, and advice on how to counteract it.

"But you must realize that in the last days the times will be full of danger. Men will become utterly self-centered, greedy for money, full of big words. They will be proud and contemptuous, without any regard for what their parents taught them. They will be utterly lacking in gratitude, purity and normal human affections. They will be men of unscrupulous speech and have no control of themselves. They will be passionate and unprincipled, treacherous, self-willed and conceited, loving all the time what gives them pleasure instead of loving God. They will maintain a facade of 'religion,' but their conduct will deny its validity. You must keep clear of people like this . . . their minds are distorted, and they are traitors to the faith . . . remember from what sort of people your knowledge has come, and how from early childhood your mind has been familiar with the holy scriptures, which can open the mind to the salvation which comes through believing in Christ Jesus. All scripture is inspired by God and is useful for teaching the faith and correcting error, for resetting the direction of a man's life and training him in good living. The scriptures are the comprehensive equipment of the man of God, and fit him fully for all branches of his work."   2 Timothy 3:1-15, Phillips

PATIENCE

Background

Patience is an admirable quality of life that few people, including Christians, seem to possess. According to God's Word, our lives are to be characterized by patience, for it is important in developing that mature, stable character which God wants to produce in His people. "Love is patient, love is kind ... it is not easily angered" (1 Corinthians 13:4,5, NIV).

Patience is the ability to absorb strain and stress without complaint and to be left undisturbed by obstacles, delays, or failures. God allows difficulties, inconveniences, trials, and even suffering to come our way for a specific purpose: they help develop the right attitude for the growth of patience. As the Christian sees these trials working to his advantage in achieving beneficial, character-building results, the stage is set for the development of a patient spirit. God the Holy Spirit will then be able to produce the fruit of patience in his life. "But the fruit of the Spirit is love, joy, peace, patience..." (Galatians 5:22, NIV).

Billy Graham comments on the lack of patience which characterizes our generation: "This is a high-strung, neurotic, impatient age. We hurry when there is no reason to hurry—just to be hurrying. This fast-paced age has produced more problems and less morality than previous generations, and it has given us jangled nerves. Impatience has produced a crop of broken homes, ulcers, and has set the stage for more world wars."

A bit of introspection and analysis on our part in regard to impatience may be revealing and helpful. What makes me impatient?

- Am I immature? Am I petty?
  "But solid food is for the mature, who by constant use have trained themselves to distinguish good from evil" (Hebrews 5:14, NIV).

- Am I selfish, legalistic or demanding? Am I able to make allowances for the mistakes and imperfections in others, remembering that God is still working on them, too?
  "...Be patient (tolerant) toward all men. See that none render evil for evil unto any man; but ever follow that which is good, both among yourselves, and to all men" (1 Thessalonians 5:14,15, KJV).

- Am I easily irked because "someone is getting away with something"?
  "Fret not thyself because of evil doers" (Psalm 37:1, KJV).

- Am I envious or jealous?
  "Be patient and stand firm. Don't grumble against each other, brothers, or you will be judged" (James 5:8,9, NIV).

- Am I materialistic? Am I dominated by the spirit of this world?
  "If ye then be risen with Christ, seek those things which are above..."
  (Colossians 3:1, KJV).

- Have I really dealt with the "secular mentality"?
  "...For I have learned to be content whatever the circumstances"
  (Philippians 4:11, NIV).

- Am I insensitive to God's attempts to deal with me by permitting adverse circumstances, irritations, and stress to buffet me in order that through His grace I might learn to transcend self and grow in love and spiritual stature?
  "My brethren, count it all joy when ye fall into divers (various) temptations; knowing this, that the trying of your faith worketh patience. But let patience have her perfect work, that ye may be perfect and entire, wanting nothing" (James 1:2-4, KJV).

Counseling Strategy

1. Tactfully ask the inquirer if he has ever received Jesus Christ as his Lord and Savior. Explain "Steps to Peace with God," page 5.

2. Treat impatience as follows:

   A. Encourage the inquirer to admit that he has a problem. Impatience is sin and should be dealt with.

   B. Encourage him to identify the areas of his impatience and the circumstances that trigger his negative response.

   C. Encourage him to pray about these circumstances daily.

      (1) Confess his impatience as sin, asking God's forgiveness (1 John 1:9).

      (2) Ask God to make him sensitive to this area of failure and to help him bring it under control.

   D. Resolve to work on the problem.

      (1) Because impatient people seem to be dominated by a mind set which causes them to respond negatively to irritations, stresses, and provocations, the inquirer should will to let God work in him to produce patience.

         The individual must resolve to bring "into captivity every thought to the obedience of Christ" (2 Corinthians 10:5, KJV) and covenant with God to be an "overcomer."

      (2) Because impatience is a characteristic of the "old nature" or "Adamic nature" (Colossians 3:9,10), the "put-off, put-on" principle should be practiced. Impatience is a response that must be "unlearned." Paul says, "But I see another law at work ... waging war against the law of my mind and making me a prisoner of the law of sin ... What a wretched man I am. Who will rescue

me from this body of death? Thanks be to God—through Jesus Christ our Lord" (Romans 7:23-25, NIV).

Thus:

- I must renounce my impatience — "Put-off."
- I must surrender a little more each day as I claim His power in faith — "Put-off" + "Put-on." (2 Timothy 1:7, Galatians 2:20.)
- I then claim His victory, His love and His patience as the fruit of the Spirit — "Put-on." (1 Corinthians 13:4,5; Galatians 5:22.)

E. Suggest that the inquirer request the help of another Christian to monitor his responses and record his victories or failures.

F. Encourage him to develop the discipline of daily Bible reading and study, Bible memorization, and prayer.

G. Encourage him to seek out other Christians of like mind in a Bible-teaching church for fellowship and Bible study.

Scripture

"Love is patient, love is kind. It does not envy, it does not boast, it is not proud. It is not rude, it is not self-seeking, it is not easily angered, it keeps no record of wrongs."   1 Corinthians 13:4,5, NIV

"But the fruit of the Spirit is love, joy, peace, longsuffering, gentleness, goodness, faith, meekness, temperance: against such there is no law."
Galatians 5:22,23, KJV

"...but we glory in tribulations also: knowing that tribulation worketh patience; and patience, experience; and experience, hope: and hope maketh not ashamed..."   Romans 5:3-5, KJV

"I am crucified with Christ: nevertheless I live; yet not I, but Christ liveth in me: and the life which I now live in the flesh I live by the faith of the Son of God, who loved me, and gave himself for me."   Galatians 2:20, KJV

"Be patient, then, brothers, until the Lord's coming. See how the farmer waits for the land to yield its valuable crop and how patient he is for the fall and spring rains. You too, be patient and stand firm, because the Lord's coming is near. Don't grumble against each other, brothers, or you will be judged. The Judge is standing at the door."   James 5:7,8, NIV

"Rest in the Lord, and wait patiently for him: fret not thyself because of him who prospereth in his way, because of the man who bringeth wicked devices to pass."   Psalm 37:7, KJV

Colossians 3:9,10
2 Peter 1:5-9, NIV

190

PEACE
Background

In our restless age there is a worldwide longing for peace. The book *Peace with God* by Billy Graham has sold millions of copies in many languages, an indication of this longing. In some languages, such as Arabic and Hebrew, the standard greeting is "Peace." But only as Jesus Christ possesses our hearts can we know true peace. In this section, we shall deal with only two aspects of the subject.

Peace With God:

Peace with God comes to us in the forgiveness of sin through the merit and suffering of our Savior.

Peace with God means a cessation of hostilities. When a person confesses his sinful pride, admits defeat, and submits to God, our war with God is over. "Being justified by faith, we have peace with God through our Lord Jesus Christ" (Romans 5:1, KJV).

Peace with God means reconciliation to Him. We are no longer alienated. "And you, that were sometime alienated and enemies in your mind by wicked works, yet now hath he reconciled in the body of his flesh through death, to present you holy and unblameable and unreprovable in his sight" (Colossians 1:21, 22, KJV).

"And, having made peace through the blood of his cross, by him to reconcile all things unto himself; by him, I say, whether they be things in earth, or things in heaven" (Colossians 1:20, KJV). "That God was reconciling the world to himself in Christ, not counting men's sins against them" (2 Corinthians 5:19, NIV).

Peace with God brings a sense of well-being and confidence "May the God of hope fill you with all joy and peace as you trust in him, so that you may overflow with hope by the power of the Holy Spirit" (Romans 15:13, NIV).

Peace Of God:

The peace of God is the legacy of Christian believers and comes as we walk in obedience to His will for our lives.

Many Christians have peace with God but have never gone on to experience the peace of God in their lives. They are torn with anxieties and fears that destroy spiritual stability and joy in the Lord. Peace is a gift from God and the rightful legacy of all believers, but far too many do not enjoy it. The peace of God flows from a full, unhindered fellowship with Him who is our peace.

Here is a simple formula from the Word of God for enjoying the peace of God.

Psalm 37:1-5 (NIV) tells us:
1. Do not fret (v.1)
2. Trust in the Lord (v.3)
3. Delight yourself in the Lord (v.4)

Philippians 4:6,7 (NIV) tells us:
1. Be anxious for nothing (v.6)
2. Be prayerful in everything (v.6)
3. Be thankful for anything (v.6)

"And the peace of God, which transcends all understanding, will guard your hearts and your minds in Christ Jesus" (Philippians 4:7, NIV).

Counseling Strategy

For the Non-Christian:

1. Explain "Steps to Peace with God," page 5.
2. Encourage him to take a firm stand for Christ, to get into the Word by daily reading and studying it andoffer to send him *Living in Christ*.
3. Counsel the inquirer to get into a Bible-teaching church for fellowship, worship, Bible study, and prayer.
4. Pray with him that the peace of God may be generously experienced in his life.

For the Christian:

Probe gently for sin in his life, worry, or emotional problems that may be hindering him. Then:

1. Counsel the inquirer to confess any known sin, wrong, irritation, anger or bitterness that might be blocking the peace of God in his life.
2. Share thoughts from the BACKGROUND on the peace of God.
3. Encourage the individual to develop a daily devotional life as a means of "delighting in the Lord" and experiencing His peace. He should:

    A. Read and study the Word daily. Offer to send him *Living in Christ*.

    B. Pray about everything; trust God to work according to Romans 8:28.

    C. Daily Commit his life into God's hands in the spirit of Proverbs 3:5,6.

4. Counsel the inquirer to get involved in a Bible-teaching church for fellowship, worship, prayer, Bible study and service.
5. Pray with him for God's peace, victory, and joy.

Scripture

John 14:27, NIV
John 16:33, NIV
Psalm 34:14, KJV
Isaiah 26:3, KJV
Romans 8:6, NIV

PRAYER
Background

Prayer is given a place of highest priority in the Bible. Some of the Scriptures' most transcendent passages deal with prayers expressing praise, worship, thanksgiving, confession and supplication. The lives of the outstanding people of God of both the Old and New Testaments, and down through the history of the Church were characterized by much prayer. All the recorded revivals of history had their beginnings in prayer. Anything of value in the Kingdom of God is initiated in and dependent upon prayer.

The Bible reveals our ignorance of prayer:
- "...we know not what we should pray for as we ought: but the Spirit itself maketh intercession for us with groanings which cannot be uttered" (Romans 8:26, KJV).
- "But when ye pray, use not vain repetitions, as the heathen do: for they think that they shall be heard for their much speaking" (Matthew 6:7, KJV).

The Bible invites us, actually commands us, to pray.
- "...but in everything by prayer and supplication with thanksgiving let your requests be made known unto God" (Philippians 4:6, KJV).
- "Let us therefore come boldly unto the throne of grace, that we may obtain mercy, and find grace to help in time of need" (Hebrews 4:16, KJV).

   "Pray without ceasing" (1 Thessalonians 5:17, KJV).

The Bible offers many guidelines for praying.
1. Through individual promises. (There are hundreds of recorded promises in the Scriptures.)
   - "But thou, when thou prayest, enter into thy closet, and when thou hast shut thy door, pray to thy Father which is in secret; and thy Father which seeth in secret shall reward thee openly" (Matthew 6:6, KJV).
   - "...ye have not, because ye ask not" James 4:2, KJV).
   - "...ask, and ye shall receive, that your joy may be full" (John 16:24, KJV).
   - "If ye abide in me, and my words abide in you, ye shall ask what ye will, and it shall be done unto you" (John 15:7, KJV).
   - "But my God shall supply all your need according to his riches in glory by Christ Jesus" (Philippians 4:19, KJV).
   - "...men ought always to pray, and not to faint" (Luke 18:1, KJV).
   - "Watch ye therefore, and pray always...." (Luke 21:36, KJV).

2. Through the prayers of Jesus Christ
   The Lord's Prayer   Matthew 6:6-14; Luke 11:1-5

His prayer for His own   John 17
His prayer at Lazarus' tomb   John 11:41-45
His prayer at the Mount of Transfiguration   Luke 9:28-36
His prayer in the Garden of Gethsemane   Matthew 26:36-46
His prayers from the cross   Matthew 27:46; Luke 23:34; Luke 23:46

3.   Through the prayers of the great spiritual leaders of the Bible

The prayer of the servant of Abraham and God's answer   Genesis 24:12-66
The prayer of Jacob and God's answer   Genesis 32:9 through chapter 33
Moses' prayer for God's presence and glory   Exodus 33:12-23
Joshua's prayer of despair and God's answer   Joshua 7:6-26
Hannah's prayer and vow, and God's answer   1 Samuel 1:1-28
David's prayer of repentance and confession   Psalm 51
David's thanksgiving, prayer for his people and for his son
     1 Chronicles 29:10-19
Solomon's prayer at the temple dedication and God's answer
     2 Chronicles 6:12-42
Hezekiah's prayer and God's answer   2 Kings 19:14-37
Elijah's prayer and God's answer   1 Kings 18:41-46 (See James 5:17,18.)
Prayers, thanksgiving and praise in the book of Psalms
Paul's prayer for knowledge and understanding   Ephesians 1:15-23
Paul's prayer for the believer's spiritual enlightenment and multi-dimensional
commitment   Ephesians 3:14-21
Paul's exhortation to Timothy   1 Timothy 2:1-8

Billy Graham emphasizes prayer:

"The Bible says, 'Pray without ceasing'! This means that we must be
always ready to pray. Prayer is like a child's communion with his father.
Because the Christian is one who has been born into the family of God
it is as natural for him to pray as it is for an earthly child to ask his father
for the things he needs. We are living in dangerous times and if there
was ever a time when we needed to pray, it's now. Because more can
be done by prayer than anything else, prayer is our greatest weapon."

Counseling Strategy

   Many people ask for prayer because they have concerns, but often know very
little about it and what language to use in approaching God. We should be ready
to offer encouragement and to pray with them about their requests. Reassure them
that you are delighted to share their concerns, because God knows about them.
He cares and has promised to answer prayer. Your prayers for others will mean
more to them than you might realize.

1. One prayer that delights God's heart is the sinner's prayer "God be merciful to me a sinner" (Luke 18:13). Do not assume that because one requests prayer that he is a Christian; often the opposite is true. Assure the individual that you are concerned for him and happy to take his request to God. However, before doing so, you would like to ask him if he has ever received Jesus Christ as his personal Savior and Lord. If indicated, share "Steps to Peace with God," Page 5, and then the follow-up steps.

2. Just previous to praying for the expressed need, encourage the individual by reading two prayer promises from the Scriptures.

   • "And all things, whatsoever ye shall ask in prayer, believing, ye shall receive" (Matthew 21:22, KJV).

   • "That if two of you shall agree on earth as touching anything that they shall ask, it shall be done for them of my Father which is in heaven" (Matthew 18:19, KJV).
   (Suggest that the person write down the references for later reading.)

3. Pray the fervent prayer of faith, and then thank God for the answer.

4. Sometimes a Christian will complain that God does not seem to answer. Encourage him to continue praying in faith, to be importunate (troublesomely persistent), as the woman in Luke 18:1-5. Also, advise him to be sure that his motives are pure, according to James 4:3.

Billy Graham offers some suggestions for Christians with unanswered prayers.

---

1. "Prayer is for God's children.

2. "Effectual prayer is offered in faith. The Bible says, 'Therefore I say unto you, what things soever ye desire, when ye pray, believe that ye receive them, and ye shall have them' (Mark 11:24, KJV).

3. "Dynamic prayer emanates from an obedient heart. The Bible says, 'And whatsoever we ask, we receive of him.'

4. "We are to pray in Christ's name. Jesus said, 'And whatsoever ye shall ask in my name, that will I do, that the Father may be glorified in the Son' (John 14:13, KJV). We are not worthy to approach the holy throne of God except through our advocate, Jesus Christ.

5. "We must desire the will of God. Even our Lord, contrary to His own wish at the moment, said, 'O my Father, if this cup may not pass away from me except I drink it, thy will be done' (Matthew 26:42, KJV).

6. "Our prayer must be for God's glory. The model prayer which Jesus has given to us concludes with, 'Thine is the kingdom and the power and the glory.' If we are to have our prayers answered, we must give God the glory."

Scripture
Encouragement to pray:

'When you pray, go into your room, close the door and pray to your Father, who is unseen. Then your Father, who sees what is done in secret, will reward you. And when you pray, do not keep on babbling like pagans, for they think they will be heard because of their many words. Do not be like them, for your Father knows what you need before you ask him."
Matthew 6:6,7,8, NIV

"Let us then approach the throne of grace with confidence, so that we may receive mercy and find grace to help us in our time of need."
Hebrews 4:16, NIV

"And pray in the Spirit on all occasions with all kinds of prayers and requests. With this in mind, be alert and always keep on praying for all the saints."
Ephesians 6:18, NIV

Prayer Promises:

"And I will do whatever you ask in my name, so that the Son may bring glory to the Father. You may ask me for anything in my name, and I will do it."
John 14:13,14, NIV

"If you remain in me and my words remain in you, ask whatever you wish, and it will be given you."
John 15:7, NIV

"In him and through faith in him we may approach God with freedom and confidence."
Ephesians 3:12, NIV

"So I say to you: Ask and it will be given to you; seek and you will find; knock and the door will be opened to you. For everyone who asks receives; he who seeks finds; and to him who knocks, the door will be opened."
Luke 11:9,10, NIV

How to Pray:

"This is how you should pray: 'Our Father in heaven, hallowed be your name, your kingdom come, your will be done on earth as it is in heaven. Give us today our daily bread. Forgive us our debts, as we have also forgiven our debtors. And lead us not into temptation, but deliver us from the evil one."
Matthew 6:9-11, NIV

"I want men everywhere to lift up holy hands in prayer, without anger or disputing."
1 Timothy 2:8, NIV

PROPHECY

Background

A helpful axiom for understanding the Scriptures is "The New is in the Old concealed; the Old is in the New revealed." We refer, of course, to the Old and New Testaments.

Prophecy was both a forthtelling within the present, and a foretelling — with events predicted decades and centuries before they actually occurred. Much of prophecy in the Scriptures has already been fulfilled. Other prophecies are being fulfilled even in our day. Peter declared, "We have also a more sure word of prophecy; whereunto ye do well that ye take heed, as unto a light that shineth in a dark place, until the day dawn, and the day star arise in your hearts: knowing this first, that no prophecy of the scripture is of any private interpretation. For the prophecy came not in old time by the will of man: but holy men of God spake as they were moved by the Holy Ghost" (2 Peter 1:19-21, KJV).

Prophecy Fulfilled:

The most convincing evidence of fulfilled prophecy concerns the Person and work of Jesus Christ, as revealed in the four Gospels. Lack of space precludes the listing of all such prophecies. The following, however, constitute powerful evidence:

He was to be of King David's family (Isaiah 9:6,7; 11:1; Psalm 89:3,4; Mark 12:36 and John 7:42).

He would be born of a virgin (Isaiah 7:14 and Matthew 1:23).

He would be born in Bethlehem (Micah 5:2 and John 7:42).

He would make a triumphant entry into Jerusalem (Zechariah 9:9 and Matthew 21:5).

He would die with criminals (Isaiah 53:9,12 and Luke 22:37).

They would cast lots for His garments (Psalm 22:18 and Matthew 27:35).

His dying words were foretold (Psalm 22:1 and Matthew 27:46).

He would rise from the dead the third day (Psalm 16:10). Jesus affirmed the resurrection by referring to past Scriptures (Luke 24:46). Peter confirmed it by quoting David's prophecy (Acts 2:25-32).

Though Isaiah prophesied 800 years before Jesus' coming, he wrote of Christ's sufferings for us (see Isaiah 53:6).

Prophecy to be Fulfilled:

The prophecies yet to be fulfilled largely concern the so-called "Blessed Hope" of the Christian believer — the imminent return of Jesus Christ —

"Which hope," says the writer of Hebrews, "we have as an anchor of the soul, both sure and steadfast. . ." (Hebrews 6:19, KJV).

Billy Graham writes: "The importance of the hope of Christ's return is established by the frequency, extent, and intensity of its mention in the Bible. It is mentioned in all but four books of the New Testament. Christ referred constantly to His return, not only to His disciples, but to others as well. He said to the high priest, 'Hereafter shall ye see the Son of man sitting on the right hand of power, and coming in the clouds of heaven' (Matthew 26:64).

One out of every thirty verses in the Bible mentions this subject. There are 318 references to it, in 216 chapters in the New Testament. One-twentieth of the entire New Testament deals with this subject. It was predicted by most of the Old Testament writers: by Moses (Deuteronomy 33:2); by Job (Job 19:25); by David (Psalm 102:16); by Isaiah (59:20); by Jeremiah (Jeremiah 23:5); by Daniel (Daniel 7:13, 14); by Zechariah (Zechariah 14:4); and by many others."

There are differing views concerning future prophecies. Instead of arguing about them, let us remember that "no prophecy of the scripture is of any private interpretation" (2 Peter 1:20, KJV). We believe, however, that the so-called pre-millennial view offers the most comprehensive explanation of coming events and list in bare outline some of its features.

1. Christ's coming is imminent: it could occur at any time (Matthew 24:42-44; 1 Corinthians 15:52; Revelation 22:12).

2. The first stage of His coming is known as the "Rapture." "We believe that Jesus died and rose again and so we believe that God will bring with Jesus those who have fallen asleep in him . . . For the Lord himself will come down from heaven, with a loud command, with the voice of the archangel and with the trumpet call of God, and the dead in Christ will rise first. After that, we who are still alive and are left will be caught up with them in the clouds to meet the Lord in the air. And so we will be with the Lord forever" (1 Thessalonians 4:14, 16-17, NIV). (See also Titus 2:13). This is the first resurrection (1 Corinthians 15:52-57; 2 Corinthians 5:4; and 1 John 3:2).

3. The Judgment seat of Christ for believers follows (see 2 Corinthians 5:10). The standard of this judgment is our faithfulness in life and service (see 1 Corinthians 3:11-15 and 4:1-5). This judgment is not for our sins. That was taken care of at Calvary (see 2 Corinthians 5:21).

4. The Great Tribulation period comes (see Daniel 12:1; Matthew 24:21,29; Revelation 7:14). The "man of sin" (Antichrist) is manifested (see 2 Thessalonians 2:3,4,8; Revelation 13:1-10).

5. Christ returns (the second stage) as King of Kings and Lord of Lords (see Revelation 19:11-21). The decisive Battle of Armageddon takes place (see Revelation 19:17-21; Joel 3:12; Revelation 16:16).

6. The Millennium (reign of a thousand years) will follow (see Revelation 20:4-6).

7. The Second Resurrection will bring together all who have rejected Christ throughout the ages. They will be judged from "the books, according to their works" (Revelation 20:12, KJV), at the Great White Throne judgment. "And whosoever was not found written in the book of life was cast into the lake of fire" (Revelation 20:15, KJV).

8. The New Heaven and the New Earth begin, the eternal home of the redeemed (see Revelation 21 and 22).

Counseling Strategy

For One Fearful of Future Events:

The only way to be confident and secure about the future is to commit our life to Him who holds the future. "We have this hope as an anchor for the soul, firm and secure" (Hebrews 6:19, NIV). Explain "Steps to Peace with God," page 5.

For the Christian Uncertain About Christ's Coming:

1. Reassure him that we can be enlightened and certain about both the present and the future. Paul said: "Brothers, we do not want you to be ignorant about those who fall asleep, or to grieve like the rest of men, who have no hope" (1 Thessalonians 4:13, NIV).

2. Share "Assurance," page 9, also emphasizing 1 John 5:13.

3. Encourage the inquirer to get into Bible reading and study and to become involved with a Bible-teaching church where he can learn to "rightly divide the word of truth" (2 Timothy 2:15, KJV). Suggest that he visit a Christian bookstore where he can purchase good books about the Christian life and witnessing, as well as Bible studies on prophecy.

For the Christian Concerned About His Standing Before God:

1. Question him about where he went astray.

2. Invite him back to Calvary for confession and forgiveness on the basis of 1 John 1:9 and 2:1. Share "Restoration," page 11.

3. Counsel him to take a firm stand for the Lord. He should:
   Get involved in Bible reading and study.
   Seek fellowship in a Bible-teaching church.
   Actively witness in life and word.
   Such action will give him assurance in Christ and lead him to know God's will for his life.

Scripture

The First Stage of His Coming: The Rapture:

"Brothers, we do not want you to be ignorant about those who fall asleep, or to grieve like the rest of men, who have no hope. We believe that Jesus died and rose again and so we believe that God will bring with Jesus those who have fallen asleep in him. According to the Lord's own word, we tell you that we who are still alive, who are left till the coming of the Lord, will certainly not precede those who have fallen asleep. For the Lord himself will come down from heaven, with a loud command, with the voice of the archangel and with the trumpet call of God, and the dead in Christ will rise first. After that, we who are still alive and are left will be caught up with them in the clouds to meet the Lord in the air. And so we will be with the Lord forever. Therefore encourage each other with these words."

1 Thessalonians 4:13-17, NIV

"Dear friends, now we are children of God, and what we will be has not yet been made known. But we know that when he appears, we shall be like him, for we shall see him as he is. Everyone who has this hope in him purifies himself, just as he is pure."

1 John 3:2, NIV

The Second Stage of His Coming: The Day of the Lord:

"In my vision at night I looked, and there before me was one like a son of man, coming with the clouds of heaven. He approached the Ancient of Days and was led into his presence. He was given authority, glory and sovereign power; all peoples, nations and men of every language worshiped him. His dominion is an everlasting dominion that will not pass away, and his kingdom is one that will never be destroyed."

Daniel 7:13,14, NIV

"But the day of the Lord will come like a thief. The heavens will disappear with a roar; the elements will be destroyed by fire, and the earth and everything in it will be laid bare . . . But in keeping with his promise we are looking forward to a new heaven and a new earth, the home of righteousness."

2 Peter 3:10,13, NIV

The Attitude of the Believer in Light of His Coming:

"These have come so that your faith — of greater worth than gold, which perishes even though refined by fire — may be proved genuine and may result in praise, glory and honor when Jesus Christ is revealed. Therefore, prepare your minds for action; be self-controlled; set your hope fully on the grace to be given you when Jesus Christ is revealed."

1 Peter 1:7,13, NIV

"If anyone is ashamed of me and my words in this adulterous and sinful generation, the Son of Man will be ashamed of him when he comes in his Father's glory with the holy angels."   Mark 8:38, NIV

"The end of all things is near. Therefore be clear minded and self-controlled so that you can pray. Above all, love each other deeply, because love covers over a multitude of sins. Offer hospitality to one another without grumbling. Each one should use whatever gift he has received to serve others, faithfully administering God's grace in its various forms."

1 Peter 4:7,8, NIV

"Preach the Word; be prepared in season and out of season; correct, rebuke and encourage — with great patience and careful instruction. For the time will come when men shall not put up with sound doctrine. Instead, to suit their own desires, they will gather around them a great number of teachers to say what their itching ears want to hear. They will turn their ears away from the truth and turn aside to myths. But you, keep your head in all situations, endure hardship, do the work of an evangelist, discharge all the duties of your ministry."   2 Timothy 4:2-5, NIV

PROSPERITY OF THE UNRIGHTEOUS

Background

Over 3,000 years ago, a humble but envious singer-priest of Israel went into God's sanctuary deeply troubled over the apparent prosperity, freedom from care, arrogance, indifference and power of the unrighteous. Why do I even bother to seek after righteousness, questioned Asaph. Why do I bother to keep my heart pure? It hardly seems worth the effort when they prosper and I don't.

What Asaph learned in the sanctuary revealed that appearances are often deceiving, and that God has truly reserved the best for those who are faithful to Him. He is always with His own and is their present strength and future portion. The prosperous wicked have their rewards, such as they are, during this lifetime, but they, themselves will perish in their unfaithfulness (see Psalm 73).

Some Christians are bothered by the apparent prosperity and success of the non-Christian in this life while they struggle on with little.

Counseling Strategy

After patiently listening to the inquirer who registers his complaint in this area, reassure him of your interest and concern. This is an area that troubles many of the Lord's people. Tell him that you are glad to share what you can and hope it will be an encouragement to him. Ask him to take the following into consideration:

1. Prosperity doesn't necessarily indicate the blessing of God. Many times wealth is ill-gotten and amassed at the expense of others. There are, however, many wealthy Christians who are thoroughly committed to Christ and attribute their wealth to the blessing of God. They joyfully support the Lord's work as faithful stewards while the former are simply enjoying "the pleasures of sin for a season" (Hebrews 11:25, KJV).

2. The inquirer is not accountable to God for the excesses of the rich, so he shouldn't assume this responsibility. God will deal with them in His own time and in His own way. Remember, God keeps the records, both theirs and ours!

3. Counsel him to avoid being envious or bitter, not coveting what another has. He should not immerse himself in self-pity. All these are displeasing to God and will destroy a person's spiritual life. Remember that most of the world's Christians are poor, especially those of the Third World. If the inquirer is a poor Christian, he is in good company! It is indicated in Scripture that God has chosen the poor of this world to be rich in faith (see James 2:5).

4. He should be objective in evaluating wealthy people. Why do they have so much? Do they have a better education or special skills he doesn't have?

Have they taken better advantage of their opportunities than he has? Did they inherit their wealth? Be sure he does not accuse all wealthy people of "getting all the good breaks" in life, or having gotten rich at the expense of others, etc.

5. Encourage him to renew his own vows of faithfulness to God, determining to love and serve Him whatever the cost. Job said, "Though he slay me, yet will I trust in him" (Job 13:15, KJV). We must seek to be rich in faith; it isn't riches that please God, it's faith. "And without faith it is impossible to please God, because anyone who comes to him must believe that he exists and that he rewards those who earnestly seek him" (Hebrews 11:6, NIV).

6. Counsel him to be always prayerful about his needs and learn to trust God to supply them. Paul said, "I know what it is to be in need, and I know what it is to have plenty. I have learned the secret of being content in any and every situation, whether well fed or hungry, whether living in plenty or in want. I can do everything through him who gives me strength" (Philippians 4:12,13, NIV).

7. Encourage him to continue to honor the Lord with his tithes and offerings. This will keep him in tune with God's eternal purposes and will witness to a committed heart.

Scripture

"Wealth and honor come from you; you are the ruler of all things. In your hands are strength and power to exalt and give strength to all."

1 Chronicles 29:12, NIV

"What good is it for a man to gain the whole world, yet forfeit his soul?"

Mark 8:36, NIV

"Then he (Jesus) said to them, 'Watch out! Be on your guard against all kinds of greed; a man's life does not consist in the abundance of his possessions."

Luke 12:15, NIV

"But God said to him, 'You fool! This very night your life will be demanded from you. Then who will get what you have prepared for yourself?' This is how it will be with anyone who stores up things for himself but is not rich toward God. But seek his kingdom, and these things will be given to you as well. For where your treasure is, there your heart will be also."

Luke 12:20,21,31,34, NIV

Joshua 1:68, NIV

REDEDICATION

Background

The Christian witness may have the privilege of praying with another Christian who wishes to rededicate his life to Christ. This rededication is usually sought by one who has already received Christ as Savior and Lord, but who seeks a deeper dimension in living for Him.

The desire to rededicate one's life could be based on several motivations:

- A lack of fulfillment coming from a feeling that "there must be more to the Christian life than I have experienced thus far."
- A search for freedom from sin and guilt resulting from carelessness in daily repentance and confession of sin to God for cleansing and renewal.
- A desire to know the will of God for a life of more dedicated service.

Counseling Strategy

1. Permit the inquirer to express fully his motive in wanting to rededicate his life. The witness who himself is experienced in the will and ways of God will be able to ask relevant questions which will help to focus on the real issue.

2. Congratulate him! Our desire to commit all to God pleases Him and is rewarded by Him. See Hebrews 11:6 and James 4:7,8.

3. If indicated, urge the inquirer to confess all known sin and to trust God for cleansing in the light of Hebrews 9:14 and 1 John 1:9.

4. Encourage him to submit himself totally to God in an act of complete obedience, using Romans 12:1,2 and Ephesians 5:15.

5. Urge him to seek the fullness of the Holy Spirit, using Ephesians 5:18 and Ephesians 3:16-19.

6. Urge him to make a serious commitment to reading the Scriptures daily and beginning to study and memorize them in a planned and disciplined way. See Psalm 119:9 and 11, and Colossians 3:16.

7. Urge him to make prayer a daily exercise according to 1 Thessalonians 5:17 and Ephesians 6:18,19.

8. Encourage him to be a witness to his faith on a daily basis:

   A. In life (see Ephesians 2:10).

   B. In word (see Romans 1:16 and Philippians 2:16).

9. Ask the inquirer to pray, making a commitment in the light of the above. Then, pray with him that his life may become a daily walk with Christ, resulting in opportunities for service.

Scripture

Joshua 24:15
1 Samuel 15:22
Psalm 43:4
Psalm 107:8,9
Matthew 6:33
Matthew 22:37,38
2 Corinthians 10:5
Philippians 1:6 and 9-11
1 Thessalonians 5:23,24
1 Peter 2:11,12

REMARRIAGE

Background

For the Christian, divorce is not an option. The couple promised before God and witnesses that the union of their two lives would be "until death do us part." "To the married I give this command (not I, but the Lord): A wife must not separate from her husband. But if she does, she must remain unmarried or else be reconciled to her husband. And a husband must not divorce his wife" (1 Corinthians 7:10, NIV).

There are, however, mitigating circumstances indicated in Scripture: when the Christian's mate is guilty of sexual immorality, such as adultery or homosexuality, and will not end such practice (see Matthew 19:9) or when the Christian's spouse deserts (see 1 Corinthians 7:15).

In both the above situations, the Scriptures encourage forgiveness and restoration which would be more honoring to God. But if no solution can be found on these grounds, then divorce is scripturally an option.

What about remarriage for the other partner? This is a matter of individual conscience; the Scriptures neither prohibit nor encourage such remarriage. It would seem, however, that if the Scriptures "permit" divorce under the above criteria, they would at the same time allow remarriage as an option. Read 1 Corinthians 7.

To the person who asks: "I am already divorced and remarried; shall I leave my present husband or wife and go to live with my first mate?" Billy Graham answers: "Under normal circumstances, I would say to stay where you are. The sins of the past cannot be undone, just as you cannot unscramble eggs. The primary thing for you to do is to confess your past sins and failures; then make sure, as far as your responsibility lies, that your home is a Christian home."

Counseling Strategy

It is possible that a number of variations to those mentioned in the BACK-GROUND will be encountered. Attempt to follow these guidelines:

For the Non-Christian:

1. The first matter of concern to be faced is not remarriage but putting oneself within the circle of the will of God. When a person does this, he or she will have a perspective on himself and remarriage that never would have been there otherwise. (See Matthew 6:33.)

   Ask if he or she has ever received Jesus Christ as personal Lord and Savior. Explain "Steps to Peace with God," page 5.

2. Encourage the inquirer to begin reading and studying the Bible.

3. Counsel the individual to learn to pray and to practice it daily, seeking God's will and guidance. NOTE: Knowledge and maturity acquired through studying the Scriptures and through praying are indispensable in making any decisions about remarriage.

4. Encourage the inquirer to unite with a Bible-teaching church for worship, fellowship, and Christian service.

5. Suggest, now that the individual is a Christian, that he or she "marry in the Lord" (1 Corinthians 7:39) and establish a truly Christian home which is both Christ- and church-centered.

For the Christian:

1. The inquirer should take into account that remarriage is not all that easy! A series of questions should be posed and answered:

   "Although I am considered to be the innocent party, did I contribute in any way to the breakup of my first marriage?"

   "Is there pride and self-centeredness which I haven't dealt with?"

   "Are there any resentments and bitterness as a result of the divorce which ought to be dealt with?"

   "Do I have the right to think that a new marriage will be a success?"

   "Am I now living in the will of God? How can I really determine if I am?"

   "Am I able to make a truly spiritual contribution to a new marriage?"

   "Is God's glory my highest aim in life?"

2. If indicated, share "Restoration," page 11.

3. Urge the caller to make sure that he or she is walking in the will of God. This can be determined by the commitment to read and study the Word of God faithfully and to rely on prayer.

4. Encourage the inquirer to identify with, and to get involved in, a Bible-teaching church.

5. Counsel the individual that, if he or she does remarry, Christ must be made the center of the marriage and the home. They should establish a daily family altar where all may read the Scriptures and pray together.

6. Pray with the inquirer for the realization of God's will and purpose in his life.

Scripture

"Be careful for nothing; but in every thing by prayer and supplication with thanksgiving, let your requests be made known unto God. And the peace of God, which passeth all understanding, shall keep your hearts and minds through Christ Jesus."   Philippians 4:6,7, KJV

"If any of you lack wisdom, let him ask of God, that giveth to all men liberally, and upbraideth not: and it shall be given him."   James 1:5, KJV

"Likewise, ye husbands, dwell with them according to knowledge, giving honor unto the wife, as unto the weaker vessel, and as being heirs together of the grace of life; that your prayers be not hindered."   1 Peter 3:7, KJV

"If we confess our sins, he is faithful and just to forgive us our sins, and to cleans us from all unrighteousness."   1 John 1:9, KJV

"He hath not dealt with us after our sins; nor rewarded us according to our iniquities. For as the heaven is high above the earth, so great is his mercy toward them that fear him. As far as the east is from the west, so far hath he removed our transgressions from us."   Psalm 103:10-12, KJV

SALVATION OF CHILDREN
Background

As children learn about Jesus, His life, His death and His resurrection, they learn to respond to God's love. Their salvation is desirable, for Jesus said, "Let the little children come to me, and do not hinder them, for the kingdom of God belongs to such as these" (Mark 10:14, NIV). On another occasion He said: "I tell you the truth, unless you change and become like little children, you will never enter the kingdom of heaven" (Matthew 18:3, NIV). A child is ready for commitment to Christ as soon as he understands the meaning of sin and that Jesus is the Savior from sin.

Billy Graham comments: "Giving yourself to Christ is the most important thing you will ever do. This could be the beginning of a new and wonderful experience... In the Gospel of John 10:10, we read where Jesus said, 'I have come that they may have life, and have it to the full' (NIV). God wants you to have a happy and useful life."

Counseling Strategy

You may explain to the child, as simply as possible, the way of salvation. Use the Bible but make sure the child understands the relevance of each Scripture in the unfolding of God's plan. If you feel that the child understands, encourage him to pray and ask Jesus to forgive him and to come into his heart as his Savior. The following outline might be of help.

1. What is God's plan for you? (Peace and life)

    This is God's world. He made it. He made you. He wants you to have peace and happiness. In the very first chapter of the Bible it says: "God saw everything that he had made, and, behold, it was very good" (Genesis 1:31, KJV). But when we read about all the trouble in the world — the unhappiness, the badness — we realize that something has gone wrong in God's world.

2. What has caused this trouble? (Sin)

    Instead of living our lives to please God, we have been pleasing ourselves. "All we like sheep have gone astray; we have turned every one to his own way" (Isaiah 53:6, KJV). This is what the Bible calls sin. Sin is insisting on our own selfish way instead of taking God's way. The Bible says that "all have sinned and come short of the glory of God" (Romans 3:23, KJV).

3. How does God solve this problem of our sin? (The Cross of Jesus.)

    When God's Son, Jesus, died on the Cross, He took the punishment for sin which we deserved. Through His death we can be forgiven. "For God so loved the world that he gave his only begotten Son, that whosoever believeth in him should not perish, but have everlasting life" (John 3:16, KJV).

4. What must we now do to please God? (Open our heart and receive Jesus.)

If you are willing to ask God to forgive your sins, and you receive Jesus as your Savior, you will become a member of God's family. "To all who received him, to those who believed in his name, he gave the right to become children of God" (John 1:12, NIV).

5. Shall we say a little prayer together? If you really want to receive Jesus, I want you to say these words after me:

"Dear God, You have said that I have sinned and need forgiveness. I am sorry for pleasing only myself instead of You. I receive Jesus right now as my Savior and Lord. Amen."

6. Encourage the child to:

A. Read his Bible every day. Tell him we are sending an interesting book, *Following Jesus,* just for him; it will help him to understand more of God's Word.

B. Learn to pray to Jesus every day.

C. Try to be loving to his parents and other people, as well as being helpful to them.

D. Go to Sunday school and church every Sunday.

Scripture

"Look! I have been standing at the door and I am constantly knocking. If anyone hears me calling him and opens the door, I will come in and fellowship with him and he with me."   Revelation 3:20, TLB

"If we say that we have no sin, we deceive ourselves, and the truth is not in us. If we confess our sins, he is faithful and just to forgive us our sins, and to cleanse us from all unrighteousness."   1 John 1:8,9, KJV

"For whosoever shall call upon the name of the Lord shall be saved."   Romans 10:13, KJV

SATAN, ORIGIN AND WORK OF
Background

Satan worship is practiced in many countries of the world and has become prevalent in America in recent years. We need to understand the enemy!

Who is Satan?

He is a fallen angel, a creation of God. He was of the highest order, anointed to cover God's throne. He was full of wisdom until iniquity revealed itself in him (Ezekiel 28:15).

God did not create Satan as an evil being; he became one when by his own free will he forfeited his position and state. He tried to make himself equal with God, even to usurp God's position. (Isaiah 14:12-14.) Pride and selfish ambition were the reasons he was put out of heaven. In his rebellion he was accompanied by millions of lesser angels who now serve as his messengers. (See "Demons," page 67.) He is known by many names in Scripture, some of which are: "the adversary (1 Peter 5:8,9), the god of this world (2 Corinthians 4:4), the prince of the power of the air (Ephesians 2:1-3), accuser of the brethren (Revelation 12:10, Job 1:6-12), the enemy (Matthew 13:39), the tempter (Matthew 4:3), a roaring lion (1 Peter 5:8-10), the father of lies (John 8:44), a deceiver (Revelation 12:9), and a murderer (John 8:44)." Satan's names in Scripture reveal something of his nature and his mission.

Where is Satan's domain?

It is not in hell with a pitchfork! He is not and never shall be the master of hell. He will some day be one of its victims, as it was made specifically for him and the fallen angels (Matthew 25:41). He goes "to and fro throughout the earth" and appears in heaven to accuse God's own. (See Job 1:6 and Revelation 12:10.) He is "the prince of the power of the air" (Ephesians 2:2).

What is Satan like?

His names in Scripture reveal something of his nature and mission. Here are three important points to remember while counseling:

- Satan deceives, transforming himself into an "angel of light" (2 Corinthians 11:14).
- Satan tempts, as seen in the contest with Jesus in Matthew 4:1-11.
- Satan blinds the minds of the unbelieving so that they may not come to the light (2 Corinthians 4:4).

The Bible contains the recorded history of the ages-long contest between Satan and the Lord Jesus Christ. Satan controls the world system as god of this world. First John 2:16 describes the spirit of this world: "For all that is in the world, the lust of the flesh, the lust of the eyes, and the pride of life, is not of the Father, but is of the world."

"Many jokes are made about the devil, but the devil is no joke," says Billy Graham. "Students today want to know about the devil, about witchcraft, about the occult. Many people do not know they are turning to Satan. They are being deluded because, according to Jesus Christ, Satan is the father of lies and the greatest liar of all times. He is called the deceiver. In order to accomplish his purposes, the devil blinds people to their need of Christ. Two forces are at work in the world, the forces of Christ and the forces of evil. You are asked to choose between them."

Counseling Strategy

For the Non-Christian:

Inquiries about the devil from non-Christians are rare; however, you may be approached by someone who asks why Christians are so preoccupied, negative, or even angry about the devil. It could be someone seeking justification for a very worldly life-style. "We accept ourselves as we are and live with it," said a representative of a Satan church.

You may also be approached by someone who will challenge the existence of Satan or the personality of Satan. In such cases proceed as follows:

1. The Bible teaches that there is a personality behind all the evil in the world; his name is Satan. Share facts about him found in the BACKGROUND.

2. Attempt to guide the conversation around to Jesus Christ as the victor over Satan. Whereas Satan is a defeated foe and will some day be cast into the lake of fire, Jesus Christ will reign as King of kings and Lord of lords (Revelation 17:14).

3. Ask the inquirer if he has ever received Jesus Christ as Lord and Savior. Share "Steps to Peace with God," page 5. Mention that part of Satan's work is to "blind the minds of those who believe not" (cf., 2 Corinthians 4:4).

4. If a commitment to Christ is made, also share the continuing steps in follow up: take a positive stand for Christ, start reading and studying God's Word, pray every day, get into a dynamic group of Christians for fellowship, worship and service.

For the Christian:

A Christian may ask one of the following questions: Just how real is Satan? Can he exercise power over my life? Is he as real as the Holy Spirit?

1. Satan is, indeed, a real person. Though limited in power, Satan is as real as

the Holy Spirit. It may be said of him that he is mighty in power and deeds, while the Holy Spirit is all mighty—possessing the attributes of God.

2. The Christian must not take lightly the designs and works of Satan. "For we wrestle not against flesh and blood, but against principalities, against powers, against the rulers of the darkness of this world, against spiritual wickedness in high places" (Ephesians 6:12, KJV).

3. The Christian must believe Satan to be a defeated foe. "Greater is he that is in you, than he that is in the world" (1 John 4:4, KJV). Jesus Christ emerged victor over Satan through His incarnation, death on the Cross and resurrection. "Forasmuch then as the children are partakers of flesh and blood, he also himself likewise took part of the same; that through death he might destroy him that had the power of death, that is, the devil" (Hebrews 2:14, KJV).

4. Satan will have no power or influence over the Christian who submits constantly to the dominion of Christ, to the authority and illumination of the Word of God, to the discipline of prayer, and who is involved with a dynamic group of Christian believers. This is what is meant by putting on the "whole armor of God that you may be able to stand against the wiles of the devil" (Ephesians 6:11, KJV).

5. Pray with the inquirer for understanding of Satan and for victory over all concerns and fears about the enemy and his influence and power.

Scripture

1 Peter 5:8-10
Ephesians 2:1-3
Revelation 12:9,10
Job 1:6-12
Matthew 4:1-11
Hebrews 2:14
Revelation 20:1-10

SATAN, RESISTING
Background

Before Jesus began His earthly ministry, He was tempted by Satan in the wilderness (Matthew 4:11). Having withstood Satan, Jesus can help us resist the devil and temptations that come from him (Hebrews 4:15,16).

Because Christ defeated Satan at the Cross, we who own Him as Savior and Lord are delivered from the power of darkness (Colossians 1:13). Yet our encounter with Satan is not over; he doesn't give up easily. He is the accuser of the brethren (Revelation 12:10), the enemy (Matthew 13:39), the tempter (Matthew 4:3), and a deceiver (Revelation 12:9).

In the hymn "A Mighty Fortress Is Our God," Martin Luther alerts us to be on our guard: "For still our ancient foe doth seek to work us woe;
> His craft and power are great, and armed with cruel hate,
> On earth is not his equal."

We are told to "stand against the wiles of the devil" (Ephesians 6:11, KJV), and to resist him (see James 4:7). Just how much power does Satan have over believers? What resources must we have in order to withstand his temptations and attacks?

The Christian must learn to rest in the finished work of Christ. Satan is a defeated foe. "They overcame him by the blood of the Lamb" (Revelation 12:11, KJV). Jesus became man "that through death he might destroy him that had the power of death, that is, the devil" (Hebrews 2:14, KJV).

The Christian enjoys a privileged position of refuge and security. According to Colossians 3:1-3, the "old you" is dead (see Galatians 2:20), and your life is now "hidden with Christ in God." The Christian is in His constant protection and care. "The one who was born of God keeps him safe, and the evil one does not touch him" (1 John 5:18, NIV).

Counseling Strategy

If a Christian feels that he is under attack by Satan or is vulnerable to his wiles or temptation, ask him to tell you about it. He may be just succumbing to selfish, sinful desires. Satan is blamed for many things for which he is not guilty.

1. Confess all known sin (1 John 1:9) with the understanding that the sin is to be abandoned. "A conscience void of offense before God and man," (cf., Acts 24:16) is the first step in confronting Satan.

2. Be vigilant, on guard. "Be sober, be vigilant; because your adversary the devil, as a roaring lion, walketh about, seeking whom he may devour" (1 Peter 5:8, KJV). Alertness to Satan's designs and intentions will help to avoid encounters with him.

3. Submit to God (James 4:7,8) with two facets:
   A. Resist the devil.
      (1) Have a psychological mind set against him. "But Daniel purposed

in his heart that he would not defile himself" (Daniel 1:8, KJV).
"Put on the Lord Jesus Christ, and make no provision for the flesh,
to gratify its desires" (Romans 13:14, RSV).

(2) Put Satan in his place. When Satan spoke to Jesus through Peter
to try to divert Him from His eternal purpose, Jesus rebuked him:
"Out of my sight, Satan! You are a stumbling block to me; you
do not have in mind the things of God, but the things of men"
(Matthew 16:23, NIV).

(3) Use Scripture (Matthew 4:1-11). In His temptation, Jesus answered
devastatingly with three pertinent Scriptures: Deuteronomy 8:3,
Deuteronomy 6:16 and Deuteronomy 6:13. A strong argument
for familiarity with Scripture is to be able to resist Satan.

B. Draw near to God and He will draw near to you. Intimate, daily devotional time with the Lord, using His Word and seeking His presence
and strength through prayer, will help us resist Satan, and result in
his fleeing. "Thy word have I hid in my heart that I might not sin against
thee" (Psalm 119:11, KJV).

4. Overcome Satan by the Holy Spirit. "Walk in the Spirit, and ye shall not
fulfill the lust of the flesh" (Galatians 5:16, KJV).

Scripture

"Put on the whole armor of God, that ye may be able to stand against the
wiles of the devil."   Ephesians 6:11, KJV

"Submit yourselves therefore to God. Resist the devil, and he will flee
from you. Draw nigh to God, and he will draw nigh to you."
                                                         James 4:7,8, KJV

"Since, then, you have been raised with Christ, set your hearts on things
above, where Christ is seated at the right hand of God. Set your minds on
things above, not on earthly things. For you died, and your life is now
hidden with Christ in God."   Colossians 3:1-3, NIV

"I am crucified with Christ: nevertheless I live; yet not I, but Christ liveth
in me; and the life which I now live in the flesh I live by the Son of God,
who loved me, and gave himself for me."   Galatians 2:20, KJV

Colossians 1:13

SEXUAL IMMORALITY
Background

Billy Graham says: "Premarital sexual relations are always a mistake ... The Bible condemns sex outside the bonds of matrimony. The fact that immorality is rampant throughout the nation doesn't make it right!"

We have become overwhelmed by the so-called sexual revolution. It has been romanticised and glorified out of all proportion. That which began in defiance of biblical principles quickly has become the battle cry of the hedonists: "If it feels right, do it — as long as nobody gets hurt"!

How ironic this maudlin defense of immorality sounds in the light of its devastating legacy to the nation; millions of illegitimate births, shattered personalities, divorce, abortions, and rampant sexual diseases — some of which are incurable.

God expressly forbids irresponsible sexual behavior, in order to spare us the disastrous consequences. "The body is not meant for sexual immorality, but for the Lord ... Flee from sexual immorality. All other sins a man commits are outside his body, but he who sins sexually sins against his own body" (1 Corinthians 6:13,18, NIV).

God condemns immorality, but He offers deliverance. In 1 Corinthians 6:9-11, the Apostle Paul states that none of the sexually immoral would inherit the Kingdom of God. But, he adds, "And that is what some of you were. But you were washed (born again), you were sanctified (cleansed), you were justified in the name of the Lord Jesus Christ, and by the Spirit of our God" 1 Corinthians 6:11,12, NIV).

As with any other sin, God deals with immorality through the Cross.

Counseling Strategy

1. Tell the inquirer you are glad he called. Project yourself as a caring, concerned person without being patronizing. Don't be judgmental.
2. Listen with sensitivity and ask questions only for understanding of the problem. Draw no conclusions nor offer any spiritual solutions until you have a complete perspective.
3. Inquire about his attitudes toward sex. How he feels about it will explain his sexual behavior. What were the contributing causes of his getting involved? Does he feel guilty about this involvement and regard it as sin?
4. Ask if you may read portions of God's Word about premarital or extramarital sex. Emphasize that the Bible is a trustworthy source in regard

to moral issues. Read some or all of the following Scriptures: 1 Corinthians 6:13,15-20; Acts 15:20; Ephesians 5:3; Colossians 3:5 and Exodus 20:14.

5. In the light of Scripture, his immoral acts are displeasing to God. To please God, he must repent of all immorality and renounce it. (Read 1 Corinthians 6:9-11.) God condemns immoral behavior, but loves us and will forgive us if we confess our sin and receive, by faith, the Lord Jesus Christ as Lord and Savior. Share "Steps to Peace with God, page 5.

6. Emphasize the importance of severing any relationships which may contribute to his immorality. "Do not be misled! Bad company corrupts good character" (1 Corinthians 15:33, NIV). The best place to form new friendships is a Bible-teaching church. Encourage him to find one and become involved. Being a committed Christian should be his goal. The lack of a vital relationship to Christ is a chief factor in this problem.

7. Counsel him to seek his pastor's encouragement and counseling. He may need serious counseling for a period of time to experience freedom from temptation and to begin to walk with the Lord.

8. Pray with him for a complete refocus of mind and life to the glory of God.

If the inquirer is a Christian, share the section on "Restoration," page 11. Encourage him to read and study God's Word for the purpose of remolding his mind and his life. As a Christian, he should become involved in a Bible-teaching church, and seek to turn his energies into serving Christ.

Scripture

"If we confess our sins, he is faithful and just to forgive us our sins, and to cleanse us from all unrighteousness ... And if any man sin, we have an advocate with the Father, Jesus Christ the righteous."
1 John 1:9 and 2:1, KJV

"But sexual sin is never right: our bodies were not made for that, but for the Lord, and the Lord wants to fill our bodies with himself."
1 Corinthians 6:13, TLB

"Let the wicked forsake his way, and the unrighteous man his thoughts: and let him return unto the Lord, and he will have mercy upon him; and to our God, for he will abundantly pardon."   Isaiah 55:7, KJV

"Wash you, make you clean; put away the evil of your doings from before mine eyes; cease to do evil ... Come now, and let us reason together, saith the Lord: though your sins be as scarlet, they shall be as white as snow; though they be red like crimson, they shall be as wool."
Isaiah 1:16,18, KJV

SPIRITUAL DOUBTS
Background:

Doubts can be debilitating. Hesitation is characteristic of the doubter. Uncertainty throws him off balance and interferes with his decision making. James mentions the "double-minded" man as being unstable in all he does. "That man should not think he will receive anything from the Lord" (James 1:7,8, NIV).

Yet it is not unusual for a person, even a Christian, to experience doubts. He may question, "Is the Bible really true?" when he hears a critic attack God's Word. In confusion over unanswered prayers, he may wonder, "Is God real? Does He really answer prayer?" When confronted with the reality of his own sinful, selfish desires, he may question, "Has God really saved me?"

Billy Graham writes: "Probably everyone has had doubts and uncertainties at times in his religious experience. When Moses went up on Mt. Sinai to receive the tablets of the Law from the hand of God, and when he had been a long time out of the sight of the Hebrews who stood anxiously awaiting his return, they finally became doubtful of his return. 'And they erected a golden calf to worship' (cf., Exodus 32:8). Their apostasy was the result of the doubting and uncertainty."

In spite of this tendency to doubt, honest questioning can become the threshold to a more solid faith and a deeper commitment to Christ.

The opposite of doubt, of course, is faith. James encouraged those who were passing through trials to ask of God and to ask in faith (James 1:5,6). We must remember that doubt can be an effective tool for Satan. He brought uncertainty to Eve by asking, "Yea, hath God said?" (Genesis 3:1, KJV). He will afflict us with doubts where we are the most vulnerable. Spiritual disobedience, disappointment, depression, illness, and even advancing years can trigger doubts.

Counseling Strategy:
Those Who Doubt Salvation:

1. Commend the inquirer for being concerned about something so important. God's Word has real encouragement for the doubter.

2. If you discern that he has been trusting in things other than a personal relationship to Jesus Christ, share "Steps to Peace with God," page 5.

3. If the inquirer is convinced that he has previously made a genuine commitment to Jesus Christ, ask him further:

A. "Are you being deliberately sinful or disobedient?" If this is the case, explain "Restoration," page 11. Emphasize 1 John 1:9.

B. "Have you been indifferent to spiritual things? Not faithful in attending church? Not reading the Bible? Not praying?" If this is the case, explain "Restoration," page 11. Emphasize 1 John 1:9 and Romans 12:1,2.

C. Encourage the inquirer to step out anew in faith, to believe God (Acts 27:25), to take a definite stand for Christ, to get into the Word of God, to learn the discipline of prayer, and to get to work for Christ in a local Bible-teaching church. Offer to send him *Living In Christ*.

D. Pray with him for a stronger relationship to God by faith.

Those Who May be Disillusioned Through Disappointments:

Disappointment can occur through divorce, a death in the family, a wayward son or daughter, unanswered prayer, betrayal by another Christian.

1. Offer a word of encouragement. God does love and care for us. He wants the inquirer also to learn to walk with Him by faith.

2. Help him to identify the source of his doubts, emphasizing that it is not wrong to ask, "Why?" in life.

3. Remind him that God has never promised freedom from adversity in life.

   It may be that he needs to get his eyes off himself and his problems and back on God. He needs to see beyond the circumstances of his life to what God is attempting to teach him through those circumstances. God is faithful. The intrusion of doubts into one's mind doesn't mean that God has ceased to care.

4. The inquirer needs to reflect on God's goodness demonstrated in the past, to remember evidences of God's faithfulness in his own life and in the lives of others. This will help to reassure him.

   A renewal of faith is in order. He needs to begin to trust God's promises again, to saturate his life with the Scriptures and to believe God. Jesus said, "Blessed are those who have not seen and yet have believed" (John 20:29, NIV).

5. Pray with him for renewal, asking that he confess his doubts to God and pray for a dynamic faith.

6. Encourage him to be faithful in worship with God's people. The cultivation of relationships with other Christians will be helpful. Getting involved in service for Christ through a local Bible-teaching church will strengthen his commitment.

Reassurance For Older Christians:

For those who due to a number of changes that accompany advancing age, need to be reassured as to their salvation and eternal relationship to God, there are three areas to remember:

1. Older people, like anyone else, can continue to trust unquestionably the

Lord Jesus Christ as their Lord and Savior. "For I am convinced that neither death nor life, neither angels nor demons, neither the present nor the future, nor any powers, neither height nor depth, nor anything else in all creation, will be able to separate us from the love of God that is in Christ Jesus our Lord" (Romans 8:38,39, NIV).

2. They can trust unquestionably their relationship to their heavenly Father. "Yet to all who received him, to those who believed in his name, he gave the right to become children of God" (John 1:12, NIV).

3. They may also trust unquestionably the Word of God. "Your word, O Lord, is eternal; it stands firm in the heavens. Your faithfulness continues through all generations" (Psalm 119:89,90, NIV).

Scripture

"But without faith it is impossible to please him: for he that cometh to God must believe that he is, and that he is a rewarder of them that diligently seek him."   Hebrews 11:6, KJV

"If any of you lack wisdom, let him ask of God, that giveth to all men liberally, and upbraideth not; and it shall be given him. But let him ask in faith, nothing wavering. For he that wavereth is like a wave of the sea driven with the wind and tossed. For let not that man think that he shall receive anything of the Lord. A double-minded man is unstable in all his ways."   James 1:5-8, KJV

"The fool hath said in his heart, There is no God."   Psalm 14:1, KJV

"Wherefore seeing we also are compassed about with so great a cloud of witnesses, let us lay aside every weight, and the sin which doth so easily beset us, and let us run with patience the race that is set before us, looking unto Jesus the author and finisher of our faith; who for the joy that was set before him endured the cross, despising the shame, and is set down at the right hand of the throne of God."   Hebrews 12:1,2, KJV

STEWARDSHIP

(Giving, Tithing)

Background

God's plan is for Christians to support the work of Jesus Christ in the world through tithes and offerings. "Upon the first day of the week let every one of you lay by him in store, as God has prospered him" (1 Corinthians 16:2, KJV).

The idea of tithing goes back to earliest biblical history. Abraham paid tithes to Melchizedek on returning from the battle of kings (Hebrews 7:6). It was ordained in the Law that the Levites should take tithes from the people (Hebrews 7:5). Though a tenth part of one's income is indicated as the tithe, this should not limit the extent of giving for those who have the means and the will to give more.

The New Testament teaches that Christians should give individually, regularly, methodically, and proportionately to support the local church, the needy, evangelism, and missions (1 Corinthians 16:2).

Giving out of a heart filled with God's love is to be a characteristic of the born-again believer. "But this I say, he which soweth sparingly shall reap also sparingly; and he which soweth bountifully shall reap also bountifully. Every man according as he purposeth in his heart, so let him give; not grudgingly, or of necessity; for God loveth a cheerful giver. And God is able to make all grace abound toward you; that ye, always having all sufficiency in all things, may abound to every good work" (2 Corinthians 9:6-9, KJV).

We have God's promise that our own needs will be supplied as we respond to the needs of His work and His servants. "But my God shall supply all your need according to his riches in glory by Christ Jesus" (Philippians 4:19, KJV).

Billy Graham comments: "We have found in our home, as have thousands of others, that when we tithe, God's blessing upon the nine-tenths helps it to go further than ten-tenths without His blessing. How you handle your money is an optional matter. God doesn't force you to distribute it one way or another. There are certain biblical principles, however, in a philosophy of Christian stewardship. For one thing, God owns everything. We are custodians, so to speak, of His property. Whatever we give is, by definition, His anyway. Secondly, one's giving ought to be prompted by love — and by a personal commitment to Christ. Thirdly, while Christian stewardship is not based on reward, it certainly recognizes that there's no better investment in terms of return. Jesus talked in Mark 4 about yields which were thirty, sixty and one-hundred fold . . . If tithing was appropriate under law, it is even more so in this age of freedom and grace . . . Try giving the tithe and more — with joy and even abandon — and you'll see, you'll see!"

Counseling Strategy

1. Determine if the inquirer is a Christian.

   The first gift God expects of us is ourselves. Explain "Steps to Peace with God," page 5. Encourage him to take a positive stand for Christ, to get into the Word of God, to cultivate habits of prayer, to become a part of a Bible-teaching church for the purposes of fellowship, Bible study and service.

2. Share the following with anyone asking advice on giving.

   A. Become an active, participating Christian in a local, Bible-teaching church. Being part of a fellowship of believers will provide challenges, along with motivation and perspective in giving.

   B. Pray for wisdom in your giving, then investigate, so that you know to whom you are giving. Many non-evangelical and even cult-type organizations receive regular gifts from evangelical Christians who lack spiritual discernment. Know before you give!

   C. To whom should the evangelical Christian give?

      (1) A substantial part of your tithes and offerings should go to your own local church.

      (2) Another portion should be set aside and used for the poor or for those with special needs. This also may be handled through your local church.

      (3) There are many ministries in evangelism, missions, and benevolences which are worthy of the Christian's support. Make provision for some of them.

Scripture

"Honor the Lord with thy substance, and with the firstfruits of all thine increase; so shall thy barns be filled with plenty, and thy presses shall burst out with new wine."   Proverbs 3:9,10, KJV

"Give, and it shall be given unto you: good measure, pressed down, and shaken together, and running over, shall men give into your bosom. For with the same measure that ye mete withal it shall be measured to you again."   Luke 6:38, KJV

"Bring the whole tithe into the storehouse, that there may be food in my house. Test me in this, says the Lord Almighty, and see if I will not throw open the floodgates of heaven and pour out so much blessing that you will not have room enough for it."   Malachi 3:10, NIV

"And my God will meet all your needs according to his glorious riches in
Christ Jesus."   Philippians 4:19, NIV

"Command those who are rich in this present world not to be arrogant nor
to put their hope in wealth, which is so uncertain, but to put their hope in
God, who richly provides us with everything for our enjoyment.
Command them to do good, to be rich in good deeds, and to be generous
and willing to share. In this way they will lay up treasure for themselves as
a firm foundation for the coming age, so that they may take hold of the life
that is truly life."   1 Timothy 6:17-19, NIV

"So when you give to the needy, do not announce it with trumpets, as the
hypocrites do in the synagogues and on the streets to be honored by men. I
tell you the truth, they have received their reward in full. But when you
give to the needy, do not let your left hand know what your right hand is
doing, so that your giving may be in secret. Then your Father, who sees
what is done in secret, will reward you."   Matthew 6:2-4, NIV

Romans 12:1

SUFFERING AND ADVERSITY
Background

Why? Why me? Why my family? What is the meaning of this suffering?

These are familiar questions which are asked by Christians and non-Christians alike. No one is immune to suffering and adversity. "Man is born unto trouble as the sparks fly upward" (Job 5:7, KJV). There are the pressures of want, need, sorrow, persecution, unpopularity, and loneliness. Some suffer for what they have done; others suffer because of what people do to them. Many suffer because they are victims of circumstances which they cannot control.

Pain is distressing. There can be nights of agony when God seems so unfair and it seems that there is no possible help or answer. Temporary relief may seem adequate, but the real solution to suffering is not to isolate it in an attempt to do away with it, nor even to grit our teeth and endure it. The solution, rather, is to condition our attitudes so that we learn to triumph in and through suffering. When the Apostle Paul sought relief from his "thorn in the flesh," God did not take it away, but reassured him with: "My grace is sufficient for thee, for my strength is made perfect in weakness" (2 Corinthians 12:9, KJV). In another encouragement to the Corinthians, he wrote, "And God is able to make all grace abound toward you; that ye, always having all sufficiency in all things, may abound to every good work" (2 Corinthians 9:8, KJV).

Except for physical pain, handling suffering seems to be a question of attitude: "What am I going to do in the face of suffering in order to learn from it and use it for my advantage as far as God's eternal purposes are concerned?"

Billy Graham comments: "Nowhere does the Bible teach that Christians are exempt from the tribulations and natural disasters that come upon the world. Scripture does teach that the Christian can face tribulation, crisis, calamity, and personal suffering with a supernatural power that is not available to the person outside of Christ."

Some of the most pathetic people in the world are those who, in the midst of adversity, indulge themselves by wallowing in self-pity and bitterness, all the while taking a sort of delight in blaming God for their problems.

Job's attitude is an inspiration: "Though he slay me, yet will I trust in him" (Job 13:15).

The sufferer will be blessed if, in the midst of great agony and despair, he can look into the face of his Heavenly Father and, because of His eternal love and presence, be grateful. Our response to suffering should lead us to look beyond it in the attempt to see God's higher purposes and what He wants to teach us.

What are Some of the Reasons for Human Suffering?

1. We may bring suffering upon ourselves. Dissipation and lack of discipline bring unhappy consequences. Long-term abuse of our bodies may bring on sickness. Wrong choices come back to haunt us.

   You may ask the caller: "Do you think this is happening to you because of your own bad judgment or intemperate actions? What can you do to alleviate your suffering?"

2. Sometimes God is taking corrective action because of sin and disobedience. God will correct and discipline His own. Through chastening He proves that He loves us and that we are truly His own (Hebrews 12:5-11).

3. God may permit suffering so we learn to respond to problems in a biblical way. Scripture tells us that Jesus "learned obedience from what he suffered" (Hebrews 5:8, NIV). Our goal should be not merely relief from suffering but rather learning to please God by being responsive and obedient to Him and to His Word (see Romans 12:1,2).

4. Sometimes God permits us to suffer to teach us that pain is a part of life. Nowhere does the Bible say that the Christian will not suffer adversity! Paul points out in Philippians 1:29, KJV, that it is "given in the behalf of Christ, not only to believe on him, but also to suffer for his sake." Adversity can be a gift from God.

   Christ did not evade the Cross to escape suffering. Hebrews 12:2 says he "endured the cross, despising the shame." Why? "For the joy that was set before him." He knew that the final word was not crucifixion (suffering); it was resurrection (victory).

   We may suffer briefly, or all our lives. But let us not give up hope or engage in self-pity or bitterness. The end-result is what we all look forward to. Being with the Lord in heaven will put all things into perspective!

5. God may permit suffering for our well-being. "And we know that in all things God works for the good of those who love him, who have been called according to his purpose" (Romans 8:28, NIV). We must accept this by faith and pray that God's highest good will come as a result of our suffering. Only through adversity are some of the deeper lessons of life learned. Trust God to work out His own will and purpose in us so that we might be more Christlike (see Romans 8:29).

   There is no redemptive merit in our suffering as there was in that of Jesus, but if we are faithful under adversity we may be able to share in "the fellowship of his sufferings" (Philippians 3:10, KJV).

6. Sometimes God permits suffering to speak through our life and testimony to comfort others. Jesus said that the sufferings of the blind man in John 9 were so "that the work of God might be displayed in his life" (NIV).

   God might work in your life through suffering to inspire others by your example in adversity. Those who endure adversity can sympathize and identify more effectively with others in their sufferings. We comfort others in the way we are comforted. "Praise be to the God and Father of our Lord Jesus Christ, the Father of compassion and the God of all comfort, who comforts us in all our troubles, so that we can comfort those in any trouble with the comfort we ourselves have received from God" (2 Corinthians 1:3,4, NIV).

Counseling Strategy

For the Non-Christian:

1. Be sympathetic. Listen carefully as the inquirer articulates his problems. Guide the conversation so that you can offer spiritual help.

2. Offer encouragement and hope. God loves the caller and knows what is happening. He is not alone. "When thou passest through the waters, I will be with thee; and through the rivers, they shall not overflow thee: when thou walkest through the fire, thou shalt not be burned; neither shall the flame kindle upon thee" (Isaiah 43:2, KJV). Tell him you are glad he called and together with him will seek answers to his problems.

3. Ask him if he has ever received Jesus Christ as his personal Savior and Lord. Sometimes God permits affliction. He wants to get our attention in order to bring us to salvation. Share "Steps to Peace with God," page 5.

4. Pray with him for salvation and deliverance.

5. Encourage the inquirer to read and study the Word of God. Praying will provide strength and perspective on the problems in life. Offer to send him *Living In Christ* which will help get him started in Bible study.

6. Encourage him to find a Bible-teaching church. Fellowship with committed Christians will have a maturing influence on his life and help him understand the ways of God. Opportunities for Bible study and for Christian service will also be provided through the church.

For the Christian:

If the inquirer is distressed because of some tragedy or suffering which has come, discuss possible reasons as to why God may have allowed it.

1. Sympathize with him. Encourage him by offering God's comfort. You may share some of the insights from the background: "Some Reasons Why God Permits Suffering." Apply those which seem suitable.

2. If restoration and rededication seem indicated, share page 11.

3. Encourage him to search God's Word and to pray sincerely that God will reveal His motives in the suffering.

    A. What is God trying to say to me?

    B. What is He trying to teach me?

    C. What steps ought I to take as a result?

4. If not already involved, encourage him to get into a Bible-teaching church. Bible study can deepen his understanding of God's will and ways.

5. Encourage him to communicate with Christian friends. It always helps to

have a listening ear. This will result in comfort, understanding, and strength.

6. Pray with him personally, asking for deliverance.

Scripture

"And we know that in all things God works for the good of those who love him, who have been called according to his purpose. For those God foreknew he also predestined to be conformed to the likeness of his Son, that he might be the firstborn among many brothers."

Romans 8:28,29, NIV

"Who shall separate us from the love of Christ? Shall tribulation, or distress, or persecution, or famine, or nakedness, or peril, or sword?"

"Nay, in all these things we are more than conquerors through him that loved us."
Romans 8:35,37, KJV

"Consider it pure joy, my brothers, whenever you face trials of many kinds, because you know that the testing of your faith develops perseverance. Blessed is the man who perseveres under trial, because when he has stood the test, he will receive the crown of life that God has promised to those who love him."
James 1:2, 3 and 12, NIV

"Let not your heart be troubled: ye believe in God, believe also in me."
John 14:1, KJV

"Beloved, think it not strange concerning the fiery trial which is to try you, as though some strange thing happened unto you: but rejoice, inasmuch as ye are partakers of Christ's sufferings; that, when his glory shall be revealed, ye may be glad also with exceeding joy."
1 Peter 4:12,13, KJV

"Yet if any man suffer as a Christian, let him not be ashamed; but let him glorify God on this behalf. Wherefore, let them that suffer according to the will of God commit the keeping of their souls to him in well doing, as unto a faithful Creator."
1 Peter 4:16,19, KJV

SUICIDE

Background

A suicidal person feels he has exhausted all his options. Life has no meaning, no purpose, no future, so why continue to endure its extreme unhappiness, anguish, hopelessness and despair? The obsession that nothing will ever change for the better leaves him feeling helpless, with the conviction that death is the only way out.

Such a person is a victim of depression, tortured with feelings of unworthiness, sin and failure, deep guilt, and the need to be punished. Many things condition this person for the depressed state that can lead to suicide or its attempt: anger, envy, jealousy, fear, guilt, self-pity, sexual deviation, drugs, alcohol, etc. It should be obvious to the counselor, then, that root causes leading to such a crisis are likely to be deep and possibly of long duration. Many of these do, in fact, reflect back to childhood and therefore point to the need for prolonged professional counseling with a Christian psychologist or psychiatrist.

In this situation we feel that although not all the problems involved are spiritual, the ultimate problem in life is separation from God, solved only through a personal relationship to Jesus Christ. Without this relationship to Christ, there can be no real solutions or healing. As a person experiences all that is involved in the "new life in Christ" (cf., 2 Corinthians 5:17)—forgiveness, freedom from guilt and fear, a sense of fulfillment and well-being, new orientations and motivations to live, etc. — forces for radical change are set in motion. This is where the counselor can be of real service: guiding the inquirer into a personal relationship with Jesus Christ.

Some persons threaten suicide in order to get attention and sympathy. They want someone to listen to their hurts and frustrations. Others are beyond this point and seriously have self-destruction in mind.

It is only natural that the counselor will feel inadequate when confronted with this kind of challenge; however, you should attempt to help, remembering that our resources come from the Lord. He will be reaching out in love and power through you. Be motivated by the promises of Scripture that "with God all things are possible" (Matthew 19:26, KJV), and "if any of you lacks wisdom, he should ask God . . . and it will be given to him" (James 1:5, NIV).

Counseling Strategy

Two main goals should be kept in mind:

- Share the Gospel as a source of hope. A new relationship to Jesus Christ can bring about change.
- Gather information about the concerned party for possible emergency procedure.

Counseling the Suicidal Non-Christian:

1. Speaking with a suicidal person demands the greatest tact and patience. Be prepared to listen! Let your caller do most of the talking until you get the complete picture. Punctuate the conversation with an occasional question to keep it flowing. If he makes a statement, ask him to explain further how he feels. Or, ask what has led him to that particular conclusion. The phrase "tell me about it" is often helpful.

2. As the conversation permits, begin to encourage him. Tell him that he has called the right place because we are friends and are willing to listen. Suggest that God can help in revealing solutions and that He really cares and loves.

3. Do not minimize any feeling or conclusion he may express about himself or his problems. He should be permitted to vent all his stored-up anger, tension, and sense of desperation. Do not contradict any statement he may make, except to disagree with his proposed "solution" to his problems.

    If he says that life is not worth living, believe him! Probably for him in his present state, it isn't. Avoid such statements as, "Oh, come now, things can't be all that hopeless," or, "You are not as bad as you would like me to think."

4. Assure the individual that there is a solution for his problems and there is hope! If he will permit God to intervene in his life, He can forgive all the past, making things right through Jesus Christ. Jesus understands suffering. He was maligned, mistreated and murdered. He truly cares about what happens to us. He loved us so much that He died for us. Christ will come to us where we are — to our level of need, sinful and hopeless perhaps — in order to lift us up and beyond our despair. He says: "Come to me, all you who are weary and burdened, and I will give you rest" (Matthew 11:28, NIV).

5. Share "Steps to Peace with God," page 5.

6. If he receives Christ, assure him that this experience can be the catalyst for bringing real change to his life. "Therefore, if anyone is in Christ, he is a new creation; the old has gone, the new has come" (2 Corinthians 5:17, NIV).

7. Tell him that to help bring about this change, he needs to begin to read and study the Bible. Offer to send him *Living In Christ* to help him get started.

8. Counsel him to pray, because communicating with God is very important in effecting change. We can turn over to God all our emotions and our problems through prayer. "Cast all your anxiety on him because he cares for you" (1 Peter 5:7, NIV). Also share Philippians 4:6. Suggest that he write the references down so he can look up the verses easily.

9. Encourage him to seek new friendships by identifying with a local Bible-teaching church. This will provide opportunities for worship, fellowship, Bible study, and service, all of which are important in his attempt to

redirect the focus of his life.

10. Unobtrusively, but as early as possible, the counselor should determine if the individual is really suicidal. Has he taken pills or poison? Does he have a loaded gun which he threatens to use?

   As the conversation develops, attempt to obtain his name, address, and telephone number, the name of a relative living in his area, and the name of a pastor and a church. Always solicit information in a casual, friendly way in order to avoid arousing suspicion.

11. If you are involved in a telephone counseling center, ask the caller if your supervisor might telephone him the following evening. With this offer, he will have something to look forward to. Ask for a convenient hour to place the call. (PLEASE NOTE: If such a promise is made, please turn over your Counselor's Report Form to your supervisor so that it is not forgotten.)

12. Ask him if he would like a visit from a pastor, if such a contact could be arranged. Do not promise, but state that we will do what we can. Perhaps he knows a local pastor and will make such a contact himself. Suicidal calls should be followed up if at all possible.

13. If the inquirer doesn't make a commitment to Christ, encourage him the best you can. Inform him that he can act on what you have told him at any time. The door of access to God is always open. Urge him to make contact with a local pastor for counseling. Immediacy is important.

Counseling the Suicidal Christian:

Christians are not immune to suicidal thoughts or attempts. Unresolved or unconfessed sin, or a crisis situation such as a deep disappointment, the death of a loved one, a divorce, loss of employment, loss of health, a nervous breakdown, etc., can precipitate depression severe enough to lead to such an attempt.

1. Remind the Christian that God always loves and cares. ". . .for he hath said, I will never leave thee, nor forsake thee" (Hebrews 13:5, KJV).

2. Remind him also that we are God's children. (Quote John 1:12.)

3. Tell him that God still forgives. Share "Restoration." Emphasize Proverbs 28:13 and 1 John 1:9. Confession results in forgiveness and restoration of fellowship.

4. Suggest that he look only to the Lord and not at the problems and circumstances around him. (See Matthew 14:27-32 and Proverbs 3:5,6.)

5. Suggest that it is important to get into God's Word: hear, read and study, meditate, and memorize.

6. Suggest that prayer is a valuable resource and forms an essential part of a Christian's life. (See 1 Thessalonians 5:17 and Philippians 4:6,7.)

7. Remind him that identity with a Bible-teaching church is an important

factor in recovering emotional stability. Such identity permits fellowship with caring people who worship and work together.

8. The telephone counselor could at this point ask if the caller would like a call from a supervisor the following evening. This will give the caller something to look forward to. Please give the Counselor's Report Form to a supervisor so that the promise is not forgotten.

9. Pray with the inquirer that God will come to him with new meaning, filling him with hope and renewed trust.

Scripture

2 Corinthians 5:17
Matthew 11:28
1 Peter 5:7
Philippians 4:6,7
Matthew 14:27-32
Proverbs 3:5,6
1 Thessalonians 5:17

TEMPTATION
Background

As the compass needle is affected by magnetic attraction, so the Christian feels a pull by sin. This is illustrated by Israel's desire to return to the "leeks and garlics" of Egypt (Numbers 11:5), and Demas, the young man the Apostle Paul mentions as "having loved this present world, and is departed..." (2 Timothy 4:10, KJV). Paul describes the Christian as having two natures, the old and the new, which constantly compete for supremacy. The Christian must understand this, and learn to confront this "magnetic pull" of his own sinful nature and Satan's wiles.

A paragraph by Billy Graham helps put this into perspective: "God never promises to remove temptation from us, for even Christ was subject to it... There is a sense of achievement and assurance that results from victory over temptation that cannot come to us otherwise. Temptation shows what people really are. It does not make us Christian or unChristian. Overcoming does make the Christian stronger and causes him to discover resources of power... In times of temptation Christ can become more real to you than ever."

Some Things to Remember About Temptation:

1. Temptation is common to all Christians. "But remember this — the wrong desires that come into your life aren't anything new and different. Many others have faced exactly the same problems before you" (1 Corinthians 10:13, TLB).
2. Temptation is of the devil (see temptation of Jesus, Matthew 4:1-11).
3. Temptation itself is not sin, but succumbing to it is.

Billy Graham says, "The sin is when we use the temptation for giving in." None of us should deliberately place ourselves in a position to be tempted. Satan will always attack where we are the most vulnerable. "But each one is tempted when, by his own evil desire, he is dragged away and enticed. Then, after desire has conceived, it gives birth to sin; and sin, when it is full-grown, gives birth to death" (James 1:14,15, NIV). A thought enters; we pamper it; it germinates and grows into an evil act.

4. God does not lead us into temptation in the sense that He purposely and personally tempts. "Let no man say when he is tempted, I am tempted of God; for God cannot be tempted with evil, neither tempteth he any man" (James 1:13, KJV).

   But, God does permit us to be tempted (see Job 1:6-12), so that we can face temptation, overcome it, and become stronger. "I have written unto you, young men, because ye are strong, and the word of God abideth in you, and ye have overcome the wicked one" (1 John 2:14, KJV). We can also be blessed in victory (see James 1:12).

5. No temptation is irresistible. "You can trust God to keep the temptation from becoming so strong that you can't stand up against it, for he has promised this and will do what he says. He will show you how to escape temptation's power so that you can bear up patiently against it" (1 Corinthians 10:13, TLB).

6. Whatever we experience, Jesus has been there before us. He "was in all points tempted like as we are, yet without sin" (Hebrews 4:15, KJV).

Counseling Strategy

1. Ask if the inquirer is a Christian, one who has received Jesus Christ as Savior and Lord. If he is not, explain "Steps to Peace with God," page 5. No one is strong enough in himself to overcome temptation, regardless of how high his ideals or motives.

2. Share ways to confront and overcome temptation.

   A. We must resist the tempter: "Resist the devil, and he will flee from you" (James 4:7, KJV).

   B. We must submit to God: "Submit yourselves . . . to God" (James 4:7, KJV). This we do by:

      (1) Committing ourselves daily to God according to Romans 12:1, and by daily confession of sin so that there is no buildup (Psalm 51:10).

      (2) Subjecting our minds to His control.
          "Be ye transformed by the renewing of your mind" (Romans 12:2, KJV).
          "Set your affection on things above, not on things on the earth" (Colossians 3:2, KJV).

      (3) The discipline of prayer
          "Let us then approach the throne of grace with confidence, so that we may receive mercy and find grace to help us in our time of need" (Hebrews 4:16, NIV).
          "Pray all the time. Ask God for anything in line with the Holy Spirit's wishes" (Ephesians 6:18, TLB).

      (4) Reading, studying and memorizing the Word of God.
          D.L. Moody used to say, "Sin will keep you from this Book (the Bible), or this Book will keep you from sin."

"The word of God is living and active . . . It judges the thoughts and attitudes of the heart" (Hebrews 4:12, NIV).

(5) Associating with the right kinds of friends: God's people.

"Do not be misled; bad company corrupts good character" (1 Corinthians 15:33, NIV).

"And let us consider how we may spur one another on toward love and good deeds. Let us not give up meeting together, as some are in the habit of doing, but let us encourage one another — and all the more as you see the Day approaching" (Hebrews 10:24,25, NIV).

(6) Putting on the whole armor of God (see Ephesians 6:13-18).

(7) Dependence upon the Holy Spirit.

"How much more shall your heavenly Father give the Holy Spirit to them that ask him" (Luke 11:13, KJV).

"And I will pray the Father, and he shall give you another Comforter (one to stand alongside), that he may abide with you forever" (John 14:16, KJV).

"When he, the Spirit of truth, is come, he will guide you into all truth . . ." (John 16:13, KJV).

Scripture

"Blessed is the man who perseveres under trial, because when he has stood the test, he will receive the crown of life that God has promised to those who love him. When tempted, no one should say, 'God is tempting me.' For God cannot be tempted by evil, nor does he tempt anyone; but each one is tempted when, by his own evil desire, he is dragged away and enticed. Then, after desire has conceived, it gives birth to sin; and sin, when it is full-grown, gives birth to death."   James 1:12-15, NIV

". . . Now have come the salvation and the power and the kingdom of our God, and the authority of his Christ. For the accuser of our brothers, who accuses them before our God day and night, has been hurled down. They overcame him by the blood of the Lamb and by the word of their testimony; they did not love their lives so much as to shrink from death."
Revelation 12:10-11, NIV

Matthew 4:1-11
Romans 8:26
Galatians 5:16

TERMINAL ILLNESS
Background

O Joy that seekest me through pain,
  I cannot close my heart to thee;
I trace the rainbow through the rain
  And feel the promise is not vain
That morn shall tearless be.

—George Matheson

Your inquirer is a very ill person. His life is threatened; in fact, he may not have long to live. Cancer, high blood pressure, heart disease, kidney failure or some other critical illness is destroying his body. He feels alone. Who else has known pain like this?

Successively, though not necessarily chronologically, he feels denial ("This cannot be happening to me"), anger ("Why me, Lord?"), depression ("There's no hope"), bargaining ("Lord, get me out of this and I'll do whatever You say"), and acceptance ("May God's will be done"). These feelings are not experienced once and then forgotten, but return again and again. They are not abnormal feelings, but are somehow characteristic of those facing the "valley of the shadow."

What do you say to such a person? How do you respond? A critical illness seems so unique to the sufferer as to resist understanding by another who can't really know what it's like.

Counseling Strategy

1. Listen! Listen with empathy to the feelings that are shared. Encourage the person to talk. You may want to probe gently for feelings, some of which lie close to the surface while others may be more deeply submerged.

2. Pass no judgment on the feelings that are shared, even though they be expressed in anger, self-pity, or bitterness. Just let the caller know that you are hearing him. Don't appear to be arrogant by saying that you understand the depth of his feelings. You can't possibly understand! But, you may tell him that you care. This can be put into words and also conveyed by the tone of your voice, your gentleness, and your capacity for feeling and identifying. "Think too of all who suffer as if you shared their pain" (Hebrews 13:3, Phillips).

   This is no time for you to introduce your own experience of pain and suffering; keep the focus on the inquirer.

3. Do not try to be a Pollyanna, even a spiritual one. Avoid clichés and platitudes. Don't tell the caller to "keep a stiff upper lip," or to be an example in suffering.

   Do not offer false hopes about healing, or tell the individual that all illness is of the devil and if he had sufficient faith he could be healed. God may or may not heal him. These are matters for the Sovereign will. What we can be sure of is that God will spiritually heal those who put their faith in Jesus Christ.

4. Don't discourage any reference he may make about death. This may be a healthy conditioning of the mind for that which is inevitable. Any references about death can prepare the way for you, as a counselor, to ask if there might be any unfinished business to attend to. This is why we witness: to help prepare persons for eternity.

You may ask the inquirer, "If you were to die tonight and find yourself at the gates of heaven confronted with the question, 'On what grounds do you seek admission to God's heaven?' what would you say?"

If indicated, explain "Steps to Peace with God," page 5. If the inquirer responds affirmatively, share "Assurance." You might also offer other portions of Scripture, such as Psalm 23; John 14:1-6; 1 Thessalonians 4:13-18.

5. The commitment to Christ should prepare the way to question if he has any other unfinished business, such as relationships (family, friends), financial matters (a will, perhaps), handling of details in regard to the process of dying, death itself, funeral arrangements, disposal of the body, etc. Encourage the inquirer to take care of all these matters, seeking either pastoral or professional advice in the process.

6. Suggest to the inquirer that he find out if his community has a hospice agency. These agencies specialize in providing reinforcement to the patient whose disease is considered terminal by health care professionals, and to their families. He may want to contact the local Hospice, Inc., and ask them to describe their services.

7. Pray for the inquirer that he might have courage and strength to be victorious in pain, committing himself to Him who bore our griefs and our sorrows.

Scripture

John 14:1-6
Psalm 23
1 Thessalonians 4:13-18
Philippians 1:21

THOUGHTS, CONTROLLING

Background

The history of man has largely centered around a battle for his mind. What we think is important. "He that ruleth his mind is greater than he that taketh a city" (Proverbs 16:32, KJV). "As a man thinketh ... so is he" (Proverbs 23:7, KJV).

The mind — or related words, such as "thoughts," "the understanding," and "the heart" (used interchangeably at times for the mind) — occupies an important place in Scripture. God wants to control our minds; so does Satan.

Billy Graham says: "What you believe is important; the development of your mind is important. We are to grow intellectually in Christ. We are to study to show ourselves 'approved unto God, a workman that needeth not to be ashamed' (2 Timothy 2:15, KJV). Jeremiah says, 'I will put my law in their minds' (Jeremiah 31:33, NIV). God said to Joshua, 'Thou shalt meditate therein day and night, that thou mayest observe to do according to all that is written therein' (Joshua 1:8, KJV). Isaiah said, 'Thou wilt keep him in perfect peace, whose mind is stayed on thee' (Isaiah 26:3, KJV). Will you surrender your mind to Christ, to the Lordship of Christ? Will you devote your mind to Him?"

The Bible mentions the unbelieving mind which is "hostile to God" (Romans 8:7, NIV), is blinded because of sin (2 Corinthians 4:4), and is morally defiled (Mark 7:20-22).

The Bible also mentions the carnal mind which is characteristic of the worldly Christian walking in the flesh (James 4:4), the unbelieving Christian (Hebrews 3:12), and the disobedient Christian (Luke 6:46 and Ephesians 2:2).

Counseling Strategy

For the Non-Christian:

1. Explain "Steps to Peace with God," page 5.

2. Encourage the inquirer to begin to read God's Word. In this way, he begins to bring his mind into subjection to God. Offer to send him *Living In Christ* to help him get started in reading and studying.

3. Encourage him to learn to pray every day. The book of Psalms is filled with the language of prayer. Also have him write down Matthew 6:9-13 and Luke 11:2-13 where the Lord's Prayer may be found. These are good examples of prayers.

4. Encourage him to seek a Bible-teaching church for worship, fellowship, Bible study, and service.
5. Pray with him for a renewed mind.

For the Carnal Christian:
1. Share "Restoration," page 11.
2. Emphasize the need for controlling the mind, using these examples:
   A. The Lord Jesus Christ: "Let this mind be in you which was also in Christ Jesus ... (he) made himself of no reputation, and took upon him the form of a servant ... and became obedient unto death, even the death of the cross" (Philippians 2:5-8, KJV).
   B. The prophet Isaiah: "Thou wilt keep him in perfect peace, whose mind is stayed on thee: because he trusteth in thee" (Isaiah 26:3, KJV).
   C. The Apostle Paul: "Be not conformed to this world: but be ye transformed by the renewing of your mind, that ye may prove what is that good, and acceptable, and perfect, will of God" (Romans 12:2, KJV)
   "Casting down imaginations, and every high thing that exalteth itself against the knowledge of God, and bringing into captivity every thought to the obedience of Christ" (2 Corinthians 10:5, KJV).

Scripture

"For my thoughts are not your thoughts, neither are your ways my ways, saith the Lord. For as the heavens are higher than the earth, so are my ways higher than your ways, and my thoughts than your thoughts."
Isaiah 55:8,9, KJV

"Finally, brothers, whatever is true, whatever is noble, whatever is right, whatever is pure, whatever is lovely, whatever is admirable — if anything is excellent or praiseworthy — THINK ABOUT SUCH THINGS."
Philippians 4:8, NIV

"The word of God is living and active. Sharper than any double-edged sword, it penetrates even to dividing soul and spirit, joints and marrow; it judges the thoughts and attitudes of the heart (mind)."
Hebrews 4:12, NIV

"Blessed is the man who does not walk in the counsel of the wicked, or stand in the way of sinners or sit in the seat of mockers. But his delight is in the law of the Lord, and on his law he meditates day and night."
Psalm 1:1,2, NIV

"Commit thy works unto the Lord, and thy thoughts shall be established."
Proverbs 16:3, KJV

238

THE TRINITY
Background

The Christian believes in the Blessed Trinity, that God is one, yet three distinct Persons: Father, Son and Holy Spirit. Each is independent, but never acts independently. Each is a distinct Person, but they are one in purpose, in essence, and in nature. The finite mind finds it difficult to comprehend this mystery; it must be accepted by faith. "And without faith it is impossible to please God, because anyone who comes to him must believe that he exists and that he rewards those who earnestly seek him" (Hebrews 11:6, NIV).

Accepted through the ages by the historical Church, the *Apostles' Creed* begins: "I believe in God, the Father Almighty, maker of heaven and earth; and in Jesus Christ, His only Son, our Lord; who was conceived by the Holy Ghost."

The *Westminster Confession* carries an eloquent defense of the Trinity: "There are three Persons in the Godhead, the Father, the Son and the Holy Ghost; and these three are one God, the same in substance, equal in power and glory."

God's redemptive work cannot be understood apart from the Trinity. The Father gave the Son (John 3:16); the Son gave Himself (Galatians 2:20); the Father gave the Holy Spirit who regenerates (John 3:8). Neither Unitarians, Jehovah's Witnesses, Christian Scientists, Spiritists, Mormons, Scientologists, nor any Eastern religion accept the Trinity.

Counseling Strategy

1. Commend the inquirer on his search for truth. Tell him that God's Word, the Bible, speaks eloquently of the reality of the Trinity.

2. Challenge him to receive Jesus Christ as his Lord and Savior. The best way to understand the Trinity is to receive eternal life through Jesus Christ. Explain "Steps to Peace with God," page 5. Some additional Scriptures you may find helpful are: "For there is one God and one mediator between God and men, the man Christ Jesus, who gave himself as a ransom for all" (1 Timothy 2:5,6, NIV). Also Titus 3:5, John 1:12 and John 3:36.

3. If the inquirer invites Christ into his life, share verses on "Assurance," pages 9 and 37, and urge him to do the following:

   A. Determine to take a strong stand for Christ.

   B. Begin to read and study the Word of God. Offer to send him *Living in Christ*, to help in starting him out.

   C. Seek a Bible-teaching church where he can fellowship with other Christians, worship, pray, witness and learn to "rightly divide the word of truth." (See 2 Timothy 2:15, KJV).

4. Pray with him for a faithful walk with Christ and for a full understanding of the Scriptures.

Scripture

The Bible makes a convincing defense of the diversity and unity of the Trinity. The following is a sampling of the more obvious texts.

The Father:

One God and Father	1 Corinthians 8:6
Father of our Lord, Jesus Christ	Ephesians 1:3
Is all powerful	Ephesians 4:6
Is unchanging	James 1:17
The author of our redemption	Galatians 1:3,4
The Father of believers	2 Corinthians 6:17,18

Jesus Christ, the Son:

Is eternal, from the beginning	John 1:1
He became incarnate	John 1:14
The author of grace and truth	John 1:17
God's Son, our Savior	John 3:16
The Father loves the Son	John 3:35
The Son loves the Father	John 14:31
The Son and the Father, One	John 10:30

The Holy Spirit:

God is a Spirit	John 4:24
He authored the Scriptures	2 Peter 1:21
He guides into all truth	John 16:13
He is sent of the Father to the world	John 14:26
He dwells within believers	John 14:17
He confirms that we are God's own	Romans 8:16
Believers can be filled with Him	Acts 4:31

The Trinity Presented Together:

Jesus was baptized; the Holy Spirit descended; the Father spoke	Matthew 3:16,17
Believers are to be baptized and discipled in the name of the Father, Son and Holy Spirit	Matthew 28:18,19

The Unique Ministries of the Trinity in redemption:

The part of the Father	Ephesians 1:3-6
The part of the Son	Ephesians 1:6-12
The part of the Holy Spirit	Ephesians 1:13,14

THE UNPARDONABLE SIN

Background

Occasionally someone will express great concern because he thinks he may have committed the "unpardonable sin." This person may, in fact, be guilty of a truly grievous sin, such as murder, adultery, incest, abortion, or even something not quite so serious. Over a period of time, he then develops an obsessive guilt, perhaps not unlike David's when he cried out, "My sin is ever before me" (Psalm 51:3, KJV). Some persons then associate this guilt with the idea that they have "sinned away the day of grace."

The admission on the part of the caller that sin is present and that he considers it serious enough to be unduly preoccupied with it is to the advantage of the counselor. The battle is partially won with such an admission.

Counseling Strategy

1. Immediately encourage the inquirer by stating that you want to help if you can. Assure him that the Scriptures maintain, in spite of what he may think, that for every temptation and sin there is an accompanying facet of the grace of God!

2. Define the unpardonable sin in the light of the Scriptures.

    When Jesus cast a demon out of a blind and mute man, the people were amazed. (See Matthew 12:22,23.) The Pharisees, however, censured Jesus, saying that He had cast out the demon by the "power of Beelzebub," the Prince of demons. Jesus answered them as follows (vs. 31,32 , KJV): "All manner of sin and blasphemy shall be forgiven unto men . . . but the blasphemy against the Holy Spirit shall not be forgiven unto men . . . it shall not be forgiven him, neither in this world, neither in the world to come."

    From this reference comes the so-called "unpardonable sin." The Pharisees, obsessed with the desire to discredit Jesus in the minds of the people, were guilty of attributing the works of the Holy Spirit (through whom Jesus worked) to the devil. This was saying, in effect, that Jesus was not of God but of Satan. This, said Jesus, would never be forgiven.

3. Ask him if he is guilty of this sin. If not, assure him that he has not committed the "unpardonable sin."

4. In emphasizing this, however, take care not to minimize the seriousness of the sin of which he is guilty. (See Galatians 5:19-21.) You need to capitalize on this admission of sin in order to emphasize the fact that "the blood of Jesus Christ, God's Son, cleanses from all sin" (1 John 1:7, KJV). In order to be enabled to experience God's grace in salvation — which includes forgiveness from sin — a person must admit that he is a sinner. See step 2 of "Steps to Peace with God," page 5.

    The next step is to confess his sin as the publican did: "God be merciful to me a sinner" (Luke 18:13, KJV). Recognizing and confessing sin is a prerequisite to all else that follows. God is in the business of forgiving sin. He sent His Son to the Cross that "we might be made the righteousness of God in him" (2 Corinthians 5:21, KJV).

Point out that now the only sin that he could consider "unpardonable" would be to reject receiving Christ as his Savior and forgiver.

Billy Graham deals with this as follows: "Perhaps I can venture a definition of what I understand the unpardonable sin to be. It seems to me, negatively, that no one has committed this sin who continues to be under the disturbing, convicting, and drawing power of the Holy Spirit. So long as the Spirit strives with a person, he has not committed the unpardonable sin. But when a person has so resisted the Holy Spirit that He strives with him no more, then there is eternal danger. In other words, the unpardonable sin involves the total and irrevocable rejection of Jesus Christ. Resisting the Spirit is a sin committed by unbelievers. But it is a sin that, when carried on long enough, leads to eternal doom. Only certain judgment remains for those who resist the Spirit."

---

5. The counselor should present "Steps to Peace with God," page 5, and urge the person to trust in Christ without delay, emphasizing that although his sin is serious, it is forgivable. "He forgiveth all our iniquities" (See Psalm 103:3).

6. If he is a Christian, emphasize that a child of God is not capable of committing the "unpardonable sin." Only unbelievers reject the Holy Spirit. Follow the counseling procedure as outlined above.

   A. Define the unpardonable sin (Matthew 12:22-31).

   B. Ask him if he is guilty of the sin described by Jesus, that of blasphemy against the Holy Spirit?

   C. In dispelling his doubts, remember not to treat lightly the sin which the inquirer thinks might be unpardonable.

   D. Assure him that the sin, no matter how terrible, can be forgiven on the basis of repentance and confession (see page 11 on "Restoration"). Emphasize especially 1 John 1:9.

      It may not be easy to convince the caller of the truth of God's Word in regard to the "unpardonable sin." Be persistent in reiterating God's love, shown in the price He paid on the Cross so that sin might be forgiven. If we confess, all sin will be forgiven.

7. Pray with the caller that he might be able to see sin from God's perspective. God hates sin, but loves the sinner and will forgive any and all sin through the Person and work of our Lord Jesus Christ.

Scripture

The Unpardonable Sin:

"He who is not with me is against me, and he who does not gather with me scatters. And so I tell you, every sin and blasphemy will be forgiven men, but the blasphemy against the (Holy) Spirit will not be forgiven."

Matthew 12:30,31, NIV

The Seriousness of Sin:

"The acts of the sinful nature are obvious: sexual immorality, impurity and debauchery; idolatry and witchcraft; hatred, discord, jealousy, fits of rage, selfish ambition, dissensions, factions and envy, drunkenness, orgies, and the like. I warn you, as I did before, that those who live like this will not inherit the kingdom of God."

Galatians 5:19-21, NIV

God's Willingness to Forgive Any and All Sin:

"If we confess our sins, he is faithful and just to forgive us our sins, and to cleanse us from all unrighteousness."

1 John 1:9, KJV

"He who conceals his sins does not prosper, but whoever confesses and renounces them finds mercy."

Proverbs 28:13, NIV

"He forgives all my sins and heals all my diseases."

"As far as the east is from the west, so far has he removed our transgressions from us."

Psalm 103:3,12, NIV

"I waited patiently for the Lord; he turned to me and heard my cry. He lifted me out of the slimy pit, out of the mud and mire; he set my feet on a rock and gave me a firm place to stand. He put a new song in my mouth, a hymn of praise to our God. Many will see and fear and put their trust in the Lord."

Psalm 40:1-5, NIV

WAR

Background

Conscientious Christians have always struggled with the problem of war and its moral implications. Some view war as incompatible with Christian teaching and spirit and therefore unacceptable under any circumstances, quoting Matthew 5:43,44: "Ye have heard that it hath been said, Thou shalt love thy neighbor, and hate thine enemy. But I say unto you, Love your enemies, bless them that curse you, do good to them that hate you, and pray for them which despitefully use you, and persecute you."

Other Christians feel that armed preparedness is necessary, and that Christian citizenship obligates us to obey those in authority, serving in the military should a war develop (See Romans 13:1; Titus 3:1 and Hebrews 13:7.)

Philosophically, war is an extension of man's struggle with sin and evil in the world. The apostle James wrote: "What causes fights and quarrels among you? Don't they come from your desires that battle within you? You want something but don't get it. You kill and covet, but you cannot have what you want. You quarrel and fight. You do not have, because you do not ask God. When you ask, you do not receive, because you ask with wrong motives, that you may spend what you get on your pleasures" (James 4:1-3, NIV).

What Should be the Attitude of a Christian in Regard to War?

1. Seek to be an instrument of God's peace, praying for it and working for it.
   "Blessed are the peacemakers, for they will be called the sons of God" (Matthew 5:9, NIV).
   "I urge, then, first of all, that requests, prayers, intercession and thanksgiving be made for everyone—for kings and all those in authority, that we may live peaceful and quiet lives in all godliness and holiness" (1 Timothy 2:1,2, NIV).

2. Seek to please God by presenting your life to Him (see Romans 12:1,2) and living in obedience to His Word. As a person finds God's will for his life, matters of conscience can be handled with perception from the Holy Spirit.

3. Seek to win others to Jesus Christ. Peace begins on the personal level and comes as one permits Him who "is our peace" to control his life. (See Ephesians 2:14.) There will be no peace on earth until the Prince of Peace, Jesus Christ, returns to establish it. We should spread the Gospel to all nations in anticipation of His return. (See Acts 1:8).

4. If a person must bear arms, he should commit himself to Christ and trust Him to keep him safe from harm and danger, and from the temptations and sins that confront the soldier. Seek to honor Christ in all ways.

Counseling Strategy

1. He is not alone in his concerns about war: any conscientious Christian is concerned. Let him know that you are happy to talk with him and share as you are able. Sometimes it is much better to confess at the outset that you are not equipped to discuss war philosophically. You are convinced, however, that God is just and does not willingly permit hurt and suffering. God is love. His greatest demonstration of this love is that He sent His Son to die for our sins. He has a plan for everyone's life, including the inquirer's. He wants to share His life, His love, His peace, with each of us. Has the caller opened his life to Jesus Christ, receiving Him as personal Lord and Savior? If indicated, share "Steps to Peace with God," page 5.

   Point out that if he will commit his life to Christ, he will gain insights and perspective in regard to his concern about war and his participation in it. The human conscience is actually only reliable when it is guided by the Holy Spirit who comes to indwell the person who receives Christ. (See 1 Corinthians 6:19,20.)

2. Reassure him that you feel his apprehensions and are glad to talk and share with him in thinking through the issues.

   You would like for the moment, however, to lay aside the concerns about war and return to them a little later. You want to ask him the most important question he will ever face in life. He is of great value and concern to God who has a plan through which he may experience a quality of life he never thought possible. Has he ever received Jesus Christ as his personal Savior? If indicated, share "Steps to Peace with God," page 5.

3. Another inquirer may raise the question: How can you believe in a God who permits war when it causes so much human suffering, destruction, and premature death? Consider:

   A. War is only one facet of the larger problem of evil which has been with the human race since the beginning. Evil is just as much present in a case of murder. This same evil tried to destroy the greatest Man who ever lived, nailing Him to a Cross.

   B. The problem boils down to one of moral choices. God wanted a world based on moral values, thus He was obligated to create a society which could respond to moral choices.

      Faced with the moral option of living selfishly or unselfishly, people can and do make wrong decisions. We are free to choose, but we reap the consequences of bad moral decisions. War is a wrong choice.

   C. War is the fruit of sin. Sin is the breaking of God's Law. We have not obeyed and do not obey this Law, thus we must face the consequences of our disobedience. We can choose to obey Him by trusting Him not only as our Savior but also as our Lord. "For God so loved the world that he gave his one and only Son, that whoever believes in him shall not perish but have eternal life" (John 3:16, NIV).

4. Another inquirer may raise the question: Why can't we just refuse to arm or to participate in wars? (No army, no defense.)

Let us reduce the problem to a very practical level in the neighborhood where we live. Would the caller be willing to stop locking the doors of his house or apartment, or his automobile? Even in our own country we must safeguard ourselves, our family, and our goods. How much more true this is for nations with conflicting philosophies and cultures! We live not in an ideal world, but a world dominated by sinful, selfish desires. Jesus said, "Thou shalt love thy neighbor as thyself" (Matthew 19:19, KJV). Applied on an international level, this would mean protecting the life, family, home and property of others as we protect our own.

Scripture

Prophecy Concerning War:

"You will hear of wars and rumors of wars, but see to it that you are not alarmed. Such things must happen, but the end is still to come."
Matthew 24:6, NIV

"And he shall judge among the nations, and shall rebuke many people: and they shall beat their swords into plowshares, and their spears into pruning hooks: nation shall not lift up sword against nation, neither shall they learn war any more."
Isaiah 2:4, KJV

"And God shall wipe away all tears from their eyes; and there shall be no more death, neither sorrow, nor crying, neither shall there be any more pain: for the former things are passed away."
Revelation 21:4, KJV

Submission to Authority:

"Everyone must submit himself to the governing authorities, for there is no authority except that which God has established. The authorities that exist have been established by God. Consequently, he who rebels against the authority is rebelling against what God has instituted, and those who do so will bring judgment on themselves."
Romans 13:1, 2, NIV

"Submit yourselves to every ordinance of man for the Lord's sake: whether it be to the king, as supreme; or unto governors, as unto them that are sent by him for the punishment of evildoers, and for the praise of them that do well."
1 Peter 2:13,14, KJV

The Reason for War:

James 4:1-3, NIV

THE WILL OF GOD, KNOWING
Background

God has a specific or direct will for the life of each Christian. It should be our highest purpose to determine just what His will is for us and then to do it, whatever the cost.

In order to know the will of God for our lives, we must first know God Himself. We can never know who we are without first knowing whose we are. We learn to know Him as we submit more and more to His authority (Lordship), are obedient to His Word, and are led by the Holy Spirit. In direct proportion to our knowledge of Him and our submission to Him, we experience the joy of walking in His will. "Trust in the Lord with all thine heart; and lean not unto thine own understanding. In all thy ways acknowledge him, and he shall direct thy paths" (Proverbs 3:5,6 KJV).

Billy Graham writes: "To know the will of God is the highest of all wisdom. Living in the center of God's will puts the stamp of true sincerity upon our service to God. You can be miserable with much if you are out of His will; but you can have peace in your heart with little if you are in the will of God. You can be happy in the midst of suffering if you are in God's will. You can be calm and at peace in the midst of persecution as long as you are in the will of God. The Bible reveals that God has a plan for every life and that if we live in constant fellowship with Him, He will lead us in the fulfillment of this plan."

Counseling Strategy

Congratulate the inquirer for desiring to seek God's highest and best. Mention, however, that only the child of God can know His direct or specific will for life.

Sometimes the non-Christian will express a desire to know the will of God about an important decision or step in life. Point out that the first step in knowing the will of God is to receive Jesus Christ as personal Lord and Savior. Explain "Steps to Peace with God," page 5.

For the Christian seeking to know the will of God, suggest some principles for knowing His will.

1. Counsel him to make right any conduct or relationships that may constitute a barrier against knowing God's will. Sometimes a relationship with a sweetheart or a business partner will have to end, or some sin must be confessed. Share the section on "Restoration," page 11.

   Emphasize that clearing the way to God must be through confession (1 John 1:9), and with others through apologies and restitution, if necessary.

"Always...have a conscience void of offense toward God, and toward men" (Acts 24:16, KJV).

2. Counsel him to be willing to do God's will, whatever it may be or may cost. "He said to them all, If any man will come after me, let him deny himself, and take up his cross daily, and follow me" (Luke 9:23, KJV).

3. Suggest that he assemble all the available facts and then filter all facets and circumstances related to knowing God's will for his life through his own intellect and common sense, his previous experience, and the counsel of godly friends. He needs to consider also his own gifts and talents.

4. Suggest that the inquirer seek God's will in the light of revealed Scripture. What principles, commands or prohibitions apply? Has the Holy Spirit given any motivating verses or promises? "Thy word is a lamp unto my feet, and a light unto my path" (Psalm 119:105, KJV).

5. Urge him to pray for God's will to be revealed, and also pray that he may be spiritually perceptive enough to discern it. Isaac's servant said, "I, being in the way, the Lord led me" (Genesis 24:27, KJV).

"Don't worry about anything; instead, pray about everything; tell God your needs and don't forget to thank him for his answers" (Philippians 4:6, TLB)

6. He must be very sensitive to the Holy Spirit's leading, asking himself: "Is He moving me toward, or away from, a particular course of action?" "But when he, the Spirit of truth, comes, he will guide you into all truth. He will not speak on his own; he will speak only what he hears, and he will tell you what is yet to come" (John 16:13, NIV).

7. Suggest that he ask himself: "Am I at peace as I consider the factors involved? Or am I restless and impatient because of uncertainty or inner conflict?" "And the work of righteousness shall be peace; and the effect of righteousness, quietness and assurance forever" (Isaiah 32:17, KJV).

8. Urge him to allow room for faith.

Is now the time to proceed, or halt, by faith? Should the individual respond to the light God has given through one or more of the above mentioned principles? "Commit thy way unto the Lord; trust also in him, and he shall bring it to pass" (Psalm 37:5, KJV).

9. As an exercise in practical monitoring of progress, counsel him to prepare a list under the headings of "pros" and "cons," and "alternatives," in order to record any insight from the Lord as to His leading.

10. Pray with the inquirer about any initial steps he should be taking to implement the above.

Scripture

"I delight to do thy will, O my God: yea, thy law is within my heart."
Psalm 40:8, KJV

"Hath the Lord as great delight in burnt offerings and sacrifices, as in obeying the voice of the Lord? Behold, to obey is better than sacrifice, and to hearken than the fat of rams."   1 Samuel 15:22, KJV

"If ye love me, keep my commandments." "If a man love me, he will keep my words: and my Father will love him, and we will come unto him, and make our abode with him."   John 14:15,23, KJV

"But be ye doers of the word, and not hearers only, deceiving your own selves."   James 1:22, KJV

"Trust in the Lord, and do good; so shalt thou dwell in the land, and verily thou shalt be fed."

"Commit thy way unto the Lord; trust also in him, and he shall bring it to pass."   Psalm 37:3,5, KJV

"For the Lord God is a sun and shield: the Lord will give grace and glory: no good thing will he withhold from them that walk uprightly."   Psalm 84:11, KJV

WITNESSING

Background

There is a clear biblical definition of witnessing:

"That which was from the beginning, which we have heard, which we have seen with our eyes, which we have looked at and our hands have touched—this we proclaim concerning the Word of life" (1 John 1:1, NIV).

The Christians of the first century "turned the world upside down" (Acts 17:6, KJV) because they had a sense of urgency about the message of Christ. Paul said, "Woe is unto me if I preach not the gospel" (1 Corinthians 9:16, KJV).

All Christians are witnesses; they are either sharing Christ by life and word, or they are not. Some are negative witnesses, others keep silent about their faith. Each of us needs to seek a more vibrant relationship with Christ so that people "will take note of us, that we have been with Jesus" (see Acts 4:13).

In witnessing, example is essential; our lives must reflect our profession. By our example we establish credibility and build confidence and trust which prepare the way for witnessing. However, we need more than just example. There is no substitute for the witness who verbalizes the facts of the Gospel:

- "That God was in Christ, reconciling the world unto himself (2 Corinthians 5:19, KJV).
- "I declare unto you the gospel which I preached unto you ... how that Christ died for our sins according to the scriptures; and that he was buried, and that he rose again the third day..." (1 Corinthians 15:1,3,4, KJV).
- "Salvation is found in no one else, for there is no other name under heaven given to men by which we must be saved" (Acts 4:12, NIV).

A Christian witnesses objectively by sharing the facts of the Gospel, and witnesses subjectively as he shares his own experiences in Christ. We should not overlook the value and potential effectiveness of our own testimony. The first real impression some people will get concerning Christ's power to transform life (2 Corinthians 5:17) will be through hearing about what Jesus has done for us. Paul shared again and again his Damascus road experience.

These are ingredients of an effective personal testimony:

- What my life was like before I received Christ.
- How I met Him and received Him (through what instrument and circumstances).
- What life has been like since I received Him.

Billy Graham writes on witnessing: "We are stewards of the Gospel. The power to proclaim the greatest news in heaven and earth was not given to the angels; it was given to redeemed men. Every Christian is to be a witness; every follower of Christ is to preach the Gospel. We can preach by sharing our experiences with others. We can preach by exalting Christ in our daily lives. Sermons which are seen are often more effective than those which are heard. The truth is, the best sermons are both heard and seen."

Counseling Strategy

1. In order to witness, an individual must know Christ personally. Ask the inquirer if he has received Jesus Christ as his personal Lord and Savior. If indicated, share "Steps to Peace with God," page 5.

2. Jesus must be real to the Christian! There will be very little for him to share with someone else if he doesn't seek and maintain a close walk with Christ through reading and obeying the Word of God and praying. We do not have to be super-Christians to witness, but we must be genuine. Counsel the inquirer to be sure he is a genuine and growing Christian.

3. Witnessing begins in prayer. Concerned prayer for those who need Christ will spiritually condition the Christian for witness. A prayer list of prospects, the people you want to reach, is a good way to start. This list may include family, neighbors, an old friend, a new friend.

4. Counsel the inquirer to make a study of each prospect to learn all he can about him. The more carefully he plans his approach, the more effectively he will witness. (An approach should be thought of in terms of rowing around an island to look for the most likely place to land.)

5. Suggest that he begin with one person. He should be natural, caring, and friendly without being patronizing. He needs to be sure he doesn't overwhelm his prospect by attempting to go too far too fast. The witness must be a good listener; most people really want to talk about themselves, their problems, their hurts, and their desires.

6. At this point, the witness may share his own experiences with Christ — how Christ came into his life and what He means to him.

7. This sharing should lead into the precise moment for the witness to explain God's plan of salvation (see "Steps to Peace with God," page 5). The facts of the Gospel must be applied in such a way that they converge at the point of the individual's need. Sin will have to be squarely faced, Christ's atoning death for sin accepted as the only way to God, and repentance and faith expressed for a person to be born again.

8. Counsel the inquirer always to witness aiming for a decision — one that is comprehensive, intelligent and definite. The witness should invite the person, lovingly but firmly, to make a decision based on the presented facts. The greatest service a Christian may render to another human being is to help him understand the all-important step of surrendering his life to Christ.

9. Encourage the inquirer to seal the decision with prayer. If his prospect is sufficiently knowledgeable, ask him to offer his own prayer of commitment. If not, perhaps the witness could guide him in a prayer.

10. Following this, the witness should review with his prospect what has acutally transpired in order to confirm the decision (see page 7).

11. The ultimate goal in witnessing and winning people to faith in Christ is so that they, themselves, may also become effective, reproducing witnesses. In order for this to develop, it will be necessary to continue to dedicate time to the prospect. Counsel the witness to instruct him on the importance of Bible reading and study, to inform him as to the value and practice of prayer, and to introduce him to committed Christians for fellowship, challenge and encouragement.

Additional Suggestions for Those Who Desire to Witness for Christ:

1. Identify with a church where the Bible is preached and taught and where emphasis is placed on personal witness and soul-winning.

2. Attempt to cultivate friendships with other witnessing Christians in order to learn from them: observe and then do. Evangelism Explosion teaches in its seminars that evangelism is better caught than taught.

3. Enroll in any courses on personal evangelism, such as Evangelism Explosion, Campus Crusade, Billy Graham Crusades, etc., that are available through your own or another church.

4. Read and study books on Scripture memory, personal evangelism and witnessing. A few that are available are:

How to Give Away Your Faith, by Paul Little	InterVarsity Press
The Art of Personal Witnessing, by Lorne Sanny	The Navigators
My Commitment and Steps to Peace with God	Billy Graham Assn.
Topical Memory System	The Navigators
Victory Scripture Memory	Word Publications
Personal Prayer Notebook	Tyndale House
Know What You Believe, by Paul Little	Scripture Press
Know Why You Believe, by Paul Little	Scripture Press
Becoming a Christian, by John Stott	InterVarsity Press

(These books are available at your local Christian bookstore or you may write to Grason, Box 1240, Minneapolis, MN 55440.)

Scripture

Acts 1:8

WORLDLINESS

Background

To be worldly, or worldly minded, is by definition to be devoted to or engrossed in worldly interests as opposed to spiritual affairs.

The worldly or carnal Christian is not concerned about those things "that pertain unto life and godliness, through the knowledge of him that hath called us to glory and virtue" (2 Peter 1:3, KJV). Rather, he is characterized by spiritual indifference, instability, and is undisciplined. He is contaminated (James 1:26) and rebellious to God (James 4:4). He is said to be a "friend of the world" (James 4:4, KJV), to have dubious spiritual identity and is a "lover of pleasures more than a lover of God" (cf., 2 Timothy 3:4, KJV).

He takes a half-hearted stand for that which pertains to the kindgom of God; therefore, he easily falls victim to almost any temptation or sect that comes along. He gives "lip service" to a form of doctrine, but ignores any real substance. "From such turn away," advises the Apostle Paul (2 Timothy 3:5, KJV).

The spiritually-minded Christian, on the other hand, is one who "seeks first the kingdom of God and his righteousness" (see Matthew 6:33). He takes a stand against the "spirit of this age" in order to establish his identity with the family of God. He enjoys a certain perception and spiritual discernment which comes from prayer and walking in the Spirit (Philippians 1:9-11).

Though far from perfect — even weak and doubtful at times — he seeks and experiences constant renewal at the foot of the cross (1 John 1:9 and 2:1). His sincere desire is to be filled with the "fruits of righteousness, which are by Christ Jesus, unto the glory and praise of God" (Philippians 1:11, KJV).

He knows that to be spiritually minded "is life and peace" (Romans 8:6, KJV).

Billy Graham comments: "The Bible teaches that we are to live in this world, but we are not to partake of the evils of the world. We are to be separated from the world of evil. When I face something in the world, I ask: 'Does it violate any principle of Scripture? Does it take the keen edge off my Christian life? Can I ask God's blessing on it? Will it be a stumbling block to others? Would I like to be there, or reading that, or be watching that, if Christ should return at that time?' Worldliness doesn't fall like an avalanche upon a person and sweep him away. It is the steady drip, drip, drip of the water that wears away the stone. The world is exerting a steady pressure upon us every day. Most of us would go down under it, if it weren't for the Holy Spirit who lives inside us, and holds us up, and keeps us."

Counseling Strategy

1. If a Christian inquires about how to be victorious over the world and how to become a spiritually-minded person, commend him for his interest in spiritual growth.

2. In order to set the stage for new attitudes and goals, counsel him to consciously renounce his sinful, selfish desires, to ask forgiveness for them, and to ask God for spiritual renewal. "...Choose you this day whom ye will serve ... but as for me and my house, we will serve the Lord" (Joshua 24:15, KJV).

   Share "Restoration," page 11, emphasizing 1 John 1:9 and 2:1. Also share Romans 12:1, asking him to make a conscious presentation of his body (life) to God.

3. Counsel him to be prepared for adversities, temptations and failures; they come to us all when we determine to keep ourselves "unspotted from the world" (James 1:27, KJV). God will not permit temptations to overwhelm us (1 Corinthians 10:13), and He will never leave us nor forsake us (Hebrews 13:5 and John 14:16).

4. Counsel him to faithfully read and study the Scriptures and to learn and practice daily prayer. There is no substitute for these if a person desires to grow in the grace and knowledge of our Lord Jesus Christ. As we practice these disciplines, a hunger and thirst for righteousness begins to develop which will send us back, again and again, to His presence for confession, renewal, growth and knowledge. "If a man is thirsty, let him come to me and drink. Whoever believes in me, as the Scripture has said, streams of living water will flow from within him" (John 7:37,38, NIV). This habitual cycle of thirsting and coming to drink will become an indispensable part of one's life.

5. It is often necessary to change one's life-style and circle of friends in order to pursue without encumbrances life in the Spirit. Counsel the inquirer to seek out dedicated Christian people for fellowship and to build new interests and outlets through service in a biblically oriented church. "And let us consider how we may spur one another on toward love and good deeds. Let us not give up meeting together, as some are in the habit of doing, but let us encourage one another — and all the more as you see the Day approaching" (Hebrews 10:24,25, NIV).

6. Pray with the inquirer for genuine commitment. Pray for immediate spiritual victories which will confirm it.

7. Finally, challenge him to set some immediate spiritual goals and to work on them, monitoring his progress from victory to victory.

Scripture

"If ye then be risen with Christ, seek those things which are above, where Christ sitteth on the right hand of God. Set your affections on things above, not on things on the earth. And whatsoever ye do in word or deed, do all in the name of the Lord Jesus, giving thanks to God and the Father by him."

Colossians 3:1,2,17, KJV

"Do not love the world or anything in the world. If anyone loves the world, the love of the Father is not in him. For everything in the world — the cravings of sinful man, the lust of his eyes and the boasting of what he has and does — comes not from the Father, but from the world. The world and its desires pass away, but the man who does the will of God lives forever."

1 John 2:15-17, NIV

"Yet every advantage that I had gained I considered lost for Christ's sake. Yes, and I look upon everything as loss compared with the overwhelming gain of knowing Christ Jesus my Lord. For his sake I did in actual fact suffer the loss of everything, but I considered it useless rubbish compared with being able to win Christ.

For now my place is in him, and I am not dependent upon any of the self-achieved righteousness of the Law. God has given me that genuine righteousness which comes from faith in Christ. How changed are my ambitions! Now I long to know Christ and the power shown by his resurrection: now I long to share his sufferings, even to die as he died, so that I may perhaps attain, as he did, the resurrection from the dead."

Philippians 3:7-11, Phillips

"Do the good things that result from being saved, obeying God with deep reverence, shrinking back from all that might displease him. For God is at work within you, helping you want to obey him, and then helping you do what he wants. In everything you do, stay away from complaining and arguing, so that no one can speak a word of blame against you. You are to live clean, innocent lives as children of God in a dark world full of people who are crooked and stubborn. Shine out among them like beacon lights, holding out to them the Word of Life."

Philippians 2:12-16, TLB

"Base your happiness on your hope in Christ . . . Live in harmony with one another . . . See that your public behavior is above criticism. As far as your responsibility goes, live at peace with everyone . . . Don't allow yourself to be overpowered by evil. Take the offensive — overpower evil with good!"

Romans 12:12-21, Phillips (Selected phrases)

"Let us therefore follow after the things which make for peace, and things wherewith one may edify another. It is good neither to eat flesh, nor to drink wine, nor anything whereby thy brother stumbleth, or is offended, or is made weak."

Romans 14:19,21, KJV

SEVEN COMMON QUESTIONS

by Paul E. Little

1. What About the Heathen?

"What about the person who has never heard of Jesus Christ? Will he be condemned to hell?" Certain things are known to God alone (Deuteronomy 29:29). On some things God has not fully revealed His plan. This is one instance. The Scripture does offer some very clear points for us to keep in mind.

a. God is just. Whatever He does with those who have never heard of Jesus Christ will be fair.

b. No person will be condemned for rejecting Jesus Christ of whom he has never heard; instead he will be condemned for violating his own moral standard, however high or low it has been. The whole world — every person, whether he has heard of the Ten Commandments or not — is in sin. Romans 2 clearly tells us that every person has a standard of some kind, and that in every culture, people knowingly violate the standard they have (Romans 2:12-16).

c. Scripture indicates that every person has enough information from creation to know that God exists (Romans 1:20, "So that they are without excuse"). Psalm 19 confirms this fact. Matthew 7:7-11 and Jeremiah 29:13 relate that if anyone responds to the light he has and seeks God, God will give him a chance to hear the truth about Jesus Christ.

d. There is no indication in the Bible that a person can be saved apart from Jesus Christ (John 14:6). Only He atoned for our sins. He is the only bridge across the chasm that separates the highest possible human achievement from the infinitely holy standard of God (Acts 4:12). We, who call ourselves Christians, must see to it that those who have not heard hear the Gospel.

e. The Bible is perfectly clear concerning the judgment which awaits the individual who has heard the Gospel. When he faces God, the issue will not be the heathen. He will have to account for what he, personally, has done with Jesus Christ. Usually someone will raise the question of the heathen as a smoke screen so he can evade his personal responsibility. We need to answer this question for him. But then, as we terminate the discussion, we should focus on the person himself and on his responsibility. What is he going to do with Jesus Christ? For a fuller discussion of the moral law inherent in the universe, see *The Case For Christianity* by C.S. Lewis.

2. Is Christ the Only Way to God?

Neither sincerity nor intensity of faith can create truth. Faith is no more valid than the object in which it is placed. The real issue is the question of truth. For example, Islam and Christianity are very similar in the moral and ethical realms, but the two faiths are diametrically opposed on the crucial question: "Who is Jesus Christ?" Islam denies that Jesus Christ is the Son of God. Both faiths cannot simultaneously be true at this point. One is correct; one is incorrect. If the crux of Christianity is false, our faith is worthless.

This question has some emotional aspects. Christians are not being bigoted, prejudiced, or presumptuous when they say that Christ is the only way to God. Christians have no other option because Jesus Christ Himself has said this. We are dealing with truth that has come to us by revelation, through the invasion into human history of God Himself in Jesus Christ.

Some laws and their penalties are socially determined. For instance, being picked up for speeding means paying a fine. But in some other aspects of life, such as in the physical realms, we find laws that are not socially determined. The law of gravity is one such law. In the moral realm, as in the physical, there are laws that are not socially determined. We discern these laws from what God has revealed about the inherent law of the universe. One such law is that Jesus Christ is the only way to God. Dorothy L. Sayers offers some further helpful thoughts on this subject in *The Mind of the Maker*.

3. Why Do the Innocent Suffer?

"If God is all-good and all-powerful, why do the innocent suffer?" Here we have to admit our partial ignorance. We do not have the full explanation of the origin and problem of evil because God has chosen to reveal only a part to us. God created the universe perfect; man, through his free will, chose to disobey. Evil came into the universe through man's disobedience. Because man disobeyed and broke God's law, evil pervades the universe.

We must not overlook the presence of evil in every one of us. If God executed judgment uniformly, not one of us would survive. Suppose God were to decree, "At midnight tonight all the evil will be stamped out of the universe." Which of us would be here at 1:00 a.m.?

After pointing out man's personal problem with evil, we need to know that God has done everything necessary to meet this problem. He came into human history in the Lord Jesus Christ, and He died to solve this problem. Every individual who willingly responds, receives His gift of love, grace, and forgiveness in Jesus Christ. C.S. Lewis has observed that it is idle for us to speculate about the problem of evil. The problem we all face is the *fact* of evil. The only solution to this fact is God's Son, Jesus Christ.

4. How Can Miracles Be Possible?

"How can miracles be possible? In this scientific age, how can any intelligent person who considers the orderliness of the universe believe in them?" The real issue here is whether or not God exists. If God exists, then miracles are logical and pose no intellectual contradictions. By definition, God is all-powerful. He can and does intervene in the universe that He has created.

Ultimately, we are being asked, "How do I know God exists?" History records many arguments for the existence of God. However, these have counter-arguments, and some evidence seems to negate them. So they are regarded as hints rather than as conclusive proof that God exists.

The greatest indication of the existence of God is His coming into human history. I know God exists, not because of all the philosophical arguments, but because He came into human history in Jesus Christ and I have met Him personally. Our answer begins with Him. His credentials substantiate His claim. The supreme credential, of course, is the fact that He rose from the dead. In helping a non-Christian think through the intellectual basis of Christianity, our best defense is a good offense. One way to stimulate his thinking is to ask, "Which of the other three possibilities about Jesus Christ do you believe, since you do not believe that He was the truth?" There are only four possible conclusions about Jesus Christ and His claims. He was either a liar, a lunatic, a legend, or the Truth.

    a. Liar. Most people believe that Jesus was a great moral philosopher and teacher. To call Him a liar would be a contradiction of terms.

    b. Lunatic. He thought He was doing right, but He suffered from delusions of grandeur. The hitch in this conclusion is that the clinical symptoms of paranoia do not fit with the personality characteristics of Jesus Christ. The poise and composure which He demonstrated are not characteristic of those who suffer from paranoid disturbances.

    c. Legend. He never made the statements attributed to Him. They were put in His mouth by over-enthusiastic followers in the third and fourth century. Modern archaeology, however, makes it difficult to maintain this theory. Recent findings confirm that the New Testament documents were written during the lifetime of the contemporaries of Jesus Christ. Development of an elaborate legend would have required a more significant time lag.

We also need to consider with the person what it means to prove or not prove God. We can never prove God by the scientific method. But that does not mean that our case is lost. The scientific method as a means of verification is limited to measurable aspects of reality. No one can measure love, hatred, or justice. However, there is a science of history. As we examine the data for Christianity, and particularly the evidence for the resurrection, we find a solid case on which to base our conviction.

These are the ideas we need to suggest to a person who takes the essentially materialistic position, based on rationalistic presuppositions, and claims that because there is no supernatural, miracles are impossible. When someone begins with this presupposition, no amount of evidence will convince him of the truth. If you started out by denying that miracles are possible, what evidence would convince you that a miracle had taken place? None. Christ dealth with this problem in Luke 16:28-31. The principle still holds today. The data we have concerning God's visitation to this planet are sufficient grounds for us to believe. When someone refuses to accept this evidence, no additional evidence will convince him.

5. Isn't the Bible Full of Errors?

"How do you reconcile your faith with the fact that the Bible is so full of errors?" The reliability of Scripture is being challenged. First, ask what particular errors the person has in mind. Ninty-nine percent of the time people cannot think of any. If the person has a specific problem and you do not have the answer, do not panic. Instead smile casually and tell him, "I don't have the answer to that one, but I will be glad to dig it up for you, "If the person has not read the Bible, that is a fair indication of his insincerity in questioning it. But do not press this point with him, and never make fun of anyone or try to argue by ridicule. This only brings the Gospel into disrepute.

The Bible does contain some apparent contradictions. But, time and time again, an apparent contradiction has been vindicated by the discoveries of modern archaeology. Dr. Nelson Glueck, an outstanding Jewish archaeologist, makes the remarkable statement, "No archaeological discovery has ever controverted a biblical reference."

Evolution may be a problem if it leads to an atheistic conclusion for someone. The real issue though is not evolution, but coming to grips with Christ Himself. Ask, "What conclusion are you drawing from your evolutionary position — that the universe happened by chance? Or are you saying that God created the universe and did so by using certain evolutionary processes? I am not convinced about that particular position, but let us assume for the moment that it is correct. What conclusion are you drawing?" From there, direct his attention to what Jesus Christ has said and done. *How* God brought the universe into being is not so important as *that* He did it. One's presupposition, and not the actual evidence, often determines his conclusion. An apparently strong case for a naturalistic position can be made by ignoring the evidence for Jesus Christ. But if a person is going to be intellectually honest, he must come to grips with Him. An amazing number of thinking non-Christians have never really thought about the evidence for Jesus Christ.

6. Isn't Christian Experience Only Psychological?

Some suggest that we have faith only because we have been conditioned since early childhood. We have been raised like Pavlov's dogs — an over-simplification. Christians have been converted from every imaginable background. Thousands have had no childhood contact with Christianity. Yet each will testify to a personal encounter with Christ that transformed his life. The Lord, Himself, is the only constant factor.

Others assert that spiritual ideals are essentially wish fulfillments. They can be traced to a person's feeling a need for God, creating an image in his mind, and then worshiping the mental projection. Objective reality is totally lacking. Religion is called a crutch of people who cannot get along in life. Religious people are self-hypnotized.

What is our objective evidence for our subjective experiences? Christianity differs from autohypnosis, wish fulfillments, and all the other psychological phenomena in that the Christian's subjective experience is securely bound to an objective, historical fact, namely the resurrection from the dead of Jesus Christ.

If the resurrection is true, it makes all the difference in the world. It is confirmation of God's revelation in Christ, an absolute truth, an historical fact outside of ourselves, an objective fact to which our subjective experience is tied. We need to hold these two facts, the objective and the subjective, in proper perspective. I need to recognize that my experience is based on the solid foundation of an objective fact in history.

Evidence For The Resurrection, by J.N.D. Anderson, is a brief and helpful summary. He discusses the evidence and the various alternatives that have been advanced to explain away the resurrection, showing why, in the light of the data, each explanation is inadequate.

7. Won't A Good Moral Life Get Me To Heaven?

A student at Duke University said, "If God grades on the curve, I'll make it." Most people will accept the philosophy that all we need to do is our best, and then everything will be all right, or at least we will be able to just get by. This is an incredible optimism about man's righteousness and appalling ignorance of God's infinite holiness. God does not grade on the curve. He has an absolute standard, Jesus Christ. Light destroys darkness. The character of God so blazes in its purity that it consumes all evil. In God's presence, we would be consumed because of the corruption in our lives. The perfect righteousness of Jesus Christ is the only basis on which we can come into fellowship with the living God.

Morality is not the answer. From the bum on Skid Row, to the Joe College type, to the tremendously moral man, all is futile. No one could swim the entire distance to Hawaii. All would drown. No swimming instructions would help. We need someone to take us to Hawaii. This is where Christ comes in.

If you can live a life that is absolutely perfect, you can make it to heaven on your own steam. But no one ever has succeeded, nor ever will succeed. All the other religions of the world are essentially sets of swimming instructions, suggested codes of ethics, for a wonderful pattern of life. But man's basic problem is not knowing *how* he ought to live; it is lacking the *power* to live as he ought. The good news is that Jesus Christ, who invaded human history, does for us what we could not possibly do for ourselves. Through Him we may be reconciled to God, given His righteousness, and enabled to have fellowship with Him in His very presence.

COMPARISON OF CHRISTIANITY WITH MAJOR CULTS AND RELIGIONS

CHRISTIANS   BUDDHISTS

God

Believe in Omniscient, Omipotent God (Job 42:2, Ps. 115:3; Matt. 19:26).

Deny existence of a personal God.

Jesus Christ

The unique Son of God who died for man's sin (Matt. 14:33; 16:16; John 1:34; 9:35-37; 1 Cor. 15:3; Rom. 5:6-8).

A good teacher, less important than Buddha.

Sin

Any thought or deed contrary to the will of God. Man is spiritually dead in sin (Rom. 3:10, 23; 5:12; Eph. 2:1)

Anything which hinders man's progress. Man is responsible for his own sin.

Salvation

Through Christ's efforts only (Acts 4:12; Titus 3:5, Eph. 2:8-10).

By self-effort only.

CHRISTIANS   CHRISTIAN SCIENTISTS

God

God is a Person. He created the universe, and created man in His own image (Gen. 1:1, 26). God, as a Person, sees, hears, speaks, remembers, knows (Gen. 6:5; Exod. 2:24; Num. 11:1; Ps. 79:8; 2 Tim. 2:19).

God is an impersonal principle, not a Person. Mary Baker Eddy, founder of the movement, writes: "God is all... that soul, or mind, of the spiritual man is God, the Divine principle of all being."

Jesus Christ

Christ is one with God. Jesus said, "I and my Father are one" (John 10:30), Christians find much evidence of Christ's deity in the Scriptures: John 1:1; Phil. 2:5-8 and 1 John 2:22, 23.

Jesus was not God. **Science and Health** states: "Jesus Christ is not God..." (p. 361). Followers of Christian Science make Christ an outstanding man, a great teacher, but deny His deity.

Matter

What man sees, touches, feels, smells and hears is real. Jesus demonstrated the reality of matter. He became flesh (John 1:14). He was hungry (Matt. 4:2). He gave others food to eat (Matt. 14:16).

Only Principle (God) exists and everything else is an "illusion." There is no matter; material things (a person's body, etc.) are not real.

Sin

Sin is real. It originates in the heart and mind of man, and separates man from God. The ultimate result of sin is death (Isa. 59:2; Mark 7:21-23; Rom. 5:12; 6:23).

Sin, evil and death do not exist. **Science and Health** states: "Since God is All, there is no room for the opposite... therefore evil, being the opposite of goodness, is unreal..." (p.234).

The Atonement and Resurrection

Christ's shed blood atoned for man's sins (1 Peter 2:24) and Christ died and rose from the dead in bodily form (John 20:16, 17, 20, 27).

Christ's shed blood on the cross did not cleanse man from sin and His disciples were fooled into thinking Him dead when he was really alive in the tomb (pp. 330 and 349, **Science and Health**).

CHRISTIANS   HINDUS

God

External, personal, spiritual Being in three persons, as Father, Son, Holy Spirit (Matt. 3:13-17; 28:19; 2 Cor. 13:14).

Brahman is formless, abstract, eternal being without attributes. Takes form in a trinity as well as **millions** of lesser gods.

Jesus Christ

Christians believe Jesus Christ to be the **only begotten Son** of God, the Father. He is God as well as man; sinless, and He died for our redemption (John 1:13, 14; 10:30; 8:46; Heb. 4:15; Mark 10:45; 1 Pet. 2:24).

Christ is just one of many incarnations, or sons of God. Christ was not **the** Son of God. He was no more divine that any other man and He did not die for man's sins.

Sin

Sin is proud, independent rebellion that separates man from God. It is falling short of the standards God has established in His Word. Sin must be punished, and its conse-

Good and evil are relative terms. Whatever helps is good; whatever hinders is vice. Man cannot help "stumbling" over these obstacles as he strives to know himself. If he can-

quence is death and eternal separation from God (Rom. 3:23; 6:23).

not succeed in this life, he may try
again in reincarnated form.

Salvation

Man is justified through the
sacrificial death and resurrection of
Jesus Christ who died in our stead
(Rom. 3:23; 1 Cor. 15:3).

Man is justified through devotion,
meditation, good works and self-
control.

CHRISTIANS

JEHOVAH'S WITNESSES

God

God is eternal, personal, spiritual
Being in three persons — the Trinity:
Father, Son and Holy Spirit (Matt.
3:13-17; 28:19; 2 Cor. 13:14).

There is one solitary being from all
eternity, Jehovah God, the Creator
and Preserver of the Universe and all
things. They deny the doctrine of the
Trinity.

Immortality

Scripture teaches that man has an
eternal, immortal soul (Gen. 1:26;
5:1; Job 32:8; Acts 7:59; 1 Cor. 11:7).

Man does not have an immortal
soul. They teach that the soul is not
separate from the body.

Jesus Christ

Christ is divine, a part of the Trinity,
God Himself (John 1:1; Col. 1:15-19;
2:9; 1 John 5:7, 8).

Christ was **not** God but God's first
created creature. They deny Christ's
deity.

Atonement

Christ's death was the complete pay-
ment for man's sins (Rom. 3:24, 25;
Col. 1:20; 1 Peter 2:24; 2 Cor. 5:20).

Christ's death provides the opportunity for man to work for his salvation: perfect human life for eternity
on an Eden-like earth.

Christ's Resurrection

Christ was bodily resurrected from
the grave (John 2:21; 20:24-29; Luke
24:43).

Christ was raised a "divine spirit."
They deny the bodily resurrection of
Christ.

Christ's Return

Christ will return to earth physically
(1 Thess. 4:16, 17; Matt. 24:30;
Zech. 12:10; Rev. 1:7).

Christ returned to earth—in-
visibly—in 1914 and now rules earth
from heaven.

Hell

There is eternal punishment for sin

There is no hell or eternal punish-

(Matt. 5:22; 8:11, 12; 13:42, 50; 22:13; Luke 13:24-28; 2 Peter 2:17; Jude 13; Rev. 14:9-11).

ment. Those who do not measure up to Jehovah's standards will be annihilated, meaning they will be or know no more.

CHRISTIANS

JEWS (ORTHODOX)

God

One God is revealed in the Scripture as Father, Son and Holy Spirit—the Trinity. Within the one "essence" of the Godhead there are three persons who are co-equally and co-eternally God (Matt. 3:13-17; 28:19; 2 Cor. 13:14).

"Hear, O Israel, the Lord our God, the Lord is one"
—The Shema

Sin

Man fell in Adam and is born in sin (Rom. 5:12; Ps. 51:5). All men are condemned before God for their sin: proud, independent rebellion against God in active or passive form (Rom. 1:18-23; 3:10,23).

Man is not born in original sin nor is he born good. Man is born free, with the capacity to choose between good and evil. Each man is accountable for himself.

Salvation

Man is justified before God and obtains salvation through the atoning death of Christ on the cross. Salvation is a gift of God through faith (Rom. 3:24; 1 Cor. 15:3; Eph. 2:8,9).

Anyone, Jew or not, may gain salvation through commitment to the one God and moral living. Judaism looks to an afterlife, however, it does not stress preparing man for the next world as much as guiding his ethical and moral behavior in this present life.

Jesus Christ

Christ is the only begotten Son of God, the Messiah predicted in Isaiah 53. He is God as well as man. He was sinless and died to redeem all men from sin (Mark 10:45; John 1:13,14; 8:46; 10:30; Heb. 4:15; 1 Pet. 2:24).

While some Jews may accept Jesus as a good teacher of ethics, they do not accept Him as Messiah because: (1) Jesus did not bring lasting peace; (2) Jesus was declared to be divine and the Jewish idea of Messiah is a man sent from God to deliver Israel from oppression, not to save individuals from personal sin.

CHRISTIANS	MORMONS

God

God is uniquely eternal and all-powerful, the only God—and He is a Spirit (Ps. 145:13; John 4:24; 1 Tim. 1:17).

God is a material creature who was once a man as we are now men. They say men can finally achieve godhood and that there are many gods.

The Bible

The Bible, given by God's Spirit is complete in itself and needs no additions. In fact, additions to the Bible are forbidden (Deut. 4:2; 12:32; Prov. 30:5, 6; Gal. 1:8; Heb. 1:1, 2; Rev. 22:18, 19).

They have "new scripture" and the writings of Joseph Smith are divinely inspired revelations — God's nineteenth century additions to the Bible.

Sin

Man is not godlike, but sinful and separated from God. Man can only have a relationship with God through faith in Christ. Man, apart from Christ, is lost. (Rom. 5:12-19; 6:23; Eph. 2:1, 3; John 1:29; Gal. 3:13.)

Man is progressively becoming a god. Mormons teach that Adam's sin in Eden was necessary in order to provide parentage for the spirit children of God who were ready and waiting for the experience of earth life.

Salvation

Salvation is a free gift provided by the grace (unmerited love) of God for all who believe and accept His plan (Eph. 2:8, 9; John 12:26; 14:1-3, 6; 1 John 3:1, 2).

Salvation comes by works and all men will spend eternity on some level of a multistoried heaven. The level will be determined by the scope of each man's good works.

CHRISTIANS	MOSLEMS

God

One God is revealed in Scripture as Father, Son and Holy Spirit. Within the one "essence" of the Godhead there are three persons who are co-equally and co-eternally God (Matt. 3:13-17; 28:19; 2 Cor. 13:14).

There is no God but Allah—the God.

Jesus Christ

Jesus is the Christ, the Son of God, one with the Father, sinless redeemer

Jesus Christ was only a man, a prophet equal to Adam, Noah,

of sinful man through His vicarious death on the cross and resurrection from the dead (John 1:13, 14; Heb. 4:15; 1 Peter 3:18; 1 Cor. 15:3).

Abraham and Moses, all of whom are below Mohammed in importance. Christ did not die for man's sins, in fact Judas, not Jesus, died on the cross.

Sin

Sin is proud, independent rebellion against God in active or passive form (Rom. 1:18-23; 3:10, 23).

Sin is failure to do Allah's will, failure to do one's religious duties as outlined in the Five Pillars of Islam.

Salvation

Christ—God's Son—died for our sins (on the cross) according to the inspired Word of God (1 Cor. 15:3, 4).

Man earns his own salvation, pays for his own sins.

CHRISTIANS   UNITARIANS

Gods

God is revealed in the Scriptures as Father, Son and Holy Spirit—the Trinity (Matt. 3:13-17; 28:19; 2 Cor. 13:14).

"God is one." They deny the doctrine of the Trinity. They also deny that God is a personal deity and use the term "God" to refer to the living processes of nature and conscience at work in mankind.

The Bible

The Bible is divinely inspired and is the sole guide and authority for faith (2 Tim. 3:15-17; 2 Pet. 1:19-21; 1 Thess. 2:13).

The Bible is a collection of "myths and legends" and philosophical writings. They deny the authority and accuracy of the Scriptures.

Jesus Christ

Christ is divine, a part of the Trinity—God Himself. Christ Himself frequently referred to Himself as God (John 8:58; 8:12-30).

Jesus was no more or less divine than any man. They deny the doctrine of the Trinity as well as the deity of Christ.

Sin

Man is inherently sinful and there is only one way that man can rid himself of his sinful nature—through faith by the grace (unmerited love) of God (Eph. 2:8, 9; 4:20-24).

Man is essentially good and he can save himself by improvement — "redemption of character."

Reprinted from *So What's the Difference?* (Regal Books) by Fritz Ridenour, ©copyright 1967 by Gospel Light Publications, Glendale, CA 91209. Used by permission. See this valuable source for further reading.

THE BILLY GRAHAM
CHRISTIAN WORKER'S HANDBOOK

SUBJECT INDEX